The Gate Breakers

The Gate Breakers

BY BRACHA HABAS

Translated from the Hebrew by **DAVID SEGAL**

Illustrated by Anna Walinska

HERZL PRESS • SHARON BOOKS

New York • THOMAS YOSELOFF • London

© 1963 by The Theodor Herzl Foundation, Inc.
Library of Congress Catalog Card Number: 63-9376

Thomas Yoseloff, Publisher
8 East 36th Street
New York 16, New York

Thomas Yoseloff Ltd
18 Charing Cross Road
London W.C.2, England

Herzl Press
515 Park Avenue
New York 22, New York

$27.9

8931

Printed in United States of America

Contents

The Gate Breakers

Content

The Gate Breakers

1

Before the Locked Gate

On a dark, rainy night the two young men stood knocking at the locked gate of the young kibbutz, Ashdot Yaakov, in the Jordan Valley. This was in the winter of 1937. Disturbances raged throughout Palestine. Settlements were attacked, fields set afire, and the wounded and the dead lay in the roads. The small kibbutz lay isolated amid stretches of barren, inimical wasteland. At nightfall the herdsmen gathered the sheep and cattle into the barbed-wire enclosure and locked the heavy gates.

The watchman on his post, keeping his ears open for every sound, suddenly gripped his rifle—one of the very few for which the kibbutz was able to receive a government permit—and lifted the sooty kerosene lamp above his head. Bundled up in an old winter coat, he plodded slowly through the sticky mud in his heavy boots, thinking: Who could it be at this hour—friend or enemy?

In a moment, however, a wide grin spread over his tanned, wind-burned face. They were friends! There were the famous boots, short leather jacket, and bobbing black hair of Berele of the Central Workers' Committee. There too were the red hair and bright, smiling eyes of Zeev Shind, better known as "Danny," from kibbutz Ayelet Hashahar, in

Upper Galilee. Wasn't he in Poland on a mission of *Hehalutz?* How did he get here so suddenly? And what madness to travel the roads at such an hour! These shlihim —emissaries—never get a moment's rest. Night, day, Sabbath, and holiday are all the same to them. Perhaps they were stopping off on their way to some meeting or conference in Galilee.

Such were the thoughts of the peasant watchman as he undid the heavy iron chain. He could not know that they were headed for *his* kibbutz this time, that they had come in the dead of night to enlist a member for a "job." This was secret, "hot" business. It couldn't wait until morning.

A delegation coming to recruit someone for a communal task was a normal occurrence in the life of the farm. But they never came like this! Such matters were usually taken care of publicly, and well in advance. A notice in the dining room would call for a general meeting and announce that "big wheels" were coming. They would arrive on the Sabbath, so that the community had time to weigh the matter, argue at length, and come to a thought-out decision.

Not so this time. There was good cause, indeed, for the uncertainty that gnawed at Danny's heart at the outset of his journey. Would his mission succeed? Who and what was he, that he should come and take a man away from the kibbutz for an unprecedented mission which was, as yet, only an idea in the minds of a few people? Moreover, who stood behind them? No institution, no recognised public body. He had spoken with some leaders that he respected, but only a few of them agreed to the idea, and half-heartedly at that. Danny, however, would take no denial. He was driven on by the enthusiasm, the misery, and the frustration of thousands of young Hehalutz members barred from entry to their historic homeland. But how, with only such forces, can one procure a ship to set out in the dead of night? How can one come to a young farm in this hostile desert and conscript one of the few members who run the entire place?

For these reasons, Danny had asked that Berele go with him that night. "Two are better than one," especially with such an important mission at stake.

It was only the day before that Danny had returned from a more distant mission, from the kibbutz training farms in Poland, where he had spent a number of months. He had gone to Poland suddenly, eager to serve the Jewish youth there, whose very existence was threatened by mounting persecution. He had plunged into his work with an intense, religious fervor.

The plan developed in his mind while he was in kibbutz Kiltz in Poland. Despite his special status as a shaliah, from the Land of Israel, he lived in the training kibbutz just like any one of its hundreds of members. With them he went hungry; with them he slept in crammed, crowded rooms on planks on wide shelves, layer upon layer, known as "internationals"; with them he would go looking for a day's work —usually in vain; and with them he sought a spark of hope for the future.

The situation of the Jews in Poland had become quite serious in recent years. Instances of anti-Semitism were on the increase. Jewish merchants were forced out of business by dint of laws, severe threats, and pogroms. Jewish students were forbidden to sit together with Poles; they were made to stand along the walls during lectures. The various Zionist youth movements were now 250,000 strong, and of this number, tens of thousands were members of Hehalutz. The requests to emigrate to Palestine that poured in from all over Poland to the Palestine Office in Warsaw had to be sent by the post office in special trucks—the regular mail service could not handle them. The number of immigration certificates designated for pioneers was almost nil. Young men sat in their kibbutzim for years and waited in vain for their turn to come. About 20,000 boys and girls were to be found on the training farms in 1935-1936. Farms composed of hundreds of veteran members got two or three visas—or "certificates," as they were called—out of each schedule. At that rate most members would have to wait twenty years or longer to get to Palestine. Moreover, there was no turning back. Jews living in small villages had always had a hard time of it, but now their situation was extremely precarious, with no prospects for improvement. On the horizon was Hitler and the Second World War, and Mussolini was dispatching his troops to Ethiopia. In Jerusalem the fanatic Mufti Amin and the Arab Higher Committee were doing all they could to further their "holy war" against Zionism. On top of all this the British Mandatory Government, concerned about its status in the Middle East, reduced with each passing year the schedule of certificates to Palestine. In 1935 the schedule allowed for 60,000 immigrants, but at the outset of 1936 it was halved.

The pioneer movement in Poland set up economic enterprises and established training farms and workshops, all on a very small scale and under adverse circumstances. Unemployment and inactivity were the lot of tens of thousands, and poverty and despair were widespread. With immigration to Palestine cut off, new blood ceased to flow to the training farms. The movement seemed paralyzed.

The pioneer spirit, however, was by no means extinguished. The very absence of alternatives led to plans and suggestions for extraordinary measures. No one, however, dared name the undertaking which they had long hoped and prayed for.

1. JEWS LIVING IN SMALL VILLAGES HAD ALWAYS HAD A HARD TIME OF IT.

The pioneer camp had not yet recovered from the Velos disaster. This small Greek ship, on a dark night in July, 1934, deposited 350 young pioneer men and women on the sandy beaches north of Tel Aviv. It was the first of the underground ships arranged for by a daring group drawn from the agricultural working community and the Hagana military leadership. On its second arrival that year, on the night of September 12, the ship was surprised by a British patrol after it had succeeded in lowering only fifty people. The remaining 300 passengers wandered from port to port for months without being able to leave the ship. The story of the incident spread and the Velos became known as the "phantom ship" and the "ghost ship." The failure of this endeavor had for three years now clouded the skies of the pioneer movement in Poland. The balance of the debt that had been incurred still hung like a sword over the leaders' heads.

Meanwhile, disturbances broke out in Palestine, bringing in their wake an economic crisis, which in turn led to greater unemployment and inactivity. At that point, however, on the threshold of despair, a daring, secret resolution was taking form.

In the summer of 1937, in the small town of Kazimir, Poland, that overlooked the green hills bordering the Vistula River, the active members of the pioneer youth organization Freiheit-Dror ("Freedom"), gathered for a long night session. The central committee of Hehalutz had called them together from all corners of Poland, hoping to bolster their morale sufficiently to enable them to hold out on the training farms. They ate bran-flour bread and diluted soup, slept on benches and on tables, and by the light of a flickering kerosene lamp wove a vision of going up to Eretz, "The Land," as Palestine was referred to by the pioneers. The emissaries from The

Land were the life breath of the convention, and the responsibility for finding a solution was laid at their feet. Principally, all looked to Shimon, a member of kibbutz Givat Hashlosha. He had been involved in the Velos affair from start to finish. Once again he was being urged to revive this venture. With him at the convention was Danny, then twenty-eight years old, who had spent eight years in The Land.

Danny was born in Vilna, a large city in Lithuania, and was brought up in a home rich in Jewish values and the love of Zion. At seventeen he left his parents' home and went off with his friends to a training farm of the youth movement Freiheit. This was in 1926, a dismal period in the history of the Zionist movement. Palestine was hard hit with a severe economic crisis, which followed upon the first widespread disillusionment with the Balfour Declaration. Immigration to Palestine was cut off and the ranks of Hehalutz thinned rapidly. Only a few hundred of its thousands of members remained loyal, and Danny was among them.

At the directive of the Warsaw branch of Hehalutz, Danny went to the small town of Rudophlin to establish a training farm in memory of the defenders of Tel Hai, one of two settlements in Upper Galilee whose members remained to fight when the district was invaded by bands of marauding Bedouins. For two months the small defense force held out until March, 1920, when Josef Trumpeldor, their leader, and five comrades were killed during an attack. The account of the heroic stand of Trumpeldor and the settlers assumed an almost legendary stature.

In the glass factory where Danny got a job, most of the workers suffered from tuberculosis as a result of the poor working conditions. Wages, moreover, were extremely low and the standard of living was deplorable. Even though kibbutz members fell sick from overwork, the number of new members increased steadily, thanks to the enthusiasm generated by the dynamic nucleus of leaders and by Danny in particular. He gladly did his share and more, helping the sick and reassuring the discouraged. After a short period of time, Tel Hai joined with two other kibbutzim and together they constituted the Union of Training Farms in Poland. Danny was chosen chairman of this new union. Although he was young, his colleagues felt that he was the right man for the job. Even then, at that early date, he was devising schemes for forcing Palestine's locked gates, but nothing practical ever resulted. Meanwhile, the Mandatory Government allocated a number of certificates for Palestine, and Danny and his friends, seizing the opportunity, were the first to go.

This was 1929, a year of violence and bloodshed in the annals of the Zionist settlement in Palestine. Numerous villages and suburbs were attacked, heavy property losses were inflicted, and many were wounded or killed. Danny arrived in Palestine and set out for Ayelet Hashahar, today a large and flourishing settlement, but then a small kibbutz numbering forty members. Without water, isolated amid the hills of Upper Galilee, and located on the outskirts of the malarial Hula swamp, the kibbutz had to struggle to survive. Danny was assigned two mules and sent to work in the fields. He ploughed, sowed the grain, and reaped the wheat like any farmer. When the disturbances broke out he participated in the defense of the farm. During the day he worked and at night he stood guard. His companions, seeing how responsible he was, entrusted him with additional duties. Soon attached to the land, he sent for his parents and entire family and brought them to Palestine.

He was invited to attend a movement seminar at Nahalal. There his outlook crystallized and his principles became firmly grounded. There too he became deeply attached to his teacher, Berl Katznelson, the leader of the seminar.

A movement cannot afford to waste its resources. An active, talented, and dedicated member like Danny was a valuable asset. After the seminar he was sent on the mission to Poland. The background that he had acquired in the past months stood him in good stead and lent a fervor to this long-awaited task.

It was during the previously mentioned night meeting in the village of Kazimir that Danny had a long talk with Shimon, the older and more experienced emissary of the two. Until dawn they walked up and down a pleasant avenue in the center of town, unaware that their conversation was to mark a turning point in the history of the pioneer movement. Slowly and with difficulty Danny perceived what this veteran emissary, respected by the pioneer movement, was suggesting: that the plan which he, Danny, had not dared to mention, could be put into effect.

And so the die was cast. From then on Danny's life became a series of daring undertakings from which there was neither escape nor respite.

This was the period of the great debate in Zionist circles over the Palestine partition plan. After the heavy blow dealt Jewish settlement by the 1936 disturbances, a glimmer of light appeared in the British House of Commons. It was conceivable that a Jewish State might be established, if it were only in one section of what then constituted Palestine. Who could be bothered with a handful of young enthusiasts at such a time? Many Jews doubted whether the final solution would be achieved through official channels, but even they felt that this was no time to annoy the authorities with underground activities.

The Revisionist group had been bringing over groups of

Jews in small craft, about twelve to a boat, and dropping them off at various points along the shore. Each departure from Europe and each arrival in Palestine constituted a small miracle; the dangers and hardships that the passengers had to undergo were formidable. No one imagined that this method could serve thousands.

In the meantime, pressures inside the Jewish youth centers in Poland continued to mount. The new plan was enthusiastically espoused by the members of the Palestinian agricultural working community and by a few public personages, primarily Hagana leaders. The latter, in arguments with other leaders of the labor movement, vehemently insisted that this new program not be prohibited.

Finally, after much heated argument, the "steering committee"—so they called themselves—decided to send two of their number to a Mediterranean port to determine whether or not the plan was feasible. So it was that two kibbutz members left Palestine for Greece. Both had taken active part in the Velos affair. Shimon, just recently returned from his mission to Poland, had organized the venture; and Levi Schwartz, from kibbutz Ramat Hakovesh, had accompanied the boat and had been in charge of the passengers.

Now everyone looked to the Greek ports as the one avenue of escape, for the underground had not yet evolved other possibilities. After the flow of arms to Spain was cut off, unemployed tramps were to be found anchored all along the Greek coast. A ship out of work means heavy losses for its owners. Agents for all sorts of ships—large, small, new, old —frantically ran around seeking business. The emissaries' problem was how to make first contact with one of these agents, and how to find one who would not cheat them or deceive them in any way. The Greeks' attitude toward the Jews was, in general, a friendly one. They seemed to understand the Jews' special problems and sympathized with them in their predicament. They disliked the British Government and its all-too-changeable policies. All these factors augured well for the success of the venture.

The two men set out with full hearts—and almost empty pockets. They had just enough money for fare to Athens and the purchase of a presentable suit of clothes. According to plan, they were joined in Athens by Danny, who had arrived from the Polish headquarters of Hehalutz as penniless as they.

In those days the boys were complete greenhorns in matters pertaining to the sea and seamanship. They hadn't the slightest notion of the ocean's complexities. Furthermore, they did not realize that the success of their venture depended not only on the vessel, but also on the man in charge of it. Boats can be had for money, but it is not easy to find honest and reliable men who will stand the test of danger. Danny and Shimon had embarked on their project lacking a common language with these foreign sailors, so unlike any men they had ever met before.

The boat too, of course, had to be examined with an eye to seaworthiness. The young Jews from Palestine scarcely knew what a boat was, much less its good and bad points. As a result they were very modest in their demands and too easily satisfied. They had not yet considered the possibility of hiring a full-sized ship. They looked for a small vessel that could carry fifty to sixty people, one whose movements would not be conspicuous. Their sailing from Europe, as well as their arrival in Palestine, would be illegal, and they did not want to arouse unnecessary questions or provoke investigations.

After a long search they finally discovered a boat that would suit their purposes. "Our boat" they labeled it in private conversations. It was a sorry-looking wooden affair with two masts, an engine, and a small hold to serve for the passengers. When Danny first saw it he was stunned. This isn't a ship, he thought, it's a washtub! a nutshell! Can this make it to Palestine? "What's the matter?" asked Shimon calmly. "Columbus crossed the Atlantic in a ship that weighed only forty-nine tons."

Next came the question of the captain. They went to a great deal of trouble before they found the right man, a sixty-year-old Greek, with six fingers on his right hand. In his youth he had been very well off, having made his fortune in smuggling and other illegal pursuits. Now, however, he had come upon hard days; the world was too peaceful, there were no smuggling jobs to be had. Except for the fact that he had spells of temper, he was a rather lethargic fellow. Sometimes he would sit for hours without stirring, sending up clouds of smoke from his pipe and fingering his beads. He was as quiet as a rock. From time to time he would emit a Greek word and the Jewish interpreter would try to explain what he meant in a garbled German that was supposed to be Yiddish. All conversations of this nature were most tedious. At long last they gave him a down payment in cash. They were overjoyed.

Now, however, the young men began to worry over the reaction at home. After long deliberation, they decided that Danny should return, meet with their friends, prepare them for the ship's coming, and win their consent.

In all that transpired in his life in later years, in all that he had to undergo in his service in the underground, Danny never confronted so difficult and decisive a trial as this. He sincerely felt that the plan could work, but how could he convince the others? And suppose it should fail? That would be the end of everything. Thousands of pioneers would be left to wither away in inactivity.

Troubled by these thoughts, Danny arrived in Tel Aviv. Unlike the typical returning organizer, he did not set out at once for his home and kibbutz in Galilee. The urgency of his mission demanded that he first see the small "steering committee." In spite of the fact that they had been informed of what was to come by urgent, coded telegrams, they were astounded. They could not believe that their dream would become a reality.

After this meeting, the crucial moment of Danny's mission arrived. Now he was to go before the three men in whose hands the moral decision lay. Now he was to confront the very men who were his teachers and mentors. The first was Berl Katznelson, spiritual leader of the labor movement, and among the first to lend moral support to the illegal immigration. He had been present on the "night of Velos" in the summer of 1934 when young men, barefoot and naked, swam into the sea and bore the human cargo from ship to shore; and the young men knew that he was close by, on a sand dune, quietly observing everything. Soon after he published in "Davar," his Hebrew daily, an anonymous article entitled "A Ship Feels Her Way in Darkness." Then, as in years to come, his words inspired all who had taken part in the venture, directly or indirectly.

Danny's heart was pounding as he knocked on the door that was always open. Berl sat immersed in his books and writings as usual, busy with affairs of the movement and the editing of "Davar"; but now, as ever, he had time for someone in need of his advice.

What a pleasure it was to be with him again! Like many young men, Danny looked upon Berl as a close friend, or even as a father. In presenting his case, Danny touched upon the Zionist political struggle, the needs of world Jewry, and the plight of the Jewish refugees from Hitler's Germany. What concerned him most deeply, however, was the need to save Hehalutz from the prevalent state of stagnation and despair. This argument carried weight with Berl. He understood and agreed.

Danny rushed to bring the good news to the "steering committee" and to recruit one of its members, Berele, for the next task. As night and the curfew approached, the two men set out in a pouring rain and headed for Ashdot Yaakov to enlist the man who would be in charge of disembarking the immigrants. For two days now Danny had been in Palestine and he wanted badly to visit his family and kibbutz; but time was short, and personal matters had to be set aside. It seemed that their undertaking now hung by a thread, that everything depended upon one man's willingness to join the venture.

That man was willing. The kibbutz too agreed that Davidka N'meri should go. Danny had not imagined that his request would be granted immediately, but his earnest and restrained words, spoken before the kibbutz council late at night, fell upon sympathetic ears. The council members, themselves having come from Russia, Poland, and Lithuania some years back, had brothers, sisters, and friends in the training farms in Europe. They were sensitive, therefore, to the needs of Hehalutz and were ready to help, despite the risks involved. True, N'meri was indispensable. He was a mainstay of the community, one who could execute any task. But how could they withhold him under the circumstances? It was decided that on the next day he should begin preparations for the undertaking.

Danny's first move upon returning to Tel Aviv was to approach David Ben-Gurion, then chairman of the Jewish

Agency, and broach the subject to him. This was a step he had long feared. "Before I went to see him, I literally shook like a leaf," wrote Danny years later in his memoirs. "I realized that if he should say no, the entire project would collapse; and after all, we didn't want to go against his will . . ."

Late at night he came to a small house in the workers' quarter in north Tel Aviv. In the library upstairs an important political meeting had just concluded, but Ben-Gurion had already immersed himself in the pages of the book that lay open before him; he seemed oblivious of his surroundings. Danny mustered all his powers of persuasion and began to speak of Hehalutz. He told of their desperate straits, of the young men and women, the majority of the Jewish youth, degenerating through inactivity and a sense of futility. So . . .since there was no choice . . . they decided to . . . to go ahead on their own. . . .

Danny had not managed to say what they had in mind to do, when Ben-Gurion jumped up and said heatedly, "Don't they understand that such rash actions taken by individuals, especially now, can damage the future of the Zionist program? What institution of the movement made the decision? When and where was the decision ratified?"

Danny blanched, but, sustained by a sense of his mission, quickly recovered. He involuntarily said things that he immediately regretted. "Operation Aliya-Bet (the secret, illegal immigration) doesn't need a decision," he said in a trembling voice. "The pioneers who came here before—did they ask permission from any committee? If they had asked, maybe the answer would have been no. They had no choice, all they could do was get up and go to Palestine. And it's no different now. We had to go ahead on our own. . . ."

Only now, it seemed, did Ben-Gurion realize that the

problem was no longer theoretical but practical. The ship in question was already at sea.

"You'll face an inquiry!" he shouted. "The movement will decide whether or not you had the right to do this! But —I will say this: any Jew who gets to Palestine by any means is "all right" as far as I'm concerned. On the night that they get here, you wake me up and I'll come and help. Whoever starts the journey will finish it. But from now on— no! We will not tolerate such goings on. Nothing will be done unless the movement decides on it first!"

Danny left the house breathing easier, even if he did feel like a wrung-out rag. Only one more job remained now, and it could not be postponed. He had to bring the matter before Eliahu Golomb, the dynamic Hagana leader, who had a hand in every pioneer undertaking and every political struggle of the Zionist movement. He too had played an active role in the Velos affair.

It was late, after midnight. This was a good time to find Eliahu at home. All day long, every day, he was to be found behind the wheel, on the roads, from Metulla in the north to Beer Tuvya in the south, checking the posts and encouraging the sentries. At times he would come home in the early hours of the morning. Even then he would find Hagana members seated at the big table, waiting to receive advice on pressing matters. The household would be awake and ready for action. Ada, his wife, would be bustling back and forth through the high-ceilinged, shadowy rooms, serving tea, listening, and delivering messages.

This night, as usual, lights were on all over the old two-story house, one of the first built on Rothschild Boulevard. Half asleep and half awake, Eliahu lay on the worn leather sofa in the corner of the wide, enclosed porch with its many tall windows. The whole house, with its heavy, old-fashioned furniture, retained the atmosphere of the period of the early Biluim—the first Zionist settlers, who came to Palestine in the 1880s. It was a beehive of activity and the source of a great many pioneering ventures.

Tonight Eliahu was exhausted, having spent a day of tense activity in Hagana affairs. However, when his visitor began to speak, he shook off his drowsiness, and with knit brows and a taut face, gave him his undivided attention. As usual he replied calmly and quietly. He too felt that they ought not have gone ahead without authorization by the movement. What would happen if every group were to do as it pleased, especially in matters so delicate and complex, and so potentially dangerous? However, since the venture was a fact, care had to be taken that it should succeed. Eliahu was fully awake now, enthused and interested in every detail, every word.

All obstacles had been overcome. Danny felt as though a weight had been lifted from his chest. However, a good deal of work remained to be done before he might return to Athens. It was not until Friday morning, a full week after his arrival in Palestine, that he was able to visit Ayelet Hashahar. This was a short visit, twenty hours in all, but it served as a restoration to the weary organizer. He bathed in the warm contact with his friends. He walked about the kibbutz, which he had not seen for months, and found that it had grown in his absence. In addition, the children's house had admitted many new "citizens." These sights had a tranquillizing effect on his strained nerves. Contented and rested, he boarded his ship and left for Athens to finish the job.

2

The First Ships

When Danny arrived at the port of Piraeus he learned that all was not going as smoothly as expected. The ship that they had discussed with the Greek was not even his; he was in the process of buying it with the money that they had advanced him. Moreover, the engine was damaged and would require a costly repair job, and even then there could be no guarantee that everything would function properly.

The boys had no choice but to lose the advance payment, cancel all the arrangements that had been made, and disappoint scores of anxious pioneers in Poland, as well as their colleagues in Palestine.

Meanwhile the news had spread like wildfire in the pioneer movement and overnight had become the main topic of discussion. Experts sprung up on all sides with free advice and admonishments. Some objected to the use of a steamship on the grounds that its smoke would give away the ship's location. Others insisted that a submarine be employed, to assure complete secrecy.

In the meantime, sixty-five impatient people waited in Warsaw with packed suitcases. But there were no funds. The pioneer movement had utilized every cent in the treasury. The prospective immigrants, by no means prosperous themselves, had somehow managed to scrape together the greater part of the required sum. However, everything that had been collected had already been spent. Only the "Iron Fund," set aside for emergencies, remained untouched, and that contained only fifteen Palestinian pounds.

No choice remained but to start all over again.

After a few days' search they found another Greek, "Black Mavros" by name, who had a small, 60-ton ship called Poseidon. His skin was dark and he was forever drunk on retsino wine. Mavros excelled not only in drinking, but in volubility as well. He was a hot-blooded fellow, spoke with his hands and feet, and possessed a self-confidence beyond the ordinary. He was not used to legal employment. He wanted a "decent" job, something he could warm to. Well then, here was their man, even if his price was outrageous!

Another Greek joined the group, one Horilo by name. He had been a captain in the Greek Army and had connections in many quarters, particularly coffeehouse circles. The young men realized that he could prove very useful. They called him "the extra," but they paid him a monthly salary— and he did a good job. With the assumption of his new duties as an agent, Horilo began to press his pants, wear a new tie, and walk very erect whenever he made an appearance in the market place. He visited Piraeus regularly and kept the young men informed of doings in the port; he kept track of food prices with an eye to buying provisions for the ship; and lastly, he served as a liason man with Black Mavros. The organizers spoke to him by gesturing, and in emergencies stammered in French with an English word or two thrown in. Horilo, however, sharing their aspirations, understood them. Once, while making his rounds, he was asked by one of the heads of the local police force, "How long will the Jewish underground go on smuggling Jews into Palestine?" "Until the Jewish State is established," he promptly replied.

Horilo wanted to convert to Judaism and settle in the Land of Israel. His burning desire was to go with the first boatload of illegal immigrants. He would show those English and those Arabs how Jews go up to their land! The young men found that his confidence was catching. When asked how he would get all the immigrants aboard ship, in view of the fact that it was illegal, he put one hand behind his back and raised the other, in accordance with Greek custom, got up from his chair and shouted. *"Me* they'll stop from loading my ship?"

Greece is dotted with numerous inlets, each inlet being a natural port with numerous anchorages, and whoever knew the sea could readily find a good anchorage. The ship might have to drop anchor a few hundred yards off shore, but small boats would be able to reach it. The organizers, realizing that their project could not suceed unless they themselves became familiar with the Greek coast and its various inlets, spent days and nights bent over maps, seeking out the best possible anchorage.

Time passed swiftly; the pioneers were to arrive in one or two days. Care had to be taken lest the history of Velos repeat itself. Three years before, hundreds of Jews arrived unexpectedly at the railroad station, and the station employees took leave of their senses. Tumult and confusion reigned, people and baggage kept colliding—and there was no one to take charge. A noisy crowd of Jews bumping into everybody around them would be noticed by Gentiles anywhere in the world, and especially in a Mediterranean seaport, with British agents about.

Danny and his friends were understandably worried. Sixty-five Jewish boys in leather jackets going on an "excursion" were likely to be suspect by secret agents—especially such pale, thin, small-town boys, whose every movement betrayed their nervousness. No one would believe that they were taking a pleasure trip or going on a sports outing.

To vex them further, an urgent cablegram arrived from Palestine telling of new difficulties and advising that everything be postponed for a while until further consultation would be possible. The members of Hehalutz in Poland rebelled. Even had they wished to obey, they would not have been able to turn back the course of events. The prospective immigrants from the training farms had long since been quietly informed of their good fortune. Each one guarded his secret zealously. One was told that he was being drafted into the army; another, that his ailing mother needed him at home; a third was given a vacation with no explanation. Everyone, of course, knew what lay behind these tactics and where it was their friends were going. Many wept for joy in private, but no one breathed a word in public. It was painful to bear in silence this promise of a new life, so long waited for. Now that the time had arrived they would have to leave for their homeland like thieves in the night, without saying a word of farewell to their closest friends.

Belongings were packed hurriedly. The parents of the young men were forbidden to accompany them to the station. The shriek of the train whistle seemed like a knife severing the past from the future.

When the sixty-five pioneers from all over Poland finally assembled, spirits were high; but the singing and dancing were short-lived. The very next day they learned that there had been a "blowout"—a term they used to cover all accidents. After having spent a torturous month of waiting with packed bags, the young people were now faced with the prospect of all becoming undone. It seemed likely that they would have to return home shamefaced. Everything

2. THEY WOULD HAVE TO LEAVE THEIR HOMELAND LIKE THIEVES IN THE NIGHT.

3. BELOW THEM IN THE PEACEFUL INLET LAY THEIR LONELY SHIP.

now depended upon the leaders, the decisions of the Hagana, and the readiness of the Yishuv, the Palestinian Jewish community. Those who had organized the undertaking were aware that a desperate situation would ensue should the departure be put off. They therefore cabled back to their Palestinian colleagues that delay was impossible.

The small band in Athens prepared for the last stages of the plan. Levi Schwartz, who was to be the immigrants' guide, accompanying the ship to Palestine, went to meet them at the station. Horilo went too, to teach them how to act like tourists.

Their arrival fell most opportunely on New Year's Eve, 1937. What with all the holiday preparations going on, everyone was fully occupied with his own affairs. The two men went to the station praying that the sea would be calm; they wanted to get their charges aboard ship without any difficulty or delay.

Fortunately, all went smoothly. The buses that were waiting outside the station filled up quickly, and when the column began to move, a tiny auto containing Danny and his friends closed up the rear. The buses stopped at a designated spot, and in a few moments fishing smacks filled with pioneers were making for the Poseidon. Danny and Levi climbed a hill to have a better look at what was happening. In the distance they saw the snow-topped Peloponnesian Mountains, and close by, mountains covered with green. Below them in the peaceful, isolated inlet lay their sorry-looking, lonely ship, swallowing one group of pioneers after another.

Now but one step remained. The owner of Poseidon had to obtain a permit from the police before the ship could sail. From atop the hill the boys saw their "black" friend confidently approach and then enter the small police station near the shore. Minutes dragged by. What was keeping him so long? The boys grew disheartened. "I'm worried," said Danny. "I don't think this is going to work out."

More time elapsed. Suddenly the door flung open and Mavros' form reappeared. However, his gait was no longer confident, but hesitant and shaky. A few minutes after he left, a policeman came running out, overtook the skipper, and returned him to the police station.

Finished! It had all come to nothing. Levi lowered his eyes. Danny felt a sharp pain in his chest, and feelings of guilt assailed him. They were right, then, when they warned us to slow up. Why didn't we calculate the risks sufficiently? What was our hurry? We've wrecked everything, ruined everything. . . .

Night fell. The boys moved their vantage point to a nearby bridge above the Corinthian Canal. Except for one lone watchman, there was no one else there. Back and forth the two men paced, their eyes following the sunset, now become a symbol of their endeavor. It grew darker. They stood on the bridge, waiting for the prearranged signal.

Finally, as the hour grew late, they decided to return to the city, gather their friends, and make a plan of action. Without looking at each other, the two walked to the road and began to thumb a ride from passing cars. Luck was with them and they arrived in Athens shortly before midnight. They sat up all night considering what to do.

It was a bitter and endless night. Danny first dozed off shortly before daybreak, but was awakened almost immediately by the sound of the doorbell. The lawyer had arrived. They got up and returned to the bay where the ship lay anchored.

The police in the meanwhile had removed the ship to another location, alongside a deserted village. Years back the village had been inhabited by miners, but when the iron-ore deposits gave out, they and the entire populace moved elsewhere. Here the ship and its precious "cargo" lay at anchor. The passengers were distraught. No one knew what lay ahead.

Then a miracle happened—one of the many miracles that took place during "Operation Aliya-Bet." Steps were taken by law officers and friends, and the injunction was lifted. It was decided that the ship should lift anchor that very evening—January 3, 1938.

Once again the young pioneers and their leaders had cause for rejoicing. But the hours dragged by very slowly. Danny, alone, paced through the ruins of the deserted village, mulling over the events of the past few days. Would he learn his lesson? Would this mark the end of their venture? As he struggled with these thoughts, he noticed a thin column rising from the galley's smokestack: dinner was being prepared. Life was going on as usual aboard the "nutshell." His mind was made up.

That night the three friends decided to spread out on three fronts. Levi would go to Warsaw and organize the next group; Danny would stay in Greece, wait for the ship to return, and prepare it for the next trip; Shimon would return to Palestine to observe the disembarkation, and to confer with their colleagues on the continuation of the operation.

Meanwhile, back in Palestine, N'meri was spending sleepless nights familiarizing himself with the country's roads, coastline, and inlets. He was trying to find both a good anchorage where the ship could lie hidden at night and a hiding place for all who were to participate in the venture.

N'meri had been taken by surprise when asked to accept this task. At the time, in an effort to work off his bitterness at the anarchic situation in Palestine, he was giving himself completely to the development of his kibbutz. Thousands of young men and women in towns and villages were appalled at the bloodshed of the 1936 disturbances and wanted to do something. However, they did not think in terms of retaliation only. "Construction and immigration" became for many a motto and a way of life promising personal fulfillment. N'meri was among the most enthusiastic adherents to this new way of life. It was no accident that he was chosen to be one of the key men in the establishment of the "Wall and Tower" settlements in the Jordan Valley, the Valley of Bet Shean, and Ein-Gev on the far side of the Sea of Galilee. N'meri was an intense and impassioned worker, and he gave the job everything he had. But a boat-load of illegal immigrants! After the Velos fiasco, past but not forgotten, it seemed absurd to him to make such an attempt. However, it upset him very much to read every morning police reports from the north of Palestine stating that "so and so many" Jews were caught in an attempt to enter Palestine via Syria, Lebanon, or Transjordan.

Each day the authorities publicized the penalties imposed upon those who attempted illegal entry and those who helped them. Many were fined and given sentences ranging from three months to a year. Some were even deported. Only recently a British judge had ruled that two Jewish women who entered Palestine from Hauran, in Arab dress, be deported. It seemed that the borders of the Jewish national homeland were open to the Bedouins of Hauran but closed to Jewish women. The chief of customs on the Syrian-Iraqi border caught three Jews hiding among sacks of Iraqi mail being taken across the desert in trucks. This was another example of the desperate measures to which Jews had to resort in order to get into Palestine.

The situation in 1934, the year of the Velos affair, was comparable. From that date on, the Yishuv waged an unceasing political struggle with the authorities on behalf of the immigration. Even prior to 1934 the police force, consisting mainly of Arabs and Englishmen, dealt harshly with any Jew suspected of being an illegal immigrant. A volunteer police force arose among the Arab youth and joined in the hunt. The Yishuv warned the Mandatory Government of the serious repercussions that would result from such actions, but the government disregarded the warning. Large sectors of the Arab population were systematically incited against the Jews, and the police encouraged this, even as they had encouraged the hunting down of immigrants. It seemed that every Jew was suspect, every Jew was fair game.

Seventeen young Jews were caught in a boat lowered from a Greek ship lying off the Palestinian coast. After ten days' confinement in the Jaffa prison, they announced that they were going on a hunger strike, and would put an end to their troubles unless a solution to their dilemma was forthcoming. They had fallen into the hands of the British without any documents and so were robbed of all protection. The police, who at first had wanted to have them tried, relented somewhat, but the lot of the prisoners was in no way improved. They had left their homes and all their possessions behind them; they had undergone an arduous danger-filled journey of forty-eight days, during which they ate no cooked food; and now that they had arrived in their national homeland, they were thrown into prison. They were closely guarded and well-isolated; no one could see them or get word to them. No wonder that they despaired and employed their one remaining weapon, a hunger strike.

This too, however, was a vain effort. On the day before the

Sukkot holiday the "criminals" were deported. Where to? No one in the Yishuv knew.

The authorities, with the imprisonment and subsequent deportation of the seventeen youths, brought charges against the captured Greek ship, the Oneon. The trial was a clear indication of the intentions of the Mandatory Government. The owner, the captain, and the three boys from Tel Aviv who had helped the immigrants were fined and given prison sentences.

During this period the British Government presented a report to the League of Nations stating that steps were being taken by the authorities, above and beyond those mentioned in earlier reports, in an effort to put a halt to the illegal immigration. Patrols had been increased along the Transjordanian border in order to stop any would-be entrants from the east and northeast. Motorized naval patrols had been set up in the ports of Jaffa and Haifa. Policemen boarded every ship arriving in Palestine to inspect the crew as well as every nook and cranny in the ship. Anyone not in possession of an immigration certificate was jailed, tried, and deported.

In February, 1935, news spread of a hunger strike declared by six Jews who had escaped the Nazi holocaust, undergone unspeakable tortures and hardships, and sought refuge in their national home. Caught in the process of immigrating, they were sentenced by the British judge to two months' confinement in Acre prison. The authorities, thinking this punishment inadequate, kept the men in prison beyond the expiration of their term until their subsequent deportation.

Another year passed. On January 2, 1936, the Palestinian Government published revisions in its immigration laws; henceforth, lawbreakers would be subject to more stringent measures. One such provision read as follows: "Anyone who aids or abets a person, knowing that said person acted contrary to this law; or having sufficient grounds to believe that said person acted contrary to this law; shall be subject to a fine not to exceed two hundred Palestinian pounds, or imprisonment not to exceed one year, or both." This new law meant that the "illegal" immigrant would now have to undergo hardship and deprivation not only on his way to the homeland, but during his stay there as well. He would be denied the right to work, stripped of all protection, and consigned to the status of an outcast. In short, he would be treated as a common criminal.

The Yishuv could no longer bear such treatment. Many were affected directly by the new enactments. Bitterness was widespread against a government that viewed unfortunate refugees and immigrants as criminals, and all who helped them as lawbreakers. The Yishuv refused to acquiesce.

The Zionist institutions submitted urgent memoranda to the British Government. The populace was enraged. To advance the cause of immigration became for many a religious duty.

The situation being what it was, N'meri cast off all reservations as to the advisability of renewing the "illegal" immigration effort, and immediately left for Tel Aviv to accept the invitation to join the venture.

He knocked on the door of room 17 in the Histadrut Executive building on Allenby Street. This was Eliahu Golomb's room, a beehive of activity day and night, buzzing with news from the various posts, and underground and defense activities. Messengers from the Hagana news service came to room 17 with all the secret information that could be obtained concerning activities among Arab bands and in the British administration. Even in this room, however, the illegal immigration effort was known to very few people.

N'meri realized that the first thing he would have to do

would be to choose the right men for the job. Since the sea was a complete mystery to him, he decided to seek advice from one of the young seamen, a rarity in the Jewish community in those days. It was only natural that he should turn to his friend, Katriel Yaffe.

Years later, when Aliya-Bet became a mass movement that employed numerous ships and conveyed thousands of immigrants across the Mediterranean, those in charge of the "illegal" immigration remembered this man and named one of their ships Katriel Yaffe. They named another ship 23 in memory of the twenty-three volunteers who, during the Second World War, when the Nazi army stood at the gates of Palestine, joined the Allied navy at the directive of the Hagana. They left Haifa on the Sea Lion on May 18, 1941, under the Middle East High Command, for the execution of an important combat mission in the Syrian campaign. They did not return. Katriel Yaffe was the head of the group.

Katriel was a bright, sensitive, and studious boy; and although he was modest and very retiring, he was always the first to volunteer for any and every new mission. He did not shake off the effects of the Velos affair easily, however. During the two months wandering on the ill-fated ship, organizers of the venture had been unable to keep their promise to support his elderly parents. As a result, he felt very guilty toward his parents and embittered toward his friends. He withdrew from further activity and kept to himself. A short while after this he joined a group of workers who were leveling the sand dunes of Tel Aviv, and became the group's unofficial leader. One day Katriel walked up to his men and said, "Let's go, fellows! To the port!" And they went, leaving behind them jobs that paid seventy piasters a day for jobs that paid only seventeen. They realized

that they were taking the first steps toward the establishment of a Hebrew port and were drunk with pride at their
pioneer task—conveying cement in small pleasure boats.
They were confident that Jaffa would one day be a thriving
port, and that its future lay in their hands.

So it was to Katriel that N'meri turned for help. He went
to the Arab courtyard on the outskirts of Tel Aviv where
Katriel lived with his parents, and after a long discussion
managed to convince him that past errors would not be
repeated. Katriel gave himself to the project wholeheartedly.
From then on he and his "boys," individually or in small
groups, would absent themselves suddenly from work, and
return after a while without a word being said.

Getting the right men for the venture presented few
difficulties, but there were other problems. The first thing
they had to do was to examine the coastline at first hand and
decide upon a debarkation point. Prior to this N'meri had
participated in a course in Kfar Vitkin for high-ranking
Hagana officers. He was very familiar with the beach there,
where he had spent many hours in day and night maneuvers.
He naturally chose to explore this area first, and preparations
got under way. He had a number of small pleasure boats
brought to the beach—their uselessness had yet to be discovered. Life preservers with ropes were prepared, and the
manifold tasks connected with getting the immigrants ashore
were apportioned among the seamen.

The date of the ship's expected arrival drew closer. In
the afternoon the young men, twenty-five in all, were informed that they had to be at the bus station at four o'clock.
From there they set out for Kfar Avihayil, a settlement of
World War I soldiers. Their first stop was "Uncle Sam's,"
the isolated house of an elderly colleague originally from
America; it served as a center of underground activity. Now

they were stopping to repair the broadcasting apparatus and get a final briefing from N'meri. They were excited and eager to begin.

While they sat in the orchard waiting for darkness to fall so that they could leave for the beach, the other parts of the plan were being carried out. At nightfall the boys boarded their boats and rowed to their appointed places. Telephone communications had been established between Kfar Avihayil and Natanya, and lookout men had been posted to observe police movements in Natanya and give warning in case any officers should head toward the watch tower. Lamp signals between ship and shore had been established long in advance. All was in readiness—but no ship came.

For days and nights on end the boys waited for the overdue ship to appear, until they almost lost hope. They feared that the "nutshell" had been wrecked in a storm. Finally, one night at nine o' clock, N'meri went up on the flat roof and saw what they had long awaited: "our ship" had arrived.

The sea was calm that night, so they signaled the ship to draw near. N'meri stood on the roof, where he could observe everything. Without aid of a telescope he made out the approaching dark hull. The activities of the various groups on shore and in the surrounding areas were carried out in complete silence and with no confusion whatever. Strict orders were given not to smoke or show any light along the shore. In the silence a churning sound could be heard: the ship, now visible at seven hundred yards, was dropping anchor. After a few minutes elapsed a dark shape pulled away from the ship and struck for shore. It was then that the first mishap occurred. The two Greek oarsmen were unfamiliar with the Palestinian coast and waters, and the boat with its ten passengers overturned. The water squad rushed to the spot, rescued the people, and brought them ashore in a matter of minutes. One man had swallowed a good deal of water and was unconscious. While the rescue was taking place, the rowers managed to right the capsized boat, bail it out, and return to the ship. A doctor and a first-aid team worked to restore the unconscious man, and it was not long before he opened his eyes, blinked, and mumbled, "Good, good, as long as I'm here in Palestine. . . ."

The immigrants were taken ashore and removed to the packing place in the Kfar Avihayil citrus grove. Sometime after midnight the seamen returned to Tel Aviv to be on their jobs in the port at six o'clock as usual. The newcomers were loaded onto a kibbutz truck which had been waiting in a corner of the citrus grove, and were sent off in the direction of kibbutz Givat Hayim. The first rays of dawn began to appear. On the road between Kfar Avihayil and Kfar Yedidya the truck hit a mud patch and bogged down. N'meri, who headed the convoy in a jeep, ordered the immigrants to get off and push. By a joint effort—their first in the home-land—they had the truck out of the mud in short order, and were safely on their way. So ended the first trip of the Poseidon. The venture had been a success.

During the remainder of the year, immigration to Palestine continued at a trickle. After Poseidon came Artemisia, a larger ship, also Greek, with a capacity of 230 tons. Again N'meri was called upon to leave his work at the kibbutz and make the necessary preparations. On the basis of his experience with Poseidon, N'meri saw the need for various improvements, particularly in communications. They had employed a one-sided system from shore to ship, and refrained from using Morse code, which probably would have been detected by the British. Their system consisted of playing recorded folk songs, such as "You have brought me to my homeland through a raging sea," "My homeland is Canaan," and the like. Each record had a special significance, such as "You may approach the shore," "The police have set up an ambush," "The sea is very rough," and so forth. The men who took part in the illegal immigration effort mention these musical communications in their memoirs in the same humorous and wistful manner in which the original settlers of Deganya, the first kibbutz, speak of their wooden shack, or of how they plowed with boards and nails fifty years ago.

One of the three men who served as guides of the Artemisia was Amiram Shohat. He perished later with the twenty-three, and an illegal ship was named after him.

By the time Amiram had reached Greece, the ship had already been hired and the contract signed by Zvi Yehieli of kibbutz Givat Hayim, a new member of the tiny group. Zvi had been delegated the job of treasurer, and his first official act had been to hire the Artemisia. Amiram's job consisted of appraising it, and examining its engines, sleeping accommodations, food-storage facilities, the condition of its tenders, and so forth. The ship lay at anchor in the sorriest-looking corner of the port of Piraeus, amid scores of filthy, dust-covered, abandoned vessels. Amiram was appalled at its appearance and condition. The immigrants who were to sail in this ship were completely inexperienced seafarers. Most likely they had never seen the sea in their lives. Amiram feared for their safety, but at the same time realized that the ship would have to do, as there was nothing else to be had.

April in the Aegean Sea is a winter month, and the tiny ship set sail in stormy waters. Waves buffeted the vessel and crashed over the deck. Many fainted. The passengers went to the lowest hold and lay down wherever they could find room. The ship sprung a leak. Shrieks resounded from below. But repairs were made and quiet returned.

After midnight the ship was forced to take refuge near one of the islands. They stayed there a full twenty-four hours. This short respite put the travelers in better spirits, even though the ship was only two hours removed from its starting point and a long journey lay ahead of them. Levi, the second guide, took advantage of the situation to call a general meeting and bolster the passengers' morale. "If you want this trip to be successful," he said, "it will be. But if you won't pitch in and do your share, it could turn out to be a nightmare. It's entirely up to you. Now we have enough food, water, and medical supplies to last us a month. You'll be in charge of it all." At his suggestion the passengers organized a "training program at sea." Committees were elected: Work, Supply, Daily Newspaper, Parties, and Sanitation. They began to function immediately. That evening the first issue of the newspaper appeared, entitled "At Sea." Morale was so high that even the sick asked that the ship proceed on its journey in spite of the storm.

And so they were on their way once more. On their third day out a party was held aboard ship. Scores of young men and women joined hands, and the dancing circles formed and reformed.

On the evening of the following day, when the ship was in the vicinity of Cyprus, they received a message telling them that arrangements on shore were all in order and that they should proceed. It was not long before the pioneers saw what they had so long waited to see—the top of Mount Carmel on the horizon.

That entire day was taken up with meticulous last-minute preparations for debarkation. The passengers were split up into groups of ten, each group having as its leader one of its members. Men were placed alongside the ladders to supervise the descent. Lifebelts were assembled in one spot in the event there might be a need for them. The boats were checked last of all. All was in readiness for a smooth debarkation. A few hours remained until nightfall, so the ship kept at a safe distance from the shore. Only after it became dark, and the prearranged signals were visible, did the ship drop anchor at a distance of 200 yards from the beach.

The first boat was to assay the situation on shore and return with the rowers. The six best swimmers from among the pioneers were equipped with lifebelts and lowered into the boat. Levi and a sailor took hold of the oars and pulled for shore. After twenty minutes the boat returned with the rowers in it, and it was full speed ahead with debarkation. The immigrants were ferried to shore, group by group, according to the prearranged schedule. After two hours the last boat returned and the crew members took their posts without delay. The anchor was lifted and the ship sailed.

1938 was a year of adversity for the Jewish people and a year of change for the Yishuv. In April, the famous "Partition Commission" published its conclusions and dealt the Yishuv a heavy blow. The unreliability of the British Government was now apparent to all. In November of the same year Hitler subjected German and Austrian Jewry to terror the like of which had never been known by the European Jewish community.

The events of November, 1938, in Germany ushered in a new era for the Yishuv and world Jewry. Every thinking Jew now knew that he could no longer be what he had been heretofore; now knew that the Jewish people had to re-examine its relationship with the rest of the world and with itself, and realize what lay ahead. The Nazi program of genocide changed the status of Zionism among world Jewry overnight. No one entertained doubts any longer: Zionism was clearly the sole hope for the Jewish people. And increasingly, immigration to Palestine came to be looked upon as the only solution.

Immediately after the November pogroms the Jewish Agency informed the Mandatory Government that the Yishuv was ready to absorb an additional 100,000 Jews immediately and unconditionally, and was prepared to absorb some hundreds of thousands more if financial aid were to be extended by the world Jewish community and the governments of the United States and Britain. It was obvious that Zionism at this point could only mean mass immigration, but it was also clear that the approval and help of the Mandatory Government would be needed. Under these circumstances, the illegal immigration effort took on a new light.

Even prior to these developments the young men in Greece had sent word that the situation there was becoming increasingly difficult. The British Government was applying pressure on the Greek Government, through its consulate in Athens, to stop the immigration to Palestine. The young men began looking for ships in the Scandinavian countries. Shimon started in Copenhagen. On the way there he stopped off at Berlin and saw how desperate the German pioneers were to get to Palestine. A similar situation existed in all other European countries.

Shimon's search took him to Copenhagen; Oslo, in Norway; and other Scandinavian ports. He learned a good deal about ships and shipping companies in the process, but he had to return to Poland with nothing to show for his efforts.

In Warsaw tensions were mounting. The members of Hehalutz began to prepare for the coming crisis. Helalutz headquarters, among other things, set up an all-girl staff in the event that the boys should be drafted.

Upon his arrival in Warsaw, Shimon found that a communication from Danny was waiting for him. It stated that there was still a chance of getting a ship and that he should come to Greece at once. The only accessible route at the time was via Germany. Shimon quickly took a train out of Warsaw and headed for Brindisi. On the way he spent a few hours in Munich, where representatives of the world's nations were gathered in conference. He walked into the city. Even though it was late at night, the entire road, stretching more than a mile to the place of the conference in "Hitlerhof" was one vast human wall. Thousands of men dressed in various Nazi uniforms jostled and shoved in the streets while hundreds of policemen stood on the street corners. "What's up?" "Is it over?" Questions were whispered on all sides. The people were anxious.

The next day, when Shimon reached the Italian border, the newspapers reported that the totalitarian states had emerged victorious from the negotiations. Among the passengers headed for Italy were crowds of Germans, most of whom were wearing Nazi emblems. They celebrated noisily and boasted of the Fuhrer's power. The man whose seat adjoined Shimon's, not thinking for a moment that this young, blue-eyed, blond-haired youth could be a Jew, addressed him as though he were one of them. "You see, my friend, our leader is very smart. He has no intention of going to war. He knows he can get what he wants by threats."

In Athens Shimon found a letter waiting for him, telling him and his companions to come to London to confer with the leaders of the Palestine labor movement, who were attending a conference of the Zionist Executive. They wished to speak with the young men of the underground about the possibilities of increasing the illegal immigration effort.

Shimon arrived in London without knowing a word of

English. It was with difficulty that he managed to 'find the
meeting place of the Zionist Executive, which had begun
its conference two days before. As soon as he entered the
auditorium Eliahu Dobkin, head of the Jewish Agency's
Immigration Department, ran over to him, took him out to
the corridor, and whispered, "Everything's all right." A sum
of money sufficient to finance the immigration of 10,000
Jews had been pledged. Jews from America had undertaken
to raise half the sum and Zionists from European countries
had pledged to raise the other half. So much would be raised
by England, so much by France, and so on—a detailed and
exact list!

Shimon listened carefully. His experience in the immigration venture had taught him to be cautious. He realized that
rejoicing at this time would be premature, for many supporters of the program had yet to be enlisted. After a few
days it became clear that even if large sums of money had
been pledged the money itself was still not in the treasury.
In the meantime the conference concluded and the delegates
began to go their separate ways, leaving no money behind
them. Shimon, desperate, turned to Berl Katznelson. The
latter set aside matters pertaining to the conference, and
listened attentively and patiently to what Shimon had to say.
At the conclusion of their talk Berl substantiated the rumor
that a group of well-to-do Jews had pledged themselves to
give seven pounds to each of the 10,000 immigrants. Berl
said that he felt it would be best to convert the sum into a
fund for the acquisition of independent means of transportation in order to avoid being exploited by self-seeking shipowners.

Shimon left Berl in an exhilarated frame of mind. He was
no longer in a hurry to leave London. Patiently and sedu-
lously he sought out every Zionist leader who was willing to

listen to him. Finally, after days of tense expectation, Berl cheerfully announced that their "friend" had two thousand pounds cash in hand. He made an appointment for Shimon to meet the man that same night.

On the following day Berl placed two thousand pounds in banknotes in Shimon's hands. The latter had never in his life held such a vast sum of money. Berl was apprehensive, as he always was when handling public funds.

"You won't lose the money, now?" he asked.

Shinon smiled and pointed to the special pouch he had sown in his belt, as was customary then among the men of Aliya-Bet.

After a few days the third ship, Atrato, set sail from Bari with 300 passengers aboard.

3

Face to Face with Eichman and the Gestapo

In the beginning of 1939 Saul Avigur joined the operation. Saul was a member of kibbutz Kinneret and had been among the defenders of Tel Hai in 1920. He was a veteran of the Velos affair and had participated in its "steering committee." Since 1933 he had been the coordinator of the Hagana, and in this capacity had been close to "Operation Aliya-Bet" from the start. During his trips abroad for the purpose of purchasing arms for the Hagana, he met with the young men occasionally and offered them advice. From 1939 on, however, he was the mainstay of the expanding operation.

The fact that he, the head of the Hagana, had taken on the task of coordinating the operation showed more than anything else the shift in attitude that had taken place in Palestine. The operation was now accepted and recognized by the more daring elements in the labor movement and the Zionist Organization. Saul was experienced in underground work and was held in high esteem for his selfless service to the movement. The young men felt that his participation in the operation presaged greater efficiency, a wider scope of activity, and a change in status for themselves.

47

Accordingly they took on a new title: "The Immigration Bureau" ("Mossad").

For a short while the main branches of the Bureau were located in Paris and London, where the Zionist Organization and the Jewish Agency had offices. Every evening at ten, Saul in London would call Shimon in Paris and the two would talk over the day's events and make plans for the following day.

In the meanwhile, relations between the Jewish Agency and the Mandatory Government had become strained. The motto of "non-cooperation" led the British to view with suspicion everyone and everything connected with the departments of the Jewish Agency. Consequently, after a short interim period, Saul moved to Paris and took up residence in a small room in an inexpensive hotel. This room served as the headquarters of the immigration underground, whose scope of activities was to branch out to all corners of the globe.

Two months prior to this, the Bureau had been enlarged by the addition of two emissaries from the Histadrut and the kibbutz movement. They were Pino Ginzburg, Hehalutz emissary in Germany who later became a member of kibbutz Ramat Hakovesh; and the Hehalutz emissary in Austria, Moshe Auerbach (Agami), who came from kibbutz Kfar Giladi. The latter had arrived in Vienna back in October of 1938, after months of effort on his part to get a visa to Nazi Austria.

The Jewish youth of Europe felt that their world was being destroyed, and they were unsure of what lay ahead. Their common predicament led them to band together about the office of the Hehalutz central committee, whose active members then included young Ehud Uberal.

All the various Zionist organizations of Vienna were still

in existence in October of 1938, and the Palestine Office held a prominent position among them. Hehalutz, sponsored by the Office, embraced all types of Jewish youth movements. The shaken Jewish populace had latched onto the new Nazi motto: *Umschulung*—transition to a productive occupation. The Nazi Government seemed interested in the lot of younger Jews and proclaimed its intention to include them along with the general population in the new programs. Three days after his arrival in Vienna the emissary from Palestine was presented to Adolf Eichmann, who then headed the Jewish Division of the SS. Eichmann had studied Judaism and Zionism somewhat, and had even circulated a false rumor to the effect that he had been born near Tel Aviv, in the German colony of Sarona. In preparation for his role he had learned a little Yiddish and picked up some common Hebrew words, had read Herzl's diaries and the records of the Zionist congresses, and had visited Palestine. He was considered by the Nazis an expert on Jews and Judaism.

The purpose of the meeting was to coordinate the training program of Hehalutz with the *Umschulung*. Eichmann greeted Agami very formally in a long bleak room in the palace on Prinz Eugen Street that once belonged to Leopold Rothschild. The emissary, coached for this unusual meeting by the Palestine Office, stopped a few yards in front of the desk and made the required military salute. The thirty-year-old Eichmann stared at him intently.

"Advance!"

The emissary took a few more steps and stopped. Again Eichmann commanded:

"Advance!"

"I am a Jew," said the emissary coldly. This bold behavior on his part was typical of him in his dealings with Nazi

officials in Vienna, and soon earned him the the title of
"der wilde Mensch von der Syrischen Grenze"—"the wild
man from the Syrian border."

The Nazi jumped up from his seat, pointed to the chair
opposite him, and said peremptorily:

"Sit down!"

He deluged Agami with questions immediately. Where
had he come from? How much time had he spent in
Palestine? Where had he been born? Who had sent him, and
why? He listened attentively to the answers.

"Hehalutz wants to teach agricultural and industrial skills
to Jewish youth," explained the emissary, "so as to bring
them to Palestine ready to work and build the land."

"So, so . . ." murmured Eichmann. "Well, good. Come
back here in three days with a plan of action."

The pioneer training farm in Austria embraced one
hundred pioneers in all, but the program that Agami brought
to Eichmann included agricultural training for one thousand
people.

"We have the people," he said. "You give us the land for
the farms and we'll do the rest."

At this meeting Eichmann designated a Nazi as a liaison
man and instructed him to keep in touch with the emissary
on all that pertained to the Hehalutz training program.

There was a threatening note in Eichmann's voice as the
meeting concluded:

"Agami, you are taking part in the *Umschulung* only.
Nothing else!"

The emissary knew very well what was meant by that.

The higher echelons of the Nazi Government had not yet
reached a final decision as to the fate of Germany's Jews.
Hitler was strongly in favor of getting them out of the
Reich as quickly as possible and by any means available.

Others in governmental circles were for mass annihilation. While Eichmann had leanings toward both viewpoints, he had a third position, his own. He believed that Germany's Jewish capital and labor should be exploited to the full; hence his *Umschulung* program, which seemed tailor-made to fit the needs of the Jewish pioneers. He was only too happy to allow the emissary from Palestine to go ahead with his training program, which he saw as a furtherance of his own ends.

The same reasoning led the Gestapo to allow Pino Ginzburg to stay in Berlin just a short while previously. With head held high and body erect, Pino had appeared before the Gestapo and compelled them to treat him with respect. He introduced himself as an emissary from Palestine and made no attempt to camouflage his aims. He implanted hope in Germany's Jewish population. He re-established the Zionist Organization at its old quarters at 10 Meinecke Street. (The Organization had disbanded after the imprisonment of its leaders). He also expanded the scope of the training-farm program and began to organize convoys of immigrants.

Similar developments were taking place in Austria. In a very short time Agami came to realize that emigration to Palestine was the only means of saving Austria's Jews. The question was, how to go about it. He knew that there were some movement members in Poland engaged in the illegal immigration effort and that they included Danny, Shimon, Levi, and Zvi. He remembered Danny from the period when they had served as treasurers of their neighboring kibbutzim, Ayelet Hashahar and Kfar Giladi. But how could he contact him? He got in touch with Eliahu Golomb at Hagana headquarters in Palestine and requested that the latter come to Vienna. Eliahu immediately agreed to include Vienna in the program. However, weeks passed before he got there and the emissary, fearful of what he saw happening nearby, began looking for other means of transporting Jews to Palestine.

The plight of European Jewry grew worse and worse. The evening of November 9, 1938, marked the outbreak of pogroms against the Jews of Germany. These pogroms were purportedly in retaliation for the murder of the Nazi von Rath in Paris by Zvi Greenshpan, a Jewish student. In Vienna, 20,000 Jews were arrested in one night, and about as many were arrested in Berlin. Heydrich, who was in charge of the Security Division of the SS, carried out this mass arrest. In a report prepared afterwards he took pride in the burning of 191 synagogues and 171 Jewish-owned homes, the plundering of 7,500 Jewish business establishments, and the killing of scores of Jews. The Jewish communities were fined approximately one billion marks, and new laws were published excluding Jews from all professions, limiting their freedom of movement, and compelling them to wear a yellow badge. After a few days all Jewish children were expelled from the schools, and Jews were forbidden to enter public parks and places of amusement.

Any Jew who could prove that he was about to emigrate was exempt from service in the forced-labor teams, recruited from Jews caught in the streets. Eichmann appointed Storper, the economic counsel, to organize the emigration of Jews from Austria. Many different kinds of emigration concerns sprung up, sponsored by the Revisionist Party, various organizations and private businessmen. These concerns would have had nothing to do with Hehalutz, whose funds were low, were it not for the fact that the pioneer organization had acquired a name for itself through its debarkation procedures in Palestine.

In the meanwhile Agami learned that the Gestapo had a

4. The Evening of November 9, 1938 marked the outbreak of pogroms against the Jews of Germany.

Jewish Division paralleling that of the SS, and he began trying to establish contacts with it. Through the good services of a Jewish woman in Austrian high society he met the Nazi official Matossiani, who was probably Italian or Greek; he had lived a long time in Vienna and was married to a Jewish woman. He was tall, dark-eyed, and handsome, and wore a distinctive, broad-brimmed artist's hat. At a time when civilized society was sinking in a flood of anarchy, he amassed a fortune through shady dealings and floated to the top. Because he wasted large sums of money, the gates of Vienna's high society were opened to him—and the gates of the Gestapo as well.

When Eliahu Golomb arrived in Vienna he saw that the emissary's fears were well-founded, and he agreed that emigration should be arranged for in any way possible. He went to Poland and assured the emissaries there of the participation of Vienna's pioneers in "Operation Aliya-Bet." The young men of the Bureau had decided that the pioneers of Germany and Austria would have to be tended to first. They chose Vienna as their headquarters since the Nazi officials responsible for ridding Austria of its Jews were to be found in that city. At first the idea of working with the Gestapo appalled the young men. As responsible movement members they did not feel qualified to make such a decision on their own. Moral reservations aside, it was difficult to determine what the Gestapo was really after. They conferred a great deal with Bureau members in London and Palestine. Saul returned to Palestine for final talks, and even though discussions in Vienna had begun in May, 1939, a decision was not reached until July of that year. Eliahu returned to Vienna with an affirmative answer. He had convinced David Ben-Gurion that the illegal immigration effort should be expanded as much as possible, since more than the interests of Hehalutz were involved. During this same period Eliahu negotiated with the "Joint" (the American Joint Distribution Committee), regarding funds for the underground. The "Joint" people finally agreed, despite their reservations and the risks involved.

The principal problem now remaining was that of land transit to a port. Agami contacted an engineer, Karthaus, who, although he had joined the Nazi Party and wore its uniform, was an exceptionally humane person. Karthaus worked for the Yugoslavian Government on the construction of highways. At a cost of twenty marks per person he obtained 20,000 visas that allowed their holders to pass through Yugoslavia. This feat was all the more incredible when it is realized that Yugoslavian transit visas were as hard to come by as gold at that time.

The Bureau decided that Shimon should go to Vienna to improve communications and coordinate activities there. Agami, through his connections, managed to get Shimon an entry permit to Vienna within three days' time. The young Halutzim were goggle-eyed at these secret goings on. To them, the emissaries from "the Land" seemed more than human. Tales spread of Levi Schwartz swimming alongside the boats, skipping across the waves, splitting the waters.

At the railroad station Shimon was met by Agami and Herr Matossiani. In the course of a long night's discussion Agami explained that the SS had established a "Department of Jewish Emigration" for the purpose of "purifying Vienna," and that the department was headed by Eichmann, who, wishing to make the best possible impression on his superiors, helped the Revisionist convoy organizers and the burgeoning private companies. Most of these companies had already gone out of business, having failed in the attempt to extort exorbitant sums from the emigrants. Some of them were apprehended for embezzlement, to the discredit of the Jewish people. A member of the board of directors of one such company had been jailed. Agami also told Shimon that Gestapo departments were doing their best to facilitate Jewish emigration. Certain Gestapo members showed a special interest in this endeavor, in hopes of impressing their superiors favorably and making a modest profit in the bargain. The head of the Gestapo's Jewish Department ordered the Prussian engineer who represented the Nazi party in Vienna to organize Jewish emigration with his unofficial consent. Matossiani was the Prussian's right-hand man.

The sign above the café entrance read "No Jews Allowed," and inside two young Jews sat with Gestapo agents discussing plans for Jewish emigration to Palestine. A Gestapo car waited outside the café to take them to other meetings that had to do with the project. Agami showed Shimon the correspondence between Berkel, the Reichskommissar (Governor) in Vienna, and the Yugoslavian consulate, wherein permission was explicitly granted for Jews to pass through Yugoslavia. The letters dealt with a treaty between the two countries whereby 20,000 Jews with visas to a South American country could pass through Yugoslavia on their way from Vienna. Transit would be granted under the condition that a seaworthy vessel would be ready and waiting at the port of embarkation before the convoy's arrival.

One point of contention between the young men and the Gestapo agents was the inclusion in the project of pioneers from Germany—the *Alt-Reich*. The Nazis were concerned with ridding Vienna of Jews and saw no reason why other areas should be included in the program. However, the two emissaries were so adamant on this point that the Gestapo agents had to capitulate. It was finally settled that approximately 4,000 pioneers from Germany be included in the program.

During these negotiations the young men never forgot for a moment how costly the price of failure would be. Thousands of lives lay in their hands. They found it difficult to sleep. They were worried over every link in the complex chain of preparations for the convoys of immigrants. To what extent could they trust the Nazi regime?

Their main concern, of course, was for the ship. Prior to this a long and arduous search had resulted in the acquisition of another, larger ship. Zvi had wandered about the bays of Athens and the port of Piraeus for weeks before he finally came to an agreement with the owner of the Colorado, a slow, undistinguished vessel with a defective propeller, suitable only for trips along the shore. It was agreed that the Colorado would pick up the passengers in the ports that it could enter and transfer them at sea to the lighter, more navigable Atrato, which would convey them to Palestine. Zvi informed his friends that the ship had been repaired and was ready to leave Piraeus for the port of Susa in Yugoslavia. Prior to his departure for Vienna, Shimon in London met Captain Demitri, who had come there to obtain legally a Panamanian flag for the Colorado. The embarkation date was set and last arrangements were underway in Vienna.

These were days and nights of feverish activity in Hehalutz headquarters in Nazi Austria. Agami's face was drawn. When all was said and done, the project was officially unauthorized. He had no documents or credentials. Once he asked the Nazis with whom he was negotiating what he should do if asked whom he was working for. Karthaus answered, "Say that Dr. Lange, the head of the Jewish Department of the Gestapo, knows of your activity. Here's his room number and telephone number." But they had never met with Dr. Lange and were not sure that Karthaus was telling the truth.

Very apprehensive, the young men began to assemble the pioneers from Germany, hire trains to convey them from the *Alt-Reich* to Vienna, and gather the pioneers of Vienna into one place. To house all these people in Nazi Vienna until their embarkation seemed an impossible task, but the young men managed to do it.

Twenty-four hours before the convoy was to set out in a specially chartered train, 280 men from the *Alt-Reich* arrived. This was the first group organized by Pino in Berlin. They had left accompanied by a Nazi, their destination ostensibly a pioneer training farm in Yugoslavia. Shimon, Agami, and the rest of the members of Hehalutz headquarters in Vienna went to meet them at dawn at the railroad station, accompanied by a Nazi sent to "assist" them. They arrived in time to see the young men and women get off the cars and line up in complete silence. Without a word being said, a multitude of knapsacks, bundles, and suitcases were passed out and placed at their feet along the length of the platform. One word, and they formed a double column behind the Nazi, who proceeded to lead them to a distant hostel. For two hours they walked in silence, carrying their luggage. The emissaries carried the baggage of the weaker ones and helped support them when necessary. The procession moved along slowly in funereal silence.

In the meanwhile the pioneers of Vienna were packed into the building that housed Hehalutz headquarters. Since they were directly opposite Gestapo headquarters, every movement demanded added precaution. When night came, bodies and baggage covered every inch of the floor. No lights were lit so as not to draw attention from the outside. The pioneers lay half awake and half asleep, bitter at not having been able to say farewell to parents and friends, who would most likely be swept away in the coming holocaust.

The emissaries and their staff stayed up all night in the narrow room at the end of the building, making last-minute preparations.

The next morning the train left. Agami and Pino accompanied the group to the border. Prior to this, Karthaus had left for the port of Susak and there met Captain Demitri, who was to take charge of the ship as soon as it should arrive in the port. It seemed that everything had been taken care of and that all would work out as scheduled.

Such was not to be the case, however.

Shimon sat by the telephone in Hehalutz headquarters in Vienna anxiously waiting to receive news from the border. Suddenly a staff member rushed in out of breath and began stammering excitedly: it seemed that the group had been stopped at the border and were not being allowed to cross to Yugoslavia. As he was speaking the telephone rang. It was Agami, calling from the border to substantiate the rumor. He told them that they had left Germany, but were being denied entry to Yugoslavia. The Yugoslavian Government insisted that the agreement be carried out to the letter. According to the agreement the emigrants were to enter Yugoslavia only after the arrival of the ship, and the ship, in spite of all the careful planning, was late.

Pandemonium broke loose. Matossiani was contacted and he rushed to the border. Telephone calls shot back and forth between the border, Vienna, and the port of Susak. Shimon, helpless, was beside himself with anger.

According to the law, Shimon had to appear that day in the offices of the Gestapo, like everyone else who had a temporary permit to stay in the city. Reluctantly he handed the telephone receiver to someone else and, accompanied by an employee of the Palestine Office, crossed the street and entered the Gestapo building. After they had completed the formalities of signing various papers and appearing before a series of guards and gatekeepers, they were taken to one of the upper stories and were left in a long hallway that had no chairs or benches in it. An hour elapsed before they were ushered into the room of one of the Assistant Directors of the Gestapo's Jewish Department. The man from the Palestine Office made the prescribed bow and quietly stated that he had brought with him Mr. So-and-so who was required to be here, and whose guarantor he was. Without raising his eyes from the papers on his desk the Assistant Director barked out Shimon's name and began asking him why he had come to Vienna, what he was doing here, and the like. In reality he knew very well why Shimon had come and what he was doing; he and his office had signed the emissary's entry permit. It seemed that this was to be a routine degradation of a Jew, not an uncommon practice at the time. Shimon did his best to answer politely: he had come to Vienna in order to acquaint himself with the situation of the Hehalutz members on the training farms, and in order to supervise the farm work. That was why he had been granted official permission to enter the country.

The Gestapo officer began to be abusive. What did he know about agriculture? Had he ever been a farmer? Was there such a thing as a Jewish farmer?

While Shimon's mind was wandering to the border and what was going on there, his body was roasting. He had to stand at attention in front of the Nazi's desk in his heavy winter coat, and he was drenched with sweat. Tired from standing so long, he put his thumbs in his pockets, but instantly the Nazi barked, "Get your hands out of your pockets!"

After he was finally released he rushed back to Hehalutz headquarters to his seat by the telephone, but good news from the border was not forthcoming. Captain Demitri's ownership papers were in perfect order, but the boat itself had not yet arrived.

In the meanwhile, the situation had grown worse. The crew of the chartered train had put in a call from the German border to the central depot in Vienna, and were instructed to give the passengers until no later than four in the afternoon, at which time they were to bring the cars back to Vienna, where they were needed. All attempts to circumvent this new obstacle had proved futile. Agami and Pino, who were at the border, reported that the situation was desperate. Failure now would mean not only that all their preparations for this convoy would come to nothing, but also that the Gestapo would most likely lose confidence in them, and see to it that the program would be completely abandoned. Once again the emissaries pleaded that the deadline be put back at least a few hours—but in vain.

At the last minute the situation was saved. At 6 p.m. the Colorado leisurely sailed into the port of Susak. However, the Yugoslavian officials on the border were not yet satisfied. They wanted signed papers from the port's police force stating that nothing was wrong with the ship and that the convoy could board it immediately. The port authorities chose this occasion to inspect the ship with more than usual thoroughness. Their intent was evident. There was nothing to do but to give them a substantial "gift." Finally word came from the border that everything was all right. This was at 7:30. At 7:29 the locomotive had been hitched to the rear of the train and was ready to leave for Vienna. The locomotive was unhitched, returned to its original place, and the train moved into the port of Susak.

The ship sailed. Pino and Agami, along with Matossiani and the four Gestapo agents who had accompanied the convoy, returned to Vienna at a late hour. The young men passed the night discussing what their next step should be. In the morning Pino and Shimon left for Berlin to contact the Jewish organizations there and enlist their aid in raising funds for the rapidly expanding operation. Agami remained at his post in Vienna. However, the Colorado incident was not yet over. Two days after the ship had sailed Agami was horrified to see the following headline spread across the top of the front page of the morning paper: "Secret Operation of Convoy of Jewish Immigrants." Following the headline came the story. On such and such a date 400 Jews left the port of Susak aboard the ship Colorado, headed for Mexico under a Panamanian flag. Two days later the ship returned to Susak with no passengers aboard. Yugoslavian authorities are investigating. . . .

As Agami was pondering this new development, a Nazi policeman appeared in his room to summon him to appear at one o'clock that afternoon in the Gestapo offices. This was not the first time he had received an invitation to Gestapo headquarters. He had connections in a few departments, and on more than one occasion had intervened in such matters as the imprisonment of pioneers, and had managed to obtain their release. However, this summons was of an entirely different nature. It had been delivered to him by a policeman, not by Matossiani, and its wording was harsh. He managed to contact Matossiani about noontime, but the latter knew nothing and could only try to reassure the emissary by saying, "Don't worry, everything will be all right. . . ."

Agami entered the building with apprehension. After he filled out some forms and signed what had to be signed, he was led by an officer into a completely empty, high-ceilinged room in an upper story of the building.

"Wait here," the officer said.

One hour passed, two hours—three—four—five—and still there was no sign of life. He approached the door and found that it was open. As he started to go out into the hallway he was immediately rebuked by the guard:

"You must wait in the room!"

After six hours had gone by and he had used up his one pack of cigarettes, he thought he heard a sound on the other side of the door. A small crack appeared. He could not see anyone, but he heard a voice say softly:

"Be quiet."

Was this his friend Matossiani looking out for him, or someone playing a vicious game of harassment?

As he tried to understand what this meant, the door closed. He wondered whether his imagination had misled him.

Not until eight o'clock, when his senses were dulled with exhaustion, hunger, and thirst, and his knees were weak, did an officer appear and say:

"Follow me!"

He was ushered into a large attractive room that was flooded with light and had easy chairs in it. Dr. Lange, seated behind a large desk, invited him to have a seat, offered him a cigarette, and asked if he would like to drink anything. Agami decided not to show the least sign of weakness and declined the proffered cigarette and drink, Once again he was subjected to a gruelling interview. Where had he been born, who were his parents, what schools had he attended, when had he gone to Palestine—there seemed to be no end to the questions. Finally he brought up Agami's connection with Eichmann and the convoy of immigrants. Casually he remarked:

"By the way, the transport to Palestine was a brilliant success . . ."

Agami mustered his will power and said quietly:

"Excuse me, the trip was to Mexico."

"Oh, yes," drawled Lange sarcastically, "to Mexico. . . . A ship leaves for Mexico Tuesday and comes back to Susak Thursday with no passengers . . ."

The interrogation recommenced. Until midnight the Gestapo chief drilled the emissary, but Agami was adamant: to Mexico! Finally the interrogator himself grew tired. He got up from his chair and said:

"Very well, it doesn't matter where they went. Let's assume it was Mexico. But the Yugoslavians have been frightened by British pressure, so I don't know what the outcome will be. In the meantime you must sign this." So saying, he handed him a typewritten sheet which read: "A citizen of Palestine, engaged in organizing the emigration of Jews to the Western Hemisphere, affirms that the above-mentioned transport is destined for Mexico."

When Agami returned after midnight to Hehalutz headquarters, his friends greeted him as though he had returned from the dead. The emissary had learned an important lesson that day. He now knew of the conflict that existed between the Gestapo and Eichmann, and he felt that he could exploit the situation to the advantage of Aliya-Bet.

At once he began to examine the possibilities of organizing a second convoy. It was a period of great confusion, and he had a hard time deciding precisely how he should go about it. Speculators and agents, scenting Jewish money, swept down on him like hawks on their prey. There was no longer any need for clandestine meetings with the Greek shipowners in the alleys of Athens. Now he could bargain with them publicly in the finest hotels in Vienna. It was evident that government officials who stood behind the project had reached an agreement with the shipowners whereby they, the officials, received a set percentage of the fee. Because of this, each official would recommend "his" shipowner to the Jewish organizations and agencies in Vienna and Berlin. As a result, Jewish institutions were being subjected to heavy pressures to speed up the emigration effort; but at the same time they were no longer able to examine the conditions of the transport agreement, the condition of the ship, and the reliability of the owners and the captain.

The leaders of the Jewish organizations in Germany, living in the shadow of the swastika, did not dare raise objections, but accepted whatever was offered them. Not so the young men from the Bureau. Once, in Berlin, when Pino was threatened with imprisonment by a shipowner unless he accepted the latter's conditions, the emissary answered heatedly:

"You can't talk to us like that! We're Jews from the Land of Israel!"

In their negotiations with the shipowners, the young men of the Bureau were resolute on the question of securing adequate breathing space for the passengers and room for them to lie down in. Their difficulties were multiplied by the fact that most of the frenetic agents, who were under the tutelage of Nazi officials, had not even seen the ships they were selling. Moreover, many of them hadn't the slightest concept of the ship trade, but were attracted to this sure-profit business, which had become a feverish exchange of sorts. Some intermediaries had dealings with many companies at the same time. On more than one occasion the young men arranged to meet with such an intermediary at night, only to find upon their arrival that he was not there, as he had already been advanced a substantial sum from other quarters.

In the meanwhile things had taken a change for the better. The shipowners had at last reversed themselves and agreed to be paid in German money or in German goods destined for Greece. This meant that large convoys would now be able to leave directly from Germany. Pino began to look into the possibilities of partially financing the operation with *"Sperrmarks,"* the vast sums of Jewish money that had been confiscated and frozen by the Nazi Government. He worked on this project hand in glove with Dr. Paul Epstein, one of the leaders of the Jewish community in Berlin, who was later made a *Judeneltester* (Jew-elder) in the camp of Theresien-stadt and was shot in another concentration camp. In those days there was no dearth of money among German Jews, who wanted to save some of their wealth. The emigration effort became an activity of the whole Jewish community of Vienna. Dr. Lebenherz, who headed the endeavor, was directly responsible to Eichmann for everything that he did. At Eichmann's directive he appointed as his representative the Jewish *Kommerzialrat* (economic adviser) Storper, who from then on played a central role in the Jewish emigration. At the outset of his new work, Storper saw that Hehalutz and the band of emissaries from Palestine would fit in with the project admirably, more so than any other group. He therefore did his best to bring them into the newly created council of all parties interested in organizing Jewish emigra-tion to Palestine. The young men, however, were wary of becoming involved with groups that had a record of embezzlement, extortion, and exploiting Jewish misfortune to their own advantage. They wished to work alone and retain their integrity, and continued to insist that they be given a voice in the management of funds and the choosing of candidates for emigration. Eichmann appointed another man to serve as a liaison between the Gestapo and the Bureau, the Nazi von Hepfner, whom the young men labeled "Ha-Von," the Von. He represented that faction of the Nazi leadership that favored Jewish emigration; for concealment's sake he was using a travel agency as a front. "Ha-Von" too wanted the emissaries from the Bureau to take part in the council.

The collaboration came off badly, but the venture was not a total loss, as far as the young men were concerned. They managed to get a contract for a new ship, with half the price payable in German currency. Shimon and Pino left Vienna for Berlin on the day after the Colorado sailed, to raise the required funds. The Jews of Berlin were still asleep, however. Unlike the Jewish population of Vienna, they were not under pressure to emigrate. Even after the events of November, 1938, they refused to deviate from their normal practices, refusing to recognize that their destruction was imminent. They saw no need for a rescue effort and would not contribute to it. After wearisome negotiations the young men asked that at least 2,000 pounds be set aside toward the organization of a second convoy from Germany, since the Jews of Berlin had contributed nothing to the first convoy. The Jewish organizations promised to comply, but only after the second convoy should be a reality.

The young men returned from Berlin deeply disappointed. They were somewhat solaced to learn that the first convoy had arrived safely in Palestine.

In the meantime, final preparations had been made for a convoy from Czechoslovakia. Zvi had traveled the length and breadth of Poland in the winter of 1938 making the

5. Hitler's army invaded Czechoslovakia that very night leaving the groups stranded at the station.

necessary preparations. The prospective emigrants were gathered together in a central place. They themselves had provided the requisite sum by paying twenty-five pounds apiece. An incredible amount of work went into obtaining right of transit through Yugoslavia. A helping factor was the agreement that had originated in Vienna, concerning the 20,000 emigrants who crossed the border at that time. In February, 1939, Zvi left Paris for Prague, whose skies were already overcast with the approaching Nazi invasion. Upon his arrival in Prague, he immediately contacted Yaakov Edelstein of the Palestine Office, another who was later executed at Theresienstadt. Edelstein, who sensed the approaching cataclysm, was enthusiastic about the idea. Their work bore fruit. On March 14, the groups that were to make up the convoy assembled at the designated railroad stations, ready to leave for the coast. However, Hitler's army invaded Czechoslovakia that very night, leaving the groups stranded at the stations. They were picked us as quickly as possible and put into two buildings—hundreds of Jewish boys and girls, whose very pressence might rouse suspicions and result in their being sent to a concentration camp. In addition, Hitler's entry into Czechoslovakia had invalidated their passports, and it would be necessary to obtain an exit permit from the Gestapo. New arrangements were also made for transfer of Czech money to London, where payments for the journey were made. However, the pressure exerted by the pioneers of Czechoslovakia grew so strong that they could no longer be restrained. After some negotiation, their Czech passports were stamped with the seal of the "protectorate" (Bohemia-Moravia) and the letter "J" *(Jude)*. Finally the 400 emigrants boarded the chartered train and were on their way.

A mishap occurred when the train arrived at the Komarno

station on the Hungarian-Yugoslavian border. The Yugoslavian authorities refused to grant them right of transit, in
spite of the fact that the immigrants had Yugoslavian visas;
they maintained that the visas had been issued to different
passports. This was the night of the first Seder, Passover.
In Zvi's room in Susak, in the hotel of a refugee from
Galicia, sat Zvi; Levi Schwartz, the guide; and the sailor, S.
Tenkus. They were stunned. The situation was all the worse
in that the pioneers had already left Czechoslovakia and
were on Hungarian soil. Zvi contacted the Bureau in Vienna.
The "engineer" (Karthaus) rushed off to the Yugoslavian
border with a letter from the Gestapo addressed to the prime
minister, Zvetkovitz, a German collaborator. Zvi set to
work through his contacts in the royal court. The king being
on vacation, his messengers turned to the queen. The young
men's principal fear was that the emigrants would be sent
directly to a concentration camp should they be returned to
Germany. To compound their difficulties, Zvi was unable to
speak with his colleagues in Paris, because telephone connections at the small border station were faulty. Danny sped to
Italy in order to be closer to Zvi and serve as a link between
the latter and Paris. Danny went from Trieste to Venice to
Fiume—cities near Susak. Due to growing political tensions
he could not stop and rest in any hotel, for the police kept
close watch on all strangers in border towns.

Immediately the organizations representing the Jewish
communities set to work, under the leadership of Rabbi
Alkalai and Spitzer, who had helped them devotedly ever
since they began their efforts to get the first ship, the Velos,
under way. The Jewish community of Belgrade sent a rail-
way dining car by means of the Jewish community of
Subotica, a town near the border. They also sent matzot and
wine for the holiday. Hungarian authorities behaved in a

humane manner. Every day a special locomotive brought the essential food rations to the pioneers, whose predicament grew worse and worse. Necessities were purchased in Yugoslavia, where they were cheaper, and brought into Hungary tax-free. In this manner several days passed. Meanwhile the Orthodox Slav Easter had arrived. The premier had left with his family to spend the holiday in Nish in southern Yugoslavia. Spitzer contacted a lawyer he knew; and Zvi, the lawyer, and the head of the Jewish community left for Nish that evening. They arrived in the town just as the church bells ushered in the Easter holiday. Through the lawyer, Zvi met the premier's daughters and managed to convince them of the gravity of the situation. They then won their mother to their side, and brought the matter to their father's attention the following morning. The premier, in a relaxed holiday mood and far removed from official Belgrade, gave a note to the lawyer to give to the Minister of the Interior. At once the three set off in their automobile to cover the hundreds of kilometers that lay between them and Belgrade.

When at last a telephone connection was established with the convoy in Czechoslovakia, and the good news was conveyed, the emissaries learned that something had gone wrong with the train's electrical system and it could not move. The torturous hours of repair were wasted ones however—it became evident that nothing had been wrong in the first place. The trainmen simply did not know how to start the train.

The convoy arrived, the ships were boarded, all the papers were at hand—and the emissaries, half out of their wits, were scouring Trieste for Captain Demitri. He had taken a holiday stroll with two attractive girls, but no one knew where. The Histadrut's emissary, Arye Shilo, who had taken part in the Prague venture and had served as a liaison man with the Yugoslavian port authorities, went looking in all the bars in the area and finally found him, dead drunk. The guides had to run the ship by themselves.

It was not long before the emissaries and Storper were at odds over the choosing of candidates for the convoys in Vienna. Storper had opened his own travel bureau and had begun organizing convoys as he saw fit. Agami became *persona non grata* as far as Eichmann was concerned. He soon received a curt note ordering him to leave Vienna within twenty-four hours. When the emissary failed to reply, he received a second blunt note, which read: "If you do not leave at once of your own free will, I will see to it that you leave against your will." So ended the emigration effort in Vienna. Agami left for Switzerland to see what could be accomplished in that country.

All the emissaries had felt for a long time the need to meet and discuss means of expanding the operation. They realized that the little they had accomplished was almost inconsequential when compared with the vast numbers of Jews desperately seeking to be rescued. The meeting was held in London in Saul's room. They all agreed that they should send more and larger convoys, but the problem was one of means. While many in the Zionist Organization realized that the illegal-immigration effort was a necessity, the financial burden still rested fully upon the shoulders of the young men of the Bureau.

An additional important decision taken at this meeting was to try to operate in an additional country, Rumania, in spite of the dangers involved. Y. Barpal (Kadmon), who had just traveled through Rumania and laid the necessary groundwork, was put in charge of this effort. After a while he was joined by Levi Schwartz.

6. Face to face with Eichmann.

4

After the White Paper

May, 1939, marked a turning point in the relationship
between the world Zionist movement and the Mandatory
Government. It saw the publication of MacDonald's "White
Paper," a proclamation of the Mandatory Government concerning its policies in Palestine. The document stirred up a
furor, the more intense in that it followed upon the tragedy
of European Jewry, three years of violence in Palestine, and
months of wearisome negotiations in London.

In cold, unequivocal language the White Paper established
the reduced immigration quota for the near future:

> Jewish immigration during the next five years will be at a
> rate which, if economic absorptive capacity permits, will bring
> the Jewish population up to approximately one-third of the
> total population of the country. Taking into account the
> expected natural increase of the Arab and Jewish populations,
> and the number of illegal Jewish immigrants now in the
> country, this would allow of the admission, as from the begin-
> ning of April this year, of some 75,000 immigrants over the
> next five years. These immigrants would, subject to the
> criterion of economic absorptive capacity, be admitted as
> follows:
>
> (a) For each of the next five years a quota of 10,000 Jewish
>   immigrants will be allowed on the understanding that a
>   shortage in any one year may be added to the quotas for
>   the subsequent years within the five-year period, if
>   economic absorptive capacity permits.

> (b) In addition, as a contribution toward the solution of the Jewish refugee problem, 25,000 refugees will be admitted as soon as the High Commissioner is satisfied that adequate provision for their maintenance is assured . . .

"Economic absorptive capacity"—there was the two-edged sword. The violent period of 1936 to 1939 had seriously undermined the country's economy. The most productive elements in the Yishuv had been diverted to the defense effort, and the new wave of immigration had not yet struck roots. The destruction of European Jewry was a shattering blow to the Jews of Palestine, who were parties to the struggle. The White Paper bluntly declared that:

> The existing machinery for ascertaining economic absorptive capacity will be retained, and the High Commissioner will have the ultimate responsibility for deciding the limits of economic capacity.

The crucial section of the document was of a political rather than of an economic nature:

> His Majesty's Government are satisfied that, when the immigration over five years which is now contemplated has taken place, they will not be justified in facilitating, nor will they be under any further obligation to facilitate, the further development of the Jewish National Home by immigration regardless of the wishes of the Arab population.

Such was the treatment accorded a nation's two-thousand-year-old dream. Any persons naive enough to have retained any faith in "His Majesty's Government" were now convinced of the error of their ways. Ben-Gurion, chairman of the Jewish Agency, renamed the document "The Paper of Betrayal." The Yishuv realized the danger to itself and to the Jewish Diaspora. In the light of this new British policy, any Zionist activity on the part of Jews of any country could be construed as a hostile act toward the British Government. All efforts to prepare young people for immigration and productive occupations in Palestine would surely fit into this category. The ultimate goal of the White Paper was the

7. Passengers were taken in trucks to prison in Haifa.

destruction of Zionism, the termination of immigration, and the disjuncture of world Jewry and the Yishuv.

The new laws were implemented immediately. The borders were now guarded more closely than ever. Additional patrol boats roamed up and down the coast and new police stations were established. A British-Arab station was set up along the coast of Ashdod.

On the first of June the Rumanian ship Lizel, sailing under a Panamanian flag, was caught off the coast of Jaffa with 900 Jews from Czechoslovakia and Austria aboard, including 350 old men, women, and children.

On June 7, a sailing ship was caught in the vicinity of Acre, and its passengers were taken in trucks to prison in Haifa.

On June 30, the ship Astir was apprehended near Migdal Gad with 724 aboard. Most of the immigrants came from Danzig. They had left their homes in early March and had headed for a small port in the neighborhood of Constanta, Rumania. From there they wandered from port to port, and wherever they stopped, remnants of refugee groups joined them. On Passover eve the ship reached the shores of Palestine, but only four sick passengers were removed— three women and one man. The ship was given enough provisions to last for a few days, and it was forced to put out to sea again. The Astir spent six weeks in the Greek Archipelago, and on June 12 set out once more for Palestine. At a considerable distance from the Palestinian shore, the passengers were transferred into a sailing ship which the Astir had pulled behind her. At a distance of twenty miles from the coast the ship turned around and pulled out to sea, while the sailboat headed for shore. After a few moments something went wrong with the engine and the boat stopped moving. Somehow they managed to get close to shore, thinking that they were in the vicinity of the Hebrew colony Rishon le-Zion. However, they were suddenly confronted with Arab and British police who asked them where they had been during the previous twenty-four hours. It seemed that the patrol had spotted them the day before. They were rowed ashore in Arab boats, and the Arabs robbed them of whatever they could on the way.

On July 2 the warship Ivanhoe halted the Los Perlos off the coast of Natanya. Three hundred and seventy immigrants were aboard, including thirty women and one girl. They too had set sail from the vicinity of Constanta and had spent a month at sea. After a week had passed, they arrived at the Greek coast and sought to replenish their water supply, but the coastal authorities drove them away. They wandered from one port to another until they managed to fill the tank half full of water. In the meantime it was discovered that the bread with which they were provisioned had become moldy, and they arrived hungry in the port of Marmaris in Turkey. Here they obtained a small quantity of water and some bread before resuming their voyage. On the way the passengers and the captain had a fallout. The latter wished to return them to Constanta. The passengers took control of the ship by force and headed her toward Palestine. Here they were spotted by a British patrol plane and were forced to withdraw. On the following day they headed for the shore again, but at the approach of a British patrol boat they again withdrew. On their third attempt they found themselves trapped in the blinding glare of a British searchlight. Once again they attempted to escape to the high sea, but the faster British warship overtook them. The captain and the sailors were imprisoned.

On July 3 the Greek sailing ship St. Nicholas was brought into the port of Haifa with 700 people aboard. The immigrants had been brought to Palestine in a large ship, but when they drew close to the shore they were transferred to the sailing vessel, which entered the port in broad daylight, at ten in the morning. It sailed towards two immigrants' ships that had been confiscated by the government, and lay tied up in the port. Port officials rushed to the ship in a motorboat and stopped it.

On July 7 the Yishuv was thrown into a furor upon hearing of a ship that burned at sea on its way from Constanta to Palestine—the ship Rim, traveling under the flag of Panama. The Italian ship Fiume saved nearly 400 of its passengers. According to reports, immigrants from Rumania possessing immigration certificates had been aboard this ship. However, there were another 115 people on board not possessing certificates, and neither their citizenship nor their countries of origin could be ascertained. When the ship arrived in Istanbul the Turkish authorities tried to remove those passengers who had no certificates or passports, and painful scenes ensued. Port authorities in Istanbul contacted Ankara for instructions. The Turkish Foreign Minister asked the Rumanian Government if it would issue the immigrants new papers. The ship was finally sent on its way, but near Rhodes it ran afoul on a reef and caught fire. The Fiume picked up the survivors, who had endured ten hours of hunger and exposure on the reef, and brought them to Rhodes.

The British Government did not soften its policies in the least. On July 13 the Colonial Secretary announced in the House of Commons that the immigration schedule would be decreased proportionate to the number of illegal immigrants remaining in Palestine. There would be no new schedule announced for the period October 1, 1938, to March 31, 1940. "The renewal of immigration schedules after this date will depend upon then prevalent conditions relating to the illegal immigration."

This was the last straw. The statement issued by the Jewish Agency Executive in Jerusalem expressed the sentiments of Palestinian and world Jewry:

> The obdurate regime designed to cut off Jewish immigration —the regime set up in Palestine by the Mandatory Government in acquiescence to Arab terrorism—lacks all moral foundations in the eyes of the Jewish people and depends solely upon force and oppression.
>
> The Jewish people has not and will not come to terms with this oppressive regime announced in the White Paper. The display of bad faith on the part of the British Government in no way invalidates the right of the Jewish people to their homeland. The return of the Jews to their homeland is their natural and historic right.
>
> The lawbreakers are not the Jewish refugees returning to their land, but rather those who seek to rob them of every man's most fundamental right—the right to survive.

The offensive launched against the illegal immigration effort exceeded all expectations. The Mandatory Government's budget for police activity grew and grew. A special department was created to combat immigration more effectively. It consisted of officers, experts and advisors, and policemen and night watchmen. Britain requested the Turkish Government to close the gates of the Bosporus to refugee ships coming from the Danube via the Black Sea. At the same time, the British judge of the district court in Jaffa sentenced the captain of the ship Astir to nine months' imprisonment, his first mate to one year, and the sailors to six months. The captain of the Lizel was also sentenced to nine months' imprisonment and was fined 1,000 pounds as well.

The British finally captured the Atrato and the Colorado. The former was caught during the night of May 29, 1939, on her seventh trip to Palestine. A British warship fired on it outside Palestinian territorial waters. On July 30, early in the morning, the Colorado was captured in the same manner, as she was making her fifth trip to Palestine. Like the Atrato, she was sailing under the flag of Panama. A warship came upon the Colorado off the coast of Herzliah with 373 aboard, and brought it to Haifa under guard.

On this occasion the two ships had sailed from Rumania. During this period painful scenes were enacted at the port of Constanta. Often Jewish refugees arrived at the port from great distances, desperate, having made no arrangements to board a ship. Many were cheated out of all their money by various tourist agencies. Once 150 people were left behind on the beach, there being no room for them on the ship sailing to Palestine. They massed around the ship and would not let it leave. Forty men and women threw themselves into the sea as those on shore shouted and wept in anger and despair.

The demand for bribery in Rumania was then at an all-time peak. No sooner would a Hehalutz convoy cross the border from Poland than all sorts of officials—important and not-so-important—would swoop down on them like vultures. A representative of the Rumanian Foreign Ministry, who accompanied the convoy, explained his "ethics" to Levi in Rumanian interspersed with Yiddish and Hebrew phrases he had acquired in his line of work.

"You see, Reb Jew," he said, "I have been responsible for thousands of your Jews getting to Palestine, legally and illegally. These illegal ones—they're human beings too, as far as I'm concerned; I don't discriminate. But—everybody has to pay, no exceptions. My associates and myself, from the stationmaster down to the lowest customs clerk, we all have to get what's coming to us. Then there will be no reason whatever, not the slightest, to delay the convoy."

Out-and-out bribery—no secrecy here. Extreme care had to be exercised lest their funds should become completely exhausted. If a high official asked for an exorbitant sum, they had to offer half or a quarter of that amount and argue until he agreed.

A group of 800 pioneers from Poland came on a chartered train fourteen cars long, including two dining cars where they all received one hot meal and a cup of tea daily. The improvement was very welcome in a two- to three-day journey. The long train, brimful of young Jews, gave the guards on the Polish border no end of pleasure. They were thrilled to see so many Jews leaving the country for good. They glanced at the passports cursorily, to have done with the matter as quickly as possible.

News of the special train spread like wildfire. From Jewish towns all along the route crowds turned out to greet the halutzim. At every station where the train stopped, Jewish delegations welcomed them and gave them candy and fruit. At the train would approach, the crowd would spontaneously burst forth with Hatikvah, the Zionist anthem. Women wept. At one stop along the line a platform had been erected and from it a local leader delivered a welcoming speech. The policemen escorting the convoy were appalled at such a public display and threatened to return the pioneers to the border unless the crowds dispersed. Only after much exhortation was Levi able to prevail upon the crowd to comply with the order.

At one town they passed by a silent gathering of men, women, and children. They did not open their mouths but their burning eyes cried out in envy and despair. Even the policemen in the area were moved by this mute protest.

The train moved across Rumania, picking up pioneers as it went. At a small seashore station not far from the Russian border it halted. In the distance the lights of Odessa were visible. The train arrived in the port towards evening, but the travelers had to spend the night in the station due to negligence on the part of the Rumanian officials. The next day half the group was taken aboard the Colorado and conveyed to the Atrato within the space of an hour. After a difficult day of transferring from one ship to the other and final preparations for embarkation, the Atrato put out to sea. The Colorado returned to port, took on the remaining half who were waiting in the closed railroad cars, and sailed away.

Levi, too, sailed on the Atrato. The ship was well provisioned with food, which had been bought with the money paid by the immigrants from Rumania. Also, several dozen new mattresses had been acquired. No other arrangements had been made, however. There were 100 extra passengers on board and the congestion exceeded all estimation. Sanitation left much to be desired. To add to their troubles, the captain took sick, just on the one voyage where he was the only man capable of running the ship. He supervised the sailing from his bed, which had been moved to the bridge. The responsibility for the ship was assumed by the sailor from the Hagana, and the ship's liaison man, who knew something about seamanship. However, both of them were greenhorns as far as their new job was concerned, and when they entered the Dardanelles the ship ran into a reef. It was only the strong engines with which the ship was equipped which enabled them to free themselves without damage.

The nights were dark and therefore vary dangerous, especially for a ship with an inexperienced captain. For safety's sake, the deafening warning whistles blew unceasingly. Nevertheless, on their third night out the ship struck another reef; but once again they managed to come away undamaged. They had to stop at a port to get some milk for the captain, whose condition had deteriorated. The ship continued on its way slowly. Finally it was overtaken by the Colorado, and the sister ships, the "navy" of the pioneer underground, dropped anchor in a Turkish bay.

Upon their arrival in Cyprus, a storm arose and they could not proceed further. Three days the Atrato lay at anchor in a sheltered bay. On the third day a cable came from Tel Aviv with the following message:

> Equip 100 men with lifebelts, approach Tel Aviv, stop at a distance of two miles, and lower them in boats. Warn them to be ready for anything!

Levi called a general meeting, read the message aloud, and added: "Whoever wants to go—can go." At once many more than 100 young men rose to their feet. And though they were warned that the venture would be highly danger- ous, only one man voluntarily withdrew; he was married and had two children.

According to instructions the ship was to come near the shore that night and lower the rest of the passengers under cover of darkness. However, due to the captain's illness, they failed to locate the area designated by the debarkation team of the Bureau.

No moon appeared that night, but the sky was full of stars. Suddenly the sharp eyes of the guide discerned in the distance two moving lights that he knew were no stars. A bulky gray shape loomed through the mist—a British war- ship hove into view. A feverish race commenced. Atrato ploughed through the waves at top speed, her engines work- ing at capacity, with the warship kept hot on her heels, chugging and quaking and sending out one warning after another. But the Atrato did not stop. A short distance more and she would be beyond the territorial waters and out of danger. The steam engines were nearly exploding. Below decks, the passengers sat in tense silence. They felt the vibrations as two cannon shots hit the water nearby.

The British ship was victorious. Her lights blazing like the eyes of a huge sea creature, she stopped alongside the Atrato, which was slowing down of necessity. Pistols in hand, white-uniformed men climbed aboard the immigrant ship and made for the captain's bridge on the upper deck. After a few moments of heated discussion one of the sailors came to Levi and told him that he would have to hand over the passengers' passports to the representatives of the British Government. At once he replied that the passports were not in his possession. He knew that if the authorities were to get hold of them, there would be no difficulty in returning the immigrants to Rumania, their country of embarkation.

He was considering what to do when the messenger came again and summoned him to appear on the bridge before the captain. Upon his arrival he found the latter in his sick-bed surrounded by the British, their pistols still in their hands. The captain turned to Levi and told him to hand over the passports of the people that he had "saved." He had told the British that he had rescued the passengers from a sinking ship, that their passports were perfectly legitimate, and that they were not headed for Palestine at all. The British officers assured him that if he could prove he was telling the truth they would release the ship at once. Levi asked to be given time to consider. He doubted that the British would keep their promise. He said that he was willing to go below and try to convince the passengers to hand over their passports. As an experiment he went to the suitcase that contained the passports and took out two Nansen passports, which were issued to persons with no citizenship and brought them up to the bridge. We'll see what their promises are worth, he thought. The officer took the passports, looked at them, and put them into his pocket.

The investigation then commenced. One of the officers addressed him in rudimentary Hebrew, which he had learned for the purpose of combatting the illegal immigration. He asked him his name and country of origin. Levi gave him a German name and said that he came from Germany, the one country to which he could not be returned. The interrogator insisted that he was lying—that he had come from Palestine and that he was the organizer of the convoy. He had the passports and had to hand them over at once! Looking as innocent as possible, Levi again asked permission to go below and try to persuade the passengers to turn in their passports. The officers granted him permission. He went below and hurriedly instructed the immigrants not to divulge their true names when questioned; and as for the passports—they were to say that they had thrown them overboard. Again he was summoned to the bridge. When he appeared empty-handed he was taken by the scruff of the neck and thrown into the radio room and a guard was assigned to keep him there. Tired from the events of the past twenty-four hours he fell into a deep sleep as though he had just returned from a gruelling day in the fields.

When he awoke early the next morning he saw through the porthole beautiful Mt. Carmel and the city of Haifa at its feet. Looking around his cell he saw that he had two companions—the Palestinian sailor and a passenger who for some reason had been taken for a leader of the group. He was astonished to find that another man was with them —a tall wireless operator who was seated in front of the radio and was broadcasting to the world this latest victory of the British Government. Levi gave a start as his eye rested on the secret code book lying open on the table, directly in

front of the British wireless operator. Levi waited for him to
be distracted. No sooner had he turned his head for an
instant than the guide whisked the book off the table and
out, and fell once more into a deep sleep.

Levi was anxious to know what was going on below deck.
The guard, however, would not let him leave the room for
any reason whatever. No food was brought into the room.
Unable to do anything, Levi experienced a new sense of
freedom. He brushed two bedbugs off the bench, stretched
out, and fell once more into a deep sleep.

At ten in the morning the various British committees
began to arrive. First to appear were the secret police,
followed closely by the health committee. They walked
about the ship whispering among themselves uninterruptedly.
One of the officials seated himself behind a desk, and all the
passengers had to pass by him and sign their names. The
immigrants met the test. Everyone invented a German name
for himself, knew the name of "his" city in Germany, his
street address, the names of the city's personages and so
forth. Before long the officers taking down this information
became so confused and tired that he simply discontinued
the procedure.

With the stir created by the activities of the various committees, the passengers began to feel good. Some of them
even dared to approach the prisoners' cell. The guard did his
best to disperse them, but no sooner would he chase them
away than they would return from the opposite direction.
They peered through the window and passed food into the
prisoners. Levi took advantage of the changing of the guard
to switch places with one of the immigrants, before the new
guard had a chance to find out who his three prisoners were.

The passengers below were overjoyed to see their guide.
They had been making plans that entire morning, and many

suggestions had been offered. Some passengers were in favor of a hunger strike. Upon Levi's arrival all gathered about him. The first thing he did was make arrangements for guarding the passports. The biggest and strongest man was stationed near the stove. In the event that they would be unable to prevent the confiscation of the suitcase, he was to throw it into the furnace. So the first day passed.

As night fell the immigrants gathered together in groups. Sentimental songs of their homelands rose from the deck of the captive ship and spilled over into the dark sea. Haifa was lovely to look at, with its myriad lights twinkling up and down Mt. Carmel. But the immigrants' slight joy was more than outweighed by longing and disappointment. They strained to distinguish signs of life behind the net of lights in the Hebrew city. Another sorry-looking blacked-out vessel lay alongside them—the Artemisia, which had been captured previously. Levi recognized it easily, for he had spent more than one night on its deck. There was a third immigrants' ship in sight. It too had been captured at sea. Alongside the neighboring pier, three British warships stood menacingly by.

The following morning Levi received a note in a cigarette pack from the Hagana debarkation team on shore. They told him that the authorities had agreed to release the girls that same day. Levi was more than pleased. Needless to say, the passport suitcase was carried ashore by one young woman to his great relief and to the passengers' relief as well. The police reappeared shortly after the girls' debarkation and combed the ship from top to bottom. They broke the partition walls, ripped mattresses, and flung baggage around—but in vain. The passports were safely ashore.

On the following day the men were taken off the ship. Levi managed to get into the first of the trucks that took them to the internment camp. At the camp they were examined, interrogated, photographed, and fingerprinted. Questions were fired at them in rapid succession: "What's your name?" "Where do you come from?" "Where were you born?" and so forth. The pioneers, experienced by now in this procedure, answered without the slightest delay: I am a Jew from Germany, I speak German, I was born in Germany, and I sailed from Germany. The ruse worked again. The official broadcast that evening told of a convoy from Germany—the one country to which Jewish refugees could not be returned.

Levi had some uneasy moments when an Arab official, acting upon instructions from a British officer, broke open the trunks and bags with crowbars. He feared that they would open his thermos and find his Palestinian passport. But luck was with him again—his fountain pen and some money were all that were pocketed by the Arab official. When the time came for photographs to be taken, he was helped out by the fellow in back of him, who had his picture taken twice. In this way he deprived the Palestine police of a prize they had long sought—a photograph of the Bureau guide Levi Schwartz.

Levi had only a short time in which to fix upon a means of setting out of the internment camp before the usual identification proceedings should take place. His opportunity presented itself with the arrival of the first truck to deliver the immigrants' luggage. He appointed himself driver's helper and in a flash was inside the truck. Fortunately the driver had been an illegal immigrant in the previous group convoy and understood at once what was going on.

They left the camp shortly before the identification began. The men were lined up in rows and the sailors were made to inspect them and point out the organizers. They looked for the head of the convoy in vain; at the moment he was in a tub of hot water in a Tel Aviv hotel. People came to warn him that the police had learned of his escape and were searching the city and that it was best for him to leave at once. Levi was unable to comply however, as he had nothing to wear. He had left the internment camp without any belongings, and the clothes that he had worn were black with filth and had been sent to be laundered. Moreover, he had no identity card, and therefore would be liable to arrest and imprisonment. He stayed in the hotel room for a week, after which he was smuggled out to his kibbutz, Ramat Hakovesh.

The haverim, members of the kibbutz, welcomed him with open arms. He was happy and proud to see how the farm had grown in spite of the disturbances of the past three years—the attacks, the burning of their fields at night, and other conditions that compelled the erection of barbed-wire fences. In the thick of this turbulent period the kibbutz, located in a dangerous sector, had acquired more land. Scores of new members had been taken in, mostly from the ranks of the illegal immigrants; they had quickly acclimated themselves to the work, and some of them held responsible posts in the various branches of the farm. Children had been born.

Levi had good reason to be happy. But he also had good reason to be sad. There were new graves. There had only been one when he left and now there were twelve more, all of them members who fell while defending their home. As he walked about the kibbutz and took in what he saw, he realized more than ever how vital was the connection between the development and defense of his own kibbutz and the illegal immigration effort. He felt compelled to cut his stay short. He soon left for Tel Aviv to rejoin his comrades in the growing Bureau.

Some new developments had taken place in the Bureau Davidka N'meri and Moishele Carmel (Chervinski) had been joined by others, among them Grisha, a member of Kfar Giladi, who became one of the mainstays of the operation in Palestine. Then there was Ephraim Dekel, who headed the southern branch of the Hagana underground news service. He was responsible for the establishment of a listening outpost which managed to crack the code used by British overseas agents to contact the Mandatory Government. As a result, the Hagana men were in a much better position to give instructions to their ships at sea, especially in matters pertaining to anchorage and debarkation. In Ephraim's small apartment in Tel Aviv, Shoshana, his wife, and Dvora, Davidka's wife, sat with their ears glued to the set, painstakingly recording and deciphering all secret messages.

S. Even-Zohar played an important role in the immigration effort. He set up a communications system with the underground ships; the system soon became known as "Gideon" and functioned most efficiently. Even-Zohar brought to the Bureau his experience as national coordinator of the Hagana's communications system, which included wireless, signaling, pigeons, and dogs. This communications department created the underground radio station called "The Voice of Israel" long before the establishment of the well-known "Telem-Shamir Boaz" station of the War of Independence. Even-Zohar himself received the first declaration of revolt from Berl Katznelson's hand and announced it over the first broadcast of the Hagana's "Voice of Israel."

This department of the Hagana was founded during the 1936 disturbances. In a small house in the workers' quarter in north Tel Aviv a wireless was installed, connecting with Jerusalem and Haifa. Eventually the system came to include all the border settlements, from Hanita in the north to Ein-

Gev in the east and Kfar Menahem in the south. Every important point among the scores of the "wall and tower" settlements, established during the 1936-1939 period, was equipped with a functioning wireless on the day after it was founded. During the War of Independence and the last years of the Hagana's existence prior to the establishment of the Israel Defense Army, the communications department set up stations outside the borders of Palestine and they served the Yishuv well. The central broadcasting station, the "nerve center" of the system, was located in one of the kibbutzim. Except for the local Hagana commanding officer and the broadcasters themselves, no one in the kibbutz knew of the station's existence.

Communicating with the illegal ships had been primitive at first—signaling with kerosene lamps and later, playing certain records. However, the system was quickly changed and improved upon. Wireless equipment was installed in the ships. Young men from the Bureau were chosen for "Gideon" and trained in Morse code, then smuggled aboard the ships. They worked so effectively that neither the crew nor the immigrants knew what they were doing. "Gideon" was always alert for the ever-changing directives from Palestine. These directives determined the ship's course at sea and along the Palestinian coast. As each ship approached, the communications men would go to the beach, set up a temporary station, and tell the men on board where to go and what to do.

By that time the underground debarkation network included many and various elements from the pioneer population, most of them Hagana members and teenagers. The young men of the Bureau acquired quite a reputation for themselves, and on more than one occasion organizers of other illegal groups turned to them and asked for help in debarking ships of their immigrants at night; such assistance was given willingly. The debarkation procedure worked as smoothly and regularly as a well-oiled machine.

The harder the British bore down on the illegal immigration effort, the more daring were the measures taken by the members of the "Shay," the secret information service. They staged criminal decoy operations in settlements in the coastal area, drawing the police away from the vicinity of debarking immigrants. They obtained advance information concerning patrol-boat movements and were able to intercept messages sent by British spies to the roving patrols. These instructions, as well as the orders given the border police and the lookout towers, greatly facilitated debarkation proceedings. "Shay" kept close track of the wireless communications between the lookout towers and the roving patrols. The young men even knew the signals intended for police airplanes and warships.

Yiddish-speaking British agents were sent to Jewish centers in the Diaspora and to ports of embarkation. The head of the Secret Service himself, two of his assistants, and many high officials in the British immigration department tried their hand at spying. "Shay" was always on guard, however, and usually found out ahead of time when such agents were to set out on their missions. They would then contact the parties concerned and supply them with official reports on the interrogation of British secret agents. These reports sometimes spread over scores of pages.

The members of "Shay" also carried out missions in Arab areas along the coast. The Mandatory Government enlisted the aid of these coastal settlements in its war against the illegal immigration. The "Fund of the Arab Nation" assisted the British by contributing money and by helping to set up roving Arab patrols along the desolate beaches in the north and south. These patrols robbed the immigrants on more than one occasion.

The immigrants themselves knew nothing of the activities of the "Shay." They could only sense the presence of a secret and efficient guiding hand. Even Levi, the first guide, who had returned to Palestine after a long period of service in the underground in Europe, now learned for the first time of all the changes that had taken place in the organization and execution of the illegal immigration.

The Bureau had been allocated an office, which they called "the roof." It was an isolated room on the second floor of the editorial offices of the daily "Davar," one of the first buildings on Allenby Road in Tel Aviv. The room had a wide porch that faced the building of the Histadrut executive committee.

When Levi attended his first meeting in the Bureau headquarters, he learned that a significant change had taken place in the Yishuv attitude toward the immigration effort. Their modest venture had become the principal national undertaking. Whereas previously the operation had been spoken of in private, in hushed tones, within a small, exclusive circle, now everyone spoke of it, openly and enthusiastically. Settlements in the coastal area were only too glad to take in the refugees. Poets and writers provided inspiration, and schoolchildren were taught the "Song of the Anonymous Immigrant."

5

The Story of Tiger Hill

One of the first events to demonstrate the maturity of the Bureau and the unity of the Yishuv as far as the illegal-immigration effort was concerned, was the Tiger Hill incident.

The Tiger Hill was rented from the same Greek ship-owning family which had supplied the movement with the Atrato. The capture of that vessel, the best of the family's ships and its chief means of support, had been a heavy loss to them. Shimon broke the news to the owners with trepidation. That evening, after they had eaten dinner, they spent some hours together and for a long time little was said. The old seaman's eyes were misty. True, the family had made handsome profits in their dealings with the Bureau but now their profits had been obliterated at a stroke. Nonetheless they agreed to continue doing business with the young men, whom they liked personally and whose cause they espoused. Repairs on the Tiger Hill were made in the Bulgarian port of Varna.

As the repairs were nearing their completion and the ship was almost ready to sail, news arrived of the capture of the Colorado. In spite of this, no changes were made in the sailing plans. The young men were prepared for all contingencies. Toward the end of July hundreds of pioneers were informed that they had been chosen to leave shortly for Palestine. Groups began flocking to Warsaw. The emigrants' hotel, which had been used to house previous groups, could not contain such large numbers. For security reasons, hotels in suburbs far removed from Jewish districts were used to accommodate the pioneers. Contact with the local Jewish community was forbidden.

In the beginning of August the convoy left the borders of Poland in a chartered train and reached Constanta by evening. However, as soon as the cars came to halt, even as the pioneers got up from their seats, packs on their shoulders—a shocking order was received: the sailing had been postponed; and they would not board the ship that evening, as planned, nor on the following evening. There was even a chance that they would be returned to Poland. All on board the train were stunned. They still did not realize how long the arm of the British Government was and how far its agents could get.

Tired and depressed, the young men took off their packs. The train was shunted to a siding outside the city and troops were assigned to guard it. The weary travelers spent a sleepless night stretched out on the benches and the floor.

At daybreak the filth in the cars was exposed to view. The stench from the refuse was stifling. There was no water and it was two days before the arrival of the first food shipment from the Palestine Office. The people were in a very weakened condition. If anyone dared to set his foot outside the car for a breath of fresh air, he was cursed and beaten by the Rumanian soldiers. The authorities relented somewhat on the third day, fearing an epidemic, and allowed the passengers to come outside while the cars were aired and cleaned. No sooner did the pioneers feel solid ground beneath

8. At daybreak the filth in the cars was exposed to view.

their feet than they placed hands on shoulders and danced the Hora—the well-known folk dance of the pioneers.

The passengers spent five days cooped up in the railroad cars alongside the port of Constanta. On the fifth day, with no advance warning, a short shrill whistle blast sounded; the train gave a jolt and was on its way.

After a half-hour's ride they stopped at the gates of the port, where the Tiger Hill lay ready and waiting to sail.

Permission to embark had not been easily procured. Barpal and his men from the Bureau worked unceasingly. The group had taken on a new member, Ruth Kluger (Eliav), better known then as the *hanum* ("lady," in Turkish). Her job was "foreign relations." At that time a distinguished British delegation was in Bucharest, at the invitation of the Rumanian Government, to negotiate a loan, with the Ploesti petroleum wells as collateral. A condition for the loan was that no more groups be allowed to pass through Constanta. Rumania was ruled at that time by the dictator Kalinesko, one of the few men who were above bribery. He was known as "the iron man" and had been authorized by the king to have the final say in all matters pertaining to the state. To meet the demands of the British delegation, he ordered that the convoy be sent back to Poland. Barpal and his group enlisted the support of Zionists as well as assimilated Jews. The latter had contacts in all governmental departments. The entire network of border employees was bribed liberally, as were the employees of the British Consulate. The *hanum* finally managed to get to the elderly scholar, Galaktian, Kalinesko's revered teacher. After much effort, her mission was accomplished. On that same day the British delegation was taken on a tour of the Tiger Hill and certified that the ship was "fit for human transport." That evening the convoy was taken to the port in locked cars and under armed guard.

Organizing the people on the ship presented problems. The pioneers from Bulgaria, who had boarded the ship in the port of Varna, had had to remain in the hold all the time that the ship lay at anchor in Constanta to avoid being seen.

That night was taken up with feverish, last-minute preparations. Among other things that required an immediate decision on the part of the guide was the matter of the "rabbits" who had by various means boarded the ship while it lay at anchor in the port. Many of them had gotten aboard by bribing the police heavily.

Maintaining an orderly daily routine was very difficult. The kitchen was small; the ovens could prepare at most fifty portions at a time; there were hardly any utensils—some thirty or forty incomplete servings in all; and there were only two cooking pots. The amount of food and medical supplies was also far from satisfactory. This was the first time that a ship had set out so poorly provisioned. They turned to one of the ship's owners who was in Istanbul at the time and asked him to buy what was needed. For some reason he did not. So the ship sailed, passed through the Dardanelles, and put out to sea as it was, with provisions to last it only one week.

During the first week of the voyage the passengers were in good spirits, hopeful of arriving in Palestine shortly, as had many of their friends before. However, as the days slipped by, their hopes faded.

Many fell sick and some were in critical condition. Hunger began to make itself felt. Finally a girl from Latvia, Zippora Levit, died. In her home she had been bed-ridden with an attack of scarlet fever; before she had recovered she received a message informing her that she had been chosen for the convoy, and she did not wish to postpone her departure. One week after her embarkation she suffered a

9. MANY FELL SICK AND WERE IN CRITICAL CONDITION. HUNGER BEGAN TO MAKE ITSELF FELT.

relapse. She grew weaker hourly and her temperature rose steadily. The ship's doctor did not have medicine for her, and there was no ice.

After she died, Levi left the cabin sick at heart and went up on deck. He wished to arrange for a burial ceremony but he knew how superstitious the sailors were. Should they learn of her death they would most likely panic and mutiny. The guide assembled the group leaders, told them of what had happened, and asked them to calm the passengers and see to it that everyone went to bed early so that it would be quiet aboard ship.

The funeral ceremony was set for 1 A.M. One by one the group leaders silently arrived. A small group entered the dead girl's room, wrapped the body in a sheet, and brought it to the dining room. Close friends said words of farewell, and the kaddish, the prayer for the dead, was recited. Then the body was tied to a wooden panel and thrown into the sea.

Shortly after this another girl died, Yonah Shimshelevitz.

The hunger problem became acute. The bread supply ran out. The biscuits became moldy. The canned food was almost gone. The meager morning coffee ration brought on nausea, as it was served in a greasy soup bowl that had not been properly washed, for want of water. The passengers stood in line for hours before they could get to the kitchen or to the ship's one faucet where the daily ration of a half-cup of drinking water was distributed

There was no choice but to get water at the island of Rhodes. A request was sent to the port authorities. The answer was a refusal and shots. The more to impress the ship, a patrol boat with a machine gun on its deck approached her.

The ship turned towards the Turkish mainland in hopes

of being more hospitably received. Upon approaching the port of Antalya the pioneers saw another immigrants' ship packed with passengers, also in need of water. As the Tiger Hill approached, its sister ship sailed away, and as the two vessels passed each other the pioneers burst out with Hatikva. However, as the Tiger Hill approached the shore it was met by a police boat and warned not to drop anchor. Levi pleaded with the police, and finally the latter brought them some sacks of flat Turkish bread, charging them excessively for it; but water and medicine were denied them.

Another night passed. When morning arrived and the ship neared a large island, the immigrants beheld a delightful sight: a waterfall bursting from the top of a hill and plunging to the sea below. Faint with thirst, the passengers crowded the deck to take in the wondrous sight.

The ship anchored. As the first boat was being lowered, a police boat approached and ordered them to leave, pointing at their machine gun for further emphasis.

Again they put out to sea. A storm came up and they headed for a wide, sheltered bay, but once more they were met by a police boat and were forced to withdraw.

Their one remaining hope was the sailboat which, in accordance with the agreement made with the owners of Tiger Hill, was to meet them at sea at a designated spot to convey the immigrants ashore. When night fell the ship came to a stop. Except for two red lamps hung on the bow and the stern as warning signals, all lights were extinguished.

The passengers were hungry. Most of them were too exhausted to wait in line for their meager ration of greasy coffee. They lay down wherever they could and tried to banish hunger with sleep. Instances of theft occurred. Food rations were found missing. People started coming to Levi to accuse one another. One young man suspected of theft, unable to bear the shame, attempted to jump overboard. On another occasion the watchman excitedly woke Levi in the early hours of the morning to report a theft in the storeroom. A few bottles of wine and other supplies set aside for the sick had been taken. He had seen the men who had broken in and was prepared to testify against them.

Levi had never come across a situation such as this, and did not know what course to pursue. He knew that tensions and bitterness were building up aboard the ship and were liable to explode at any minute, but he also knew that he could not let the matter go by. He called a general meeting and brought up the topic of the "night operation." No sooner had he related the incident than one of the pioneers jumped up and shouted, "We're hungry! I join the accused!" Speaking slowly and in a low voice, Levi addressed himself to the young man:

"Can a few bottles of wine set aside for the sick cure hunger? On top of everything else that's happened to us are we going to let ourselves turn into bandits and rob one another?" He went on to speak at length and the group listened in silence.

No more thefts occurred. But then a new crisis arose. Sickness spread throughout the ship, and there was no medicine left. Critically ill passengers writhed in pain and nothing could be done for them. To complicate matters further, fights broke out among the sailors and particularly among the stokers. The latter were opium smokers and in their drunken state began fighting with knives. Levi set a watch over them from among the immigrants, and sent some men to work with them and learn how to stoke the furnaces so that the convoy would not be dependent upon drunkards.

Finally the sailboat appeared on the horizon to the great joy of all aboard ship. It came nearer and soon Kosta, one of the ship's owners, clambered aboard amid a rousing reception and gave the Hebrew greeting of "Shalom, haverim"—"Greetings, friends!"

It was immediately decided that a celebration was in order that night. The barrel of herring that had been guarded as though it were gold was brought up from below. The news spread like wildfire, and everyone began to get ready for the feast. However, when the barrel was opened, all the fish were found to be rancid. The celebration was held notwithstanding. Kosta himself accounted for the major part of the artistic program with his Greek songs. Hovever, the morale was still very low. The immigrants went to bed on empty stomachs, as there was nothing whatsoever left to eat.

Levi was very disturbed and angry at himself and his colleagues for not having delayed the ship's embarkation until such time as they could have obtained adequate provisions. He could not help but think of what had happened five years before, when the Velos wandered from port to port with hundreds of young refugees on its deck. He remembered how he had distributed the water. Two bucketsful were all he had to give out to the long line of hundreds of hungry, tired, parched young people. Each person received only half a cup. Five years had passed since then, and he and his colleagues had accomplished much, but it seemed likely that the Tiger Hill would suffer the same fate as the Velos.

When morning came the ship was met by boats bearing food and medicine. Water and coal were also brought on board. The leaders of the group spent most of their remaining funds on these supplies. The ship anchored in the port of Beirut in Lebanon and stayed there for three days, during which time the passengers and crew ate and drank their fill, and rested in preparation for whatever lay ahead.

On the third day they left Beirut and headed for Palestine.

They stopped a good distance outside Palestinian territorial waters. According to the prearranged plan, 300 immigrants were to be taken ashore by night in the ship's one tender. They began lowering the people at 11 P.M. The weak and the sick were the first to go. One hundred and fifty people were packed inside the tender; the rest were to be placed on its deck. However, after 180 persons had been lowered, the organizers discovered that a leak had sprung in the bottom of the boat. Soon it was one-quarter filled with water. Careful not to exhibit the least amount of excitement, the organizers quietly announced to those on board the tender that there had been a change in plans and that they would have to return to the ship. Hours passed before the retransfer was completed.

From the deck of the ship Levi and his companions watched the tender sink below the waves. The Tiger Hill made for the open sea once more.

The night had been particularly trying for the sick passengers, whose condition had been aggravated by the transfer to and from the tender. Many had cried out in pain. However, when morning arrived, prospects brightened. A message was received from the shore stating that the Trumpeldor, the famous boat of the Histadrut's sports federation "Hapoel," was on its way to the Tiger Hill, with men from the Hagana debarkation team aboard. While it was yet morning the boat arrived and its passengers climbed aboard, bringing with them sacks of bread, and a small quantity of special food for the children. They were greeted by hundreds of cheering voices. Immediately the newcomers and the leaders of the ship sat down to make a plan of action. Shortly after midnight the group leaders were summoned to the dining room. There they were informed of the new attitude in the Yishuv toward the debarkation of illegal immigrants, and were instructed to tell the members of the convoy that a state of "stand-by" readiness had been declared and that they should be prepared for anything. On the next day the debarkation group returned to Palestine leaving behind them Aaron Leshevsky and Katriel to reinforce the leadership of the Tiger Hill for what lay ahead. That evening the ship received a directive from the shore to proceed northward to Beirut and take on the passengers of another immigrants' ship that lay anchored in that port.

The 658 people on board the Prosula were refugees from Czechoslovakia who had originally intended to debark at Beirut and make the rest of the journey by land. Their ship had been arranged for by a private company. The men of the Bureau, when asked to give their help, conferred with Eliahu Golomb and decided to do whatever they could to save the convoy—and it proved to be no easy task.

The transfer of passengers from one ship to another at sea required first of all that the Prosula be equipped with a wireless. Yosef Fein of Deganya was assigned the delicate task of acquiring the wireless in Beirut. Menahem from Kfar Giladi, one of the most talented communications men in the Bureau, was sent to Beirut, and with Yosef's help he was able to get on board the Prosula.

Communications were established between the two ships and they began to approach one another and get ready for the operation in spite of the protests of the Tiger Hill's captain, who was unwilling to take on more passengers. He and his uncooperative crew were finally placed on board the Prosula and Katriel took charge of the ship. The transfer of the refugees took up the entire night. When morning came the men on shore were informed that the Tiger Hill, with 1,189 aboard, awaited further instructions.

It was decided to direct the ship to Nebi Yunis in the

southern part of Palestine, near the Suhrir River. This was a bold move in view of the fact that the coast of Ashdod was desolate and that there were no Jewish settlements nearby. N'meri realized how difficult it would be to have the immigrants march four to five miles. He was also aware of security conditions on the beach. Nonetheless he chose Nebi Yunis in the hope that they would not run into any patrols in that area.

Many helping hands were recruited from distant settlements for the debarkation night. All the necessary supplies—wireless equipment, first aid, and provisions—were carried to the beach on the shoulders of the participants.

By 11 P.M., all was in readiness. The communications team set to work and the lookouts began to discern the shape of the approaching ship. Suddenly, however, two bright searchlights shot through the darkness, and a British patrol boat opened fire. To the men on shore it seemed that nothing could prevent the ship's capture. Fortunately, they were mistaken. Katriel managed to get the Tiger Hill out of territorial waters before the patrol boat could overtake them. The police ambush had not been entirely ineffective, however; two men lay dead on the deck of the immigrant ship.

This was the first time that anyone had been killed on board ship. The immigrants were terrified, particularly those who had come from the Prosula and had not undergone training in Hehalutz. They openly demanded that the ship surrender to the authorities and not risk another attempt at an illegal debarkation. The debarkation men realized that the time had come for a bold maneuver. They decided to run the Tiger Hill openly onto a sandbank opposite the Histadrut building on Yarkon Street in north Tel Aviv.

The operation got under way. According to instructions

the two bodies and the wireless were to be sent ashore on the first boat, and as soon as the anchor was to be dropped, Katriel and the sailors were to swim northward to the Moslem cemetery, to avoid arrest. Hagana patrols were set up all along the beach to the north and to the south. The men of "Shay" carefully kept track of police activities. Groups of sailors stood on the beach, ready to establish connections with the ship by means of boats and ropes. Large and small boats from sea-sport organizations were standing by.

The ship ran onto the sandbank and the anchor was dropped. Within minutes the beach was swarming with thousands of people offering assistance, and this with no prior announcements having been made. However, willing as the people were, they only managed to interfere with the sailors.

Connection with the ship was established as planned, and the immigrants began to descend rapidly, one after another. Hundreds got ashore and were led away immediately to the houses of the people who had gathered on the beach. Tel Aviv welcomed them with open arms, although no prior preparations had been made.

The debarkation had proceeded for half an hour when the police began to arrive. At first there were only a few unarmed policemen and they were chased away and hooted at from the windows and rooftops of the Mahlul slum quarter. The people had been enraged by the sight of the emaciated refugees, and the two dead men who had been immediately removed to the Hadassah Hospital in the center of the city. They set upon the police with a vengeance. Whoever had nothing to throw or wield, scooped up sand and threw it in their faces.

British reinforcements arrived shortly and the battle was

terminated. Armed policemen pushed the crowds back from the shore and at the same time tried to locate the organizers of the debarkation in the crowds. N'meri, however, was no longer in the area. He had hurried northward to meet Katriel and the sailors at a prearranged spot. The immigrants remaining on board the Tiger Hill were taken to the army camp in Sarafand.

The date was September 2, 1939, one day after Germany's invasion of Poland, which heralded the beginning of the Second World War.

6

One Disaster after Another

The Twenty-First Zionist Congress, assembled in Geneva in August of 1939, provided the Zionist world with its first opportunity to debate publicly the illegal immigration question.

A hush settled over the large auditorium. All the doors were shut. The young ushers stood rigidly at their posts in the corners.

The hall and the galleries were filled to capacity, even though it was only a regular morning session. Thousands of eyes were focused on the gray-haired figure on the platform wearing a faded dark suit and an open-collared shirt—Berl Katznelson—who was about to speak in defense of the illegal-immigration effort. During the previous evening session the delegates had heard Rabbi Abba Hillel Silver, President of the Zionist Organization of America and a leader of the Reform movement there, speak out sharply against those people who had entered and were entering Palestine in opposition to the will of the Mandatory Government. Berl had taken to the rostrum to make a reply.

Yesterday (he began) words were spoken from this platform that I cannot permit myself to ignore. They constituted an unscrupulous attack upon our immigrants at sea and a stab in the back to the Zionist program. . . .

I will frankly say that I took offense last night. Aren't we all immigrants? And if there are any among us fortunate enough to live in their countries fully secure, can they say that their ancestors were not immigrants? . . .

Were our leaders to have first-hand knowledge of what is happening, I believe they might experience a change in outlook. Some years back I spent a night on the beach of Tel Aviv and watched groups of young men and women row ashore. I watched them as they struggled through the water, with their hands linked so that no one might be swept away. Now from an aesthetic point of view the scene left much to be desired. I can well imagine that had a British swimming team been placed in the same situation, things would have taken on an entirely different appearance. But as far as I was concerned, those young people linked together were part of a chain that stretches from Yehuda Halevi and the Golden Age of Spain down to this very day. And what is more, I believe that the day is not far off when songs will be sung about these people and perhaps prayers will be written in their behalf. And who knows? Perhaps these prayers will be recited even in the "Temples" in America. . . .

The illegal immigration effort has a special role to play in our battle for statehood. Every ideal requires a particular social group to achieve realization. There was a time when the small Jewish storekeeper kept the love of Zion alive. Then Herzl came. Later, there were periods when the standard was borne by doctors, lawyers, students. Many look upon those days as a golden era. Then there came new standard bearers, young men without university degrees, who worked in the orange groves of Petach Tikva and in the fields of Galilee. And when I ask myself, Who today is the natural standard bearer in Israel's war for existence, and where is he to be found? I reply,—On the sea, bearing aloft the banner of Jewish persecution. These men and women will not let the gates of The Land to be closed upon them. They will give the world's conscience no rest. They will not allow Mr. Malcolm MacDonald to perpetrate his White Paper. The Jewish refugee has advanced to the front lines, and we must close ranks behind him. . . .

This is a question of Jewish solidarity; it is a question of the strength of resolve of those responsible for bringing about united Jewish action; and finally, it is a question of the honor of the Zionist movement. . . .

It is neither the fault of Israel nor is it the fault of the refugees that we have become lawbreakers. That government that has transgressed the fundamental law of the Land of Israel makes lawbreakers of us. Being law abiding people, we wished to work within the framework of the law. We even submitted to laws that were none too friendly to us. But there can be no submission to a law that deprives men of their right to exist! . . .

After the conclusion of the session, the sweat-soaked speaker stood in the corridor of the large building and hundreds of people approached him to shake his hand in gratitude for his having expressed what they themselves felt. Among them were the men of the Immigration Bureau.

The small group had gathered in Geneva in order to sum

up past activities and set policies for future action. On their
agenda was the question of their relationship with the various
Zionist institutions. In the months preceding the Congress
there had been a marked change of attitude on the part of
the Zionist leaders as far as the illegal immigration effort
was concerned, and both sides felt the need to arrive at a
mutual understanding regarding details of the immigration
program and means of implementing it.

The likelihood that they would expand the scope of their
activities gave the young men added incentive to intensify
their search for suitable ships. Once again, during the
summer months, they made their weary rounds through
Europe, contacting and meeting with the various agents and
companies large and small, reputable and otherwise.

Saul, who until that time had had almost no direct contact
with shipowners and middlemen, began to take part in these
meetings in hopes of speeding up the tempo of the operation.
Once he went with Shimon to a meeting with two owners of
a well-known shipping company in the luxury Hotel
George V in Paris. Prior to the meeting Shimon called Saul's
attention to the patch on the latter's pants, even though his
own shirt was shiny from use. On more than one occasion
Saul had been urged by his colleagues to take some money
and buy a new suit, but he would have none of it: "How
can I waste five or six pounds for some clothes that I'll never
use back home, when I don't even know how much longer
I'll be staying here?" All during the meeting with the shipowners Saul sat with his hand covering the patch, and for a
long time afterwards Shimon jokingly twitted him about the
patch, claiming that it had been responsible for the subsequent poor relations they had with that company.

The Twenty-first Zionist Congress was clouded over with

the portents of approaching war. While no one foresaw even dimly the extent of the horror that was to come, it was clear to all that Hitler would wreak havoc on the Jews. The atmosphere during the last days of the Congress was particularly somber and tense. The Works Committee continued its meetings long into the night, as the packed hall listened attentively to the speeches of veteran leaders and younger members. Strong sympathies were evidenced toward those who were to return to the danger zones—the delegates from the countries dominated by Hitler, and the emissaries from Palestine who were to go to the Jewish communities in Germany, Austria, Czechoslovakia, and Poland, countries that were likely to turn into blood baths at any minute. In emotional and sometimes vague speeches delegates expressed their fears concerning the fate of the Yishuv during the coming war, when it would be cut off from world Jewry, its chief means of support. The Congress ended on this troubled note, and the delegates hurried home to their respective countries.

The men of the Immigration Bureau, however, did not rush off to their homes and kibbutzim in Palestine. The Zionist Congress had been a period of deliberation for them, wherein past activities were reviewed and plans for the future were discussed.

The Bureau had an impressive record of achievement. Since the sailing of the Poseidon in January, 1938, with sixty-five immigrants aboard, until the Zionist Congress of August, 1939, the young men had brought fifteen ships to the shores of Palestine. If one adds to the sum of immigrants brought by those ships the 700 people that the Velos carried during its two trips in 1934; the 1,189 people aboard the Tiger Hill, then nearing the Palestinian coast; and the 470

passengers of the Asimi, organized by others but debarked
with the help of the young men of the Bureau—one arrives
at a total of 6,821 people. On the one hand such a number
was almost infinitesimal when compared with the millions
of Jews who were seeking to be rescued. On the other hand,
the very fact that such an idealistic group of men existed, and
had the courage and capability to break through the barriers
that had been erected to halt immigration, was enough to
give hope to Europe's Jewish youth. They felt that there was
a reason to struggle, that there was a chance, however slight,
of reaching the Homeland.

With the outbreak of the Second World War, the young
men of the Bureau hurriedly left the Zionist Congress and
other places where they were then active, and rushed to a
meeting in Saul's cramped quarters in the Ceramic Hotel
in Paris. They had to decide whether or not to call a halt to
the operation just when new possibilities were presenting
themselves as a result of the experience they had acquired
and the new methods that they had developed. The young
men did not conceive of the possibility of an extended war.
They assumed that they were entering upon a short interim
period, one which they would utilize to lay the groundwork
for an expanded operation that would incorporate new and
more efficient methods.

On that morning of September, as millions were descend-
ing upon the army enlistment offices in France, Saul and his
colleagues were crowded together in the small hotel room
arranging their own "troops." The room had two doors, and
Saul, standing between them, gave the young men their
orders by pointing to one or the other. Those assigned to the
right were to go home on the Cairo City, the Egyptian ship
that provided the delegates to the Congress with their only

means of returning to Palestine. Those assigned to the left were to remain in the Diaspora.

Years later, when Saul and his colleagues, individually and collectively evaluated what they had accomplished, they took themselves to task bitterly for their short-sightedness in those first days of September, 1939. How, they asked themselves, how could they have failed to realize that they should have stayed at their posts and attempted to work in spite of the war? And indeed, while it is most likely that they would have been unable to organize emigration groups under the circumstances, who can say for certain that the concentration camps and Hitler's ghettos would not have taken on a different aspect had these young men from the Bureau remained in the Diaspora to exert a vital influence?

On the first day of the war, the representative of the Jewish communities of Prague, Vienna, and Berlin were summoned to appear before the Nazi authorities and were informed of the creation of the *Reservat*. Even at that early date plans had been made for the annihilation of the Jews, not on German soil but outside the country's borders. The suggestion of Lublin as a "Jewish National Home" was a snare that trapped a few leaders of the Jewish communities. Eichmann suggested to Y. Edelstein, director of the Palestine Office in Prague, that he head the *Reservat*. When Edelstein refused, the Nazi said sarcastically, "You are a capable fellow, but it seems that you are not a natural leader." On another occasion Eichmann remarked, "We don't care if the Jews emigrate or die out, as long as we get rid of them." A few weeks after the first meeting, the shipments to Lublin commenced, and the first convoy, which Edelstein was forced to lead, contained scores of pioneers from Austria. On a rainy autumn day they arrived at a swampy area on the

new border between that part of Poland annexed by the
Germans and that annexed by the Russians. The Gestapo
officer led them off the train onto the swampy ground devoid
of any house or shelter and said sarcastically, "Now you
have arrived at your national home." Edelstein managed to
escape and worked toward halting these shipments in con-
junction with the *Wehrmacht,* the German Army, whose war
plans would be disrupted by the creation of Jewish districts
on the border.

The men of the Bureau did all that was in their power to
bolster the illegal immigration effort, not merely because
they wished to save a few more people, but primarily because
they wanted to strengthen that element in the Nazi hierarchy
that favored emigration. They felt that every Jew who left
Nazi-dominated lands increased the possibility of a mass
exodus. Holding this point of view, Hehalutz headquarters in
Vienna continued to oppose the shipments to Lublin and
continued to send emigrant groups down the Danube under
the pressure of the Nazi authorities, even as late as mid-
November, at which time the river usually froze over, making
it impossible for boats to pass.

Thus it was that convoys of pioneers from Vienna arrived
at the Yugoslavian-Rumanian border in November and were
detained at Kladovo because they did not have transit
permits.

The name Kladovo is a memorable one in the annals of the
illegal immigration effort. Kladovo provided the setting for
the Hilda incident. The Hilda was the first ship to arrive in
Palestine after the outbreak of the war, in the beginning of
1940. Its passengers comprised 726 adults and two infants
that had been born on the ship. The outcome of the Hilda
incident shed a much-needed ray of light at that dark period.

The pioneers were scheduled to leave Berlin in the

beginning of September, 1939, but with the outbreak of the war, a new date, October 13, was set. They left for Vienna by train in a pouring rain. Each person was allowed to take along no more than eighteen pounds of luggage. At the station the newsboys were shouting that the French had blown up the Rhine bridge. The train was met in Vienna by the secret police. They lined the travelers up and led them off to be questioned. Luck was with the pioneers and on the next day they were given permission to embark in their small ship—a steamboat of sorts, resembling the kind to be found on the "blue" Danube. Four hundred people were jammed into the tiny ship for six weeks. They lived on cabbage and occasional noodles. When they arrived in Sulina they had to wait for weeks for the arrival of the ship that was to take them to Palestine. The port of Sulina was under military rule, and the boat had to be taken to another Danube port. The ship, lying at anchor alongside something resembling a pier, was frozen to the wooden bridge. The ship weighed only 1,200 tons. Some of the passengers had to be on the deck at all times, for there was not enough room for everyone inside the ship. Refuse lay everywhere and the air was stifling. The passengers for the most part either sat on their luggage or stretched out on the mattresses. Weeks passed while all anxiously awaited the arrival of the convoy held up in Kladovo, only two days' distance away. The Danube had frozen over, and the land border was closed to the immigrants.

Rations consisted of frozen bread, sausage, and cheese sent by the Palestine Office in Rumania. The passengers refused to obey the two representatives of the Bureau, who shared their lot in everything. Then Ruth Kluger (Eliav) arrived for a visit, after a ten-hour drive on the smooth and partially frozen road. She came upon a frightful scene. The

majority of the crew, who resembled pirates more than
sailors, were drunk and wounded from a knife fight. Even
the captain was stone drunk. There was no drinking water,
as the water had frozen in the pipes, and a few days passed
before water was brought in a cart and was distributed to
the passengers, half a cup per person. One girl, unable to
bear the strain, jumped overboard and was rescued with
difficulty. The passengers had not washed themselves or
their clothing for days. The first thing Ruth did was to repair
Kladoro's Turkish bath, which had not been used for years.
When she succeeded in getting it to work, the townspeople
could scarcely believe their eyes. The neighboring villagers
rushed over to see the miracle of the smoke rising from the
old building. The water boiled for twenty-four hours, and
the people bathed to their hearts' content. They presented a
somewhat strange sight, dancing and singing their way back
to the filthy ship.

The pregnant women presented a serious problem. The
ship's doctor refused to accept responsibility for them and
insisted that they be taken ashore. They and their husbands,
however, refused to comply. The emissary finally prevailed
upon the drunken captain to turn over his room to the
women. The room required a great deal of cleaning before
it was fit to be used. An elderly Rumanian woman in the
village donated two sheets that she had kept hidden in her
chest; she had spun them herself before her marriage. Some
utensils, too, were obtained—a bowl, a tub, and the like. The
two babies were born on the very eve of the ship's departure.

More troubles lay ahead, however. One of the pioneers
mistakenly took benzene from the storeroom instead of oil,
to light the candelabra, and a fire broke out. A girl from
Germany was severely burnt and died as a result. The
passengers had not yet recovered from this disaster when on

the following night a violent storm arose. The ship was
buffeted about and almost smashed on the pier, for the
anchor chains had ripped out of their rings. The small boat
sounded its distress sirens but they were drowned out by the
noise of the storm. The immigrants' defense force worked
together with the crew for hours and barely averted disaster.

Days passed and Hanukkah arrived. Some of the immigrants built a huge wooden candelabrum and topped it with
electric candles. They held a party with traditional singing
and dancing and speeches.

They finally sailed. However, no sooner did they approach
Istanbul than they were discovered by British warships. A
group of British soldiers led by two captains boarded the
ship at sea, took command of it, and brought it into Haifa
on January 23, 1940.

Then the struggle commenced.

The Mandatory Government intended to send the boat
to Paraguay, the country officially designated as the immigrants' destination on their passports. This was the first time
that the British had dared to take such a step. The captain
was ordered to lift anchor and sail, but he convinced the
authorities that "some repairs" would be necessary first.

In the meantime the Yishuv organized for action. Overnight Haifa was plastered with proclamations demanding
the release of the immigrants. The Council of the Jewish
Community of Haifa assembled and chose a delegation to
bring the Yishuv's demands to the representative of the
Mandatory Government. They met with him on Saturday.
He asked that the Council calm the populace no matter
what the Government should decide. David Hacohen
answered for the delegation:

> The Yishuv does not like to engage in demonstra-
> tions and strikes and unnecessary contention. Even

10. FINALLY, AFTER 107 DAYS, THE IMMIGRANTS WERE ALLOWED TO DEBARK.

though the Yishuv is fully aware of what is happening to the Jews under Hitler's domination and at sea, it has remained silent. Just as parents and brothers in England carry on their daily affairs with an outward calm, while their sons and relatives are dying in the war, so we go about our business quietly while our brothers are being killed. But it's another thing entirely when the battle reaches our front doorstep. When a man finds himself under fire, he acts. Do you believe that there will be a single Jew who will not seek revenge if this ship is sent away? This is a delicate matter, and you can't compare it with any other incidents involving illegal immigration. You British had better be careful now.

Days passed, weeks, and months. Finally, after 107 days the immigrants were allowed to debark.

No such happy fate, however, awaited the convoy that had been held up at Kladovo in November, 1939.

Kladovo is an isolated village on the Yugoslavian side of the Danube and is a few miles from the river. The nearest railroad station is thirty-three miles away. The only way to reach the spot in winter is by sleigh. Supplying the convoy with food and medicine was therefore a major problem. In addition, the size of the group necessitated a strict internal regime. Despite this situation, the morale was high. Everyone looked forward to the end of winter when the snow would melt and they would be able to embark. The health situation was not bad. After one man died as a result of a serious illness, an agreement was reached with the authorities of the Rumanian border city whereby seriously ill persons were to be brought to the hospital that was located in the city.

The local authorities also showed their consideration by

helping to alleviate the immigrants' boredom. In contravention of orders that they had been given, they allowed 100 persons to go to the beach daily to take part in sports and games.

Camp life became well organized. Cultural activities were instituted. Hebrew study groups were formed, parties were held, lectures were given, and bulletins were put out. The camp was subdivided into groups of twenty, with one member representing each group and serving as a liason with the small directorate. As the end of winter approached a growing impatience was evident in the camp. Classes and games no longer held people's interest. One question prevailed in everyone's mind: When will the day arrive?

When the snows had melted sufficiently, Agami set out for Yugoslavia to visit the camp. The Danube was overflowing its banks and only by means of a cart yoked to a team of oxen was he able to get to the three river boats that housed the refugees. Agami came upon a formidable sight—a black cluster of boats on the water with hundreds of heads packed together on the decks. These youngsters were the cream of the Hehalutz movement, and some of them were his personal friends. Some were leaders of the movement and had participated in the Zionist Congress in Geneva. When the war broke out they did not feel free to save themselves, but chose to return to Vienna. Strangely enough, no one spoke as Agami came on board, although they had eagerly waited all winter long for a visit from a member of the Bureau. Their silence was frightening.

When the emissary entered one of the ship's cabins that night he saw the floor completely covered with people. It was a long time before he could thread his way through the thick mass of bodies.

By the time he left he was thoroughly depressed. He went

directly to the "Joint" director in Europe, described to him what he had just seen, and urged him to give him some money before it was too late—but in vain.

At this time Eliahu Golomb was on his way to the United States in an effort to raise money for the operation. He was traveling on a freighter, as there were no other means of transportation available. Agami got to him and asked for his immediate help. Golomb did his best. He tried to buy a Rumanian tugboat but failed for lack of sufficient funds.

In the meanwhile Italy had entered the war, but still no one thought that it would last very much longer. Nonetheless, the need was felt to establish camp life on a new basis. A huge steamer that could accommodate 1,000 passengers was brought over from Rumania. The camp began to lead an independent existence. Job openings were discovered, to the relief of the long idle immigrants. Many found employment in services and work projects within the camp. The authorities treated them kindly. They agreed to transfer them during the summer to a small port near Belgrade. Bunkhouses were built and tents were erected. The immigrants organized themselves in different groups according to their countries of origin and the movements to which they belonged. After a while their poor circumstances became very taxing, but they adjusted in hopes that the day would soon come when they would leave for Palestine.

That day never came. They remained in their new location two years, until Hitler's army invaded the region. The camp was destroyed and its inhabitants were killed. Groups of Nazis hunted them down to a distance of two miles from the camp and shot them down one by one. Not a single person remained alive.

During this period Dr. Chaim Weizmann, Chairman of the Jewish Agency, publicly defined the illegal immigration effort as the "only means" of rescue. In February, 1940, he wrote:

> "Our minds cannot grasp nor can our hearts comprehend the extent of the calamity that has blotted out Jewish life on the continent of Europe. Great communities have perished, and among them the Jewish community of Poland, which despite famine and persecution, nurtured and guarded with its life the faith of the Jewish people. Now it is ground into the dust. . . . We must not acquiesce, we must not accept the lot that is meted out to us as refugees. Acceptance of such a lot would mean the destruction of our state and the end of our existence as a people. . . . At this very moment ships bearing our young immigrants are making their way to Palestine through mined and submarine-infested seas, and they will reach their destination in spite of all the dangers that lie in wait for them.

His prophecy was only partially fulfilled. Some ships that started out in early 1940 did reach Palestine, but only after they underwent many dangers.

On July 17 the coast guard caught the Libertad, a 90-ton boat flying the flag of Uruguay, off the coast of Zikhron Ya'akov. The 390 refugees aboard were from the Balkan countries and had spent over a month at sea. Most of them were discouraged, middle-aged and older people whose families had been destroyed. There were only a few young people aboard, who looked to the future with hope.

There was a large bunker on board the Libertad, a long and narrow corridor-like affair only two yards wide. Three levels were built into it and 300 people were put inside. Benches were brought in and each person was allocated a space 27 inches wide and 5 feet long. Most passengers had to sleep with their feet doubled up. Very little air and light entered the one doorway that stood at the top of the steps that led to the deck. At night this opening was almost completely sealed off by a net that hung over it to provide a sleeping place for ten people. The few oil lamps did little to dispel the darkness, but did increase the closeness; and the amount of filth and refuse was appalling.

At long length they arrived at the port of Burgas. By that time it was evident that the ship would never survive a journey at sea; the engine was almost falling apart. When the Jews of Burgas heard of the immigrants' situation they came out to them in boats and brought them drinking water, and promised to do their best to bring them ashore. However, they were soon approached by a mine layer. The tug crept up on them in the darkness and burst suddenly into sight, its deck manned by officers holding rifles aimed at the refugees. The tug's captain demanded that the Libertad's ropes be thrown to him so that the boat could be pulled out of Bulgarian waters. He threatened to shoot unless his order was obeyed. No one spoke. Suddenly a woman shouted:

"Go ahead and shoot then, you murderers! Better that than we should drown!"

Apparently the outcry had its effect on the captain of the tug. He promised to haul the boat to Turkish waters, but the people on the Libertad did not believe him. Only after he took a seaman's oath that he would hold to his promise did the crew tie a rope to the mainmast and throw the other end to him. The captain was as good as his word, and only when they approached the Turkish coast, before dawn, did he untie the rope and disappear.

They were met at the entrance of the Bosporus by the Turkish police. After they spent one night in the port of Istanbul, another tug came along, tied the boat to itself with ropes, and took it out to sea. The wind carried the Libertad along the Sea of Marmara to Canak Kale at the mouth of the Dardanelles. One of the local Jews brought them bread, water, olives, and cheese, and his gift came not a moment too soon. There was not a drop of water to be found aboard the boat and the supply of stale biscuit that they had been living on for three days was almost exhausted. Once again, however, the police appeared and ordered them to leave at once. As they were on their way, drinking water was hoisted up from the boat that was accompanying them.

At nightfall they sailed into a calm Aegean Sea. Here the boat anchored for twenty-four hours until a storm arose and began pushing it toward the island of Mytilene. In vain they waved flags and sent out SOS signals. Fortunately the storm subsided and the captain managed to get close to the shore. A Greek sailor came over in his boat and showed them how to enter the bay, and soon they arrived at the town of Sigri where they were warmly received. The police permitted them to stay there, and to go ashore and bathe in the sea; they even placed a small boat at their disposal to enable them to get to shore and back. They were also given permission to buy fresh fruit and vegetables. Last of all a mechanic from the neighboring village repaired the engine. This took a long time as the engine was very old, and some of its parts were rust-eaten and worn away. Two weeks passed, during which time the town continued in its hospitable treatment of the refugees.

When they put out to sea once more the repaired engine was running smoothly. Swiftly the Libertad sailed past the Dodecanese Islands, conquered by the Italians. Joy was short-lived, however. A case of typhus was discovered, the engine broke down again, and the water ran out. Yet, in spite of everything, the boat finally reached Palestine.

Other boats were not so fortunate.

At the end of 1940 many disasters occurred at sea. The first was that of the Pencho, a 245-ton ship that flew the

Bulgarian flag and carried 509 Slovakian refugees. Almost all of them were capable of physical labor and many of them were artisans.

The ship sailed from Bratislava on May 18 down the Danube, and in ten days' time arrived at the Yugoslavian town of Bezdan. Here they stayed for fourteen days and took on 100 German refugees. From Bezdan they sailed to Moldova where, however, the Rumanian guard forced them to return to Yugoslavian waters. For two months they lay at anchor on the Danube between the two countries until the Yugoslavian Government sent a motor boat that took the immigrant ship through the "Iron Gate" and left them at Vidin on the Yugoslavian-Bulgarian border. However, no sooner did the ship lower the Bulgarian flag than they were chased away and were forbidden to drop anchor even to take on provisions. From Vidin they sailed to another Bulgarian port, and from there down the river to the Rumanian port of Giurgiu, where they stocked up on food and fuel. Finally they arrived at Sulina. On September 21, after repairs had been made on the ship, they sailed toward Istanbul, on the Black Sea. Turkish coastal authorities did not allow them to drop anchor in Turkish waters, so they could not stop until they arrived at the Greek island of Mytilene, where they took on provisions of bread and water. In the vicinity of the island of Stampalia they were set upon by an Italian warship. The travelers were taken ashore and searched, and only on the next day were they allowed to continue their journey.

Their trials were far from finished however. On October 9, the pipe leading from the steam boiler burst and the ship was incapacitated. For two days it drifted about at sea until it arrived in the vicinity of the Greek island of Khamili, which was then in Italian hands. They had but one lifeboat on board and they used it to convey the passengers to the desolate, rocky island where they were forced to spend eleven days. Four of the immigrants were responsible for saving the entire group. With the help of a Turkish crew member they put to sea in the rickety lifeboat to seek help. They hoped to reach the island of Crete by the light of the towers on the shore. For two days they pulled through stormy waters, but the elements proved too much for them and they were driven in the opposite direction, out to sea. Then a patrol plane passed over them, followed by a fleet of twenty-six British ships. They were brought aboard one of the ships in a state of unconsciousness. As soon as they revived, they told of the abandoned refugees on the island.

The rocky island was only two miles long and a few hundred yards wide and was completely barren of trees or shrubs. The emigrants collected stones and piled them layer upon layer to make shelters against the wind. They built two mounds, and atop one they placed the former mast of the Pencho with a white flag attached to it, in hopes that it might be seen from the sea. They also built a fire and set a twenty-four hour watch over it to make sure that it would not go out. Then they made a huge kite from pieces of wood and strips of linen. Some of the younger immigrants managed to get into the slowly sinking ship and salvage whatever food was left, some wood for fuel, and some cooking utensils. Many managed to save their personal belongings. To their great joy, the emigrants discovered water pouring from a crevice in the rocks; and even though the water tasted foul, they looked upon the incident as an act of providence. This was the eve of the Day of Atonement. As the sun sank into the sea, the camp stood massed together for the Kol Nidre prayer. They prayed with a fervor that they had never known.

Each passing day brought on new problems, and hunger was the most pressing problem of all. They wove a net in hopes of catching some fish. They made a large wooden raft with SOS written on it in bold letters, as well as a description of the island and its location. Everyone gathered around to see it sent out to sea.

After they despaired of being rescued quickly and their hunger became acute, they began gathering sea plants and snails. Everything was thrown into one big pot that stood on the fire. Since the matches were almost exhausted by that time and had to be saved for signaling purposes at night, the lens of a magnifying glass was employed to kindle the fire. Everyone gathered about the pot and carefully dipped into the strange concoction with spoons that had been salvaged from the Pencho, which by that time had sunk into the sea.

October 19 was the last day of their travail. A violent storm attacked the island, and the refugees could not go to the shore and gather food. They assembled inside a cave and lay down wherever they could, hungry, thirsty, cold, and afraid. Some prayed. One man lost control of himself and began screaming hysterically.

Most of the night went by. Suddenly a voice shouted out: "A ship!"

It was an Italian warship that had come in answer to the plea of the four emigrants who had been picked up by the British warship. The rescue ship came equipped with everything that was needed—blankets and clothes, food and water. Even Chianti wine had been brought.

The ship took the emigrants to Rhodes and from there they were taken as prisoners of war to Feremonti in Italy. Only after the conclusion of the war did they reach Palestine.

A worse fate befell the Salvador, a ship that carried 325 emigrants and flew the flag of Uruguay. It was an old, dilapidated Bulgarian sailing ship that weighed only 100 tons. It was owned by two Jews of Sofia who were engaged in the profitable business of smuggling Jewish refugees who could afford to pay well. The boat lacked the most essential nautical tools; there wasn't a map, a compass, or barometer aboard. The crew consisted of two old sailors and a Bulgarian captain. The passengers were too heavy a load for the weak vessel, and the owners, who had only profit in mind, had not even bothered to equip the vessel with a lifeboat.

The Salvador left the Bulgarian port of Varna and on December 6 arrived in Istanbul. A violent storm was then raging and port authorities allowed the ship to anchor in the outer Bosporus. They stayed there for five days and the city of Istanbul supplied them with food and medical care. After the storm abated the port authorities sent a guide and sanitation supervisor on board the boat with orders to remain on it until it should leave the Dardanelles.

The boat set sail in the afternoon, but after a few hours passed, a storm wind arose from the opposite direction. It increased in force and became a raging snowstorm. The boat was buffeted about all night on the stormy waves. Early in the morning, as the intensity of the storm increased, the skipper decided to return to Istanbul, but he was unable to turn the boat around. The sail ripped and they smashed on a reef. One hundred and three bodies were cast up on the shore. Many had been swept away by the waves even before the boat crashed. A few bodies remained aboard the sunken vessel, and only after days passed were they recovered by divers. Among those who perished were sixty-six children and one of the two officials that the port authorities in

Istanbul had sent to accompany the boat. Most of the survivors were treated at the hospital in Istanbul.

The world was not overly upset by the incident, however. The war was claiming its attention, and the disaster went by relatively unnoticed.

7

S.S. Patria—Symbol of Resistance

The Patria disaster was one of the most shocking incidents in the history of the Yishuv, and a turning point in its struggle with the Mandatory Government.

Over two hundred men, women, and children died aboard the Patria when the ship was scuttled by the immigrants themselves with the aid of the Hagana. The immigrants took this desperate step after learning that the Mandatory Government intended to banish the ship to Mauritius, a British colony off Africa, near Madagascar. The incident caused an uproar in the Jewish world and united the Yishuv in its struggle against the British. The name Patria became a rallying cry for the pioneer youth.

Before Second World War the Patria had been a regular passenger liner, but with the outbreak of the war it became a transport ship for French troops. After France succumbed to Hitler's army the ship was taken over by the British Navy. It arrived in Haifa in the beginning of 1940 and lay idle in the port, with no crew to look after it. The Mandatory Government chose the Patria to house three immigrant groups recently arrived in Palestine from Nazi Europe aboard three ships: the Pacific, the Milos, and the Atlantic. These were three of Storper's *Sondertransporten*, or "special shipments."

126

Storper, then in his fifties, behaved very servilely in Eichmann's presence. His assiduity in carrying out his superior's orders soon earned him the role of *Sonderkommissar*—"Special Commissar"—of Education. He had acquired most of his wealth by supplying the German Army with provisions during the First World War, but both that wealth and his close connections with the Gestapo were of no help to him when the time came for him to pay for his crimes. From the beginning of the Second World War he openly opposed the demands of the Hehalutz emissaries and disregarded agreements made with them concerning joint activities. Y. Edelstein tried to warn the "Joint" people about what was really going on so that they should not give Storper large sums of money without first examining whether the funds were really being used for the rescue effort or whether they were being pocketed by Nazi officials. The councils of the Jewish communities, subjected to pressures by Storper, sent telegrams urging that the "Joint" continue to send the money unconditionally and not endanger them by angering Eichmann.

The members of the Bureau who were in Geneva felt that they were caught between the frying pan and the fire. They finally accepted Storper's invitation to meet with him in Geneva in May, 1940. Prior to this meeting, Dr. Nahum Goldmann and Zvi Yehieli flew to London to meet with David Ben-Gurion and E. Kaplan. At this meeting it was decided that the rescue effort took precedence over everything else. Even if it became clear that Storper was but a tool of Eichmann, interested only in stuffing his pockets and the Nazi treasury with American dollars, they were still to cooperate with him. Their position was in agreement with that taken by Dr. Chaim Weizmann. At the advice of the young men of the Bureau, the "Joint" appointed their friend Shmarya Tzameret to represent them in the talks with Storper. Shmarya and Agami went to Athens and hired three ships: the Pacific, the Milos, and the Atlantic.

The meeting took place at a time when the Nazi Army was drunk with victory; it had just conquered Poland and was about to enter Paris. Storper said to them: "The Allies have lost the war, but I have power. Just leave everything to me." He wished to allay their fears and free himself of any Zionist supervision of his work.

Two months before the meeting with Storper, Eichmann called together the representatives of the various Jewish organizations to consider the problem of Jewish emigration to Palestine. The meeting, held in the Special Department for Jewish Emigration on the Kurfürstendamm in Berlin, was attended by eight representatives from various levels of the German administration as well as representatives of the Jewish communities of Vienna, Prague, and the Reich. Erich Frank represented the pioneer youth movement. They were ushered into a large hall, at the end of which sat Eichmann, flanked by his adjutants. They were not offered seats, but remained standing, waiting to hear what he would say. He looked at them intently and then, in a loud voice, announced that at that meeting he would tell them how many Jews would leave Germany in the near future. He announced a large number, knowing as well as they did that they would be unable to handle emigration on such a large scale, cut off as they were from the world Jewish community. Eichmann repeated emphatically that this would be their last chance to get Jews out by emigration, and that should they fail to do it—the Jews would be taken to eastern Europe for the *Umsiedlung*.

At that time the German border was still open. Jewish

emigration was not prohibited entirely until 1942. At that meeting in March, 1940, it was already obvious that Eichmann had decided to do something about the troublesome leaders of Hehalutz and the emissaries of the Bureau, who were still struggling to retain their slight degree of freedom in the organization of the emigration to Palestine and the selection of candidates. Their concern for the emigrants interfered with Eichmann. Storper was given the authority to organize shipments as he saw fit, and he gave preference to Jews who had been released from concentration camps. The Gestapo began to release people purposely in order to get them off their hands, and compelled Storper to give these people priority. This method had a direct and adverse effect on the number of pioneers included in the illegal immigration. Also, one of the reasons that Hehalutz wanted to screen the prospective immigrants was to prevent Nazi agents from infiltrating the groups, and so deny the British Government one of their excuses for combatting the illegal immigration.

Immediately after the meeting with Eichmann, Storper sent Erich Frank a note with the following message: "Leave at once, tonight, or you will regret it!" The next day he was summoned by the Nazis, who deprived him of his passport, warned him never to come before them again as a representative of a public body, and all but threw him out bodily. Shortly after this he joined one of the three emigrant groups that were eventually placed on board the Patria. He was given permission to do so after representatives of Jewish bodies told Eichmann that without him they would not be able to organize and supervise such a large group of emigrants.

The groups brought together on the Patria came from different countries. A large portion of them had gathered previously in Bratislava. There they lived for months in large Czech Army barracks.

The ships that were to take them to Palestine did not arrive on schedule. These people knew what it meant to be despised and persecuted under a hostile regime. They contrasted sharply with the emigrants from Berlin, Vienna, and Prague who arrived in August, 1940, hale and hearty, from comfortable city dwellings or pioneer training farms. The people from the Reich knew what group discipline meant, and they were well organized. The immigrants were divided up into groups, each group having a leader and his helper. The entire group had a commander and his helper, and they were assisted by the committee of group leaders. Every person who wished to take the trip signed a document stating that he was aware of the dangers involved and that he was willing to subject himself to the rule of the group.

Every German emigrant was allowed to take ten marks out of the country. The money was gathered into one fund, and the "Union of the Jews of the Reich" added its contribution of 20,000 marks to provide for the ship during its journey down the Danube. With this money a great deal of provisions were purchased later in the Balkan countries. Two hundred and eighty members of the German contingent had completed their pioneer training, and seventy of them were boys and girls of the Youth Aliya, an organization formed in 1933 for the purpose of saving the young from the Nazi terror. The rest were Zionists of long standing and parents who had children in Palestine.

When the emigrants arrived in Vienna and the ships that were to convey them down the Danube had not yet arrived, the Gestapo arranged to have them accommodated at first-class hotels. However, as time passed and still the ships did not come, they were ordered out of the hotels and moved into Jewish school buildings, where they learned for the first time what it meant to live like emigrants. Fortunately their discomfort did not last long, and after a few days they were on a train to Bratislava. There three luxury liners were waiting to take them to the Black Sea, where they would transfer to other ships that would take them the remainder of their journey. They were accompanied by a Nazi officer who saw to it that they were not held up by passport and baggage inspections at the Hungarian, Bulgarian, and Rumanian borders.

In Tulcea, a port on the Danube, they were transferred to three pitiable, battered Greek ships that flew the flag of Panama: the Atlantic, weighing 1,000 tons; the Pacific, weighing 500 tons; and the Milos, weighing even less. There they lay at anchor for a month.

The immigrants from Bratislava were put on board the Pacific, where the living conditions were wretched. Wooden tables served as beds, there were few lavatories, and there was no kitchen at all. They even lacked a captain. Nevertheless, they had to transfer to the wretched ships, because the German liners were needed to convey to Germany *Volksdeutsche* who had left Russia. Due to the overcrowded conditions a skin disease broke out among the children. Morale was low. Of necessity, however, life was organized somehow. A stove was obtained for cooking, provisions were bought, and service rooms were set up.

After a few days had passed, captains and crews arrived for each of the three ships. The captain of the Pacific was an old Greek who had acquired his underground experience in smuggling arms to Spain during the Spanish Civil War. Because of his socialistic leanings he had been banished from Greece.

Just as the ships started to sail, they were suddenly

surrounded by boats full of Jews who had been waiting for that moment to force their way on board—and some of them managed to do it.

As soon as they were out on the Black Sea all of the Pacific's weak points, disregarded by Storper and his lieutenants, quickly became apparent. The water that was drawn from one of the tanks for the first breakfast was found to be muddy and unfit for use. The tank had a leak and sea water had gotten in. There was nothing to do but resort to rationing at once. Watches were set over the water tanks, but even at that it was clear that their water supply would not last them till Palestine. They also soon learned that the compass did not function properly, and to top off their troubles, the ship had not been sufficiently provisioned with coal.   After a conference with the captain and the Bulgarian mechanic who was his assistant, it was decided to head for the Bulgarian coast and there obtain a new compass and some coal. En route they were met by a Bulgarian warship and were ordered to follow it to port as punishment for entering the country's territorial waters. The ship was led to Varna and was ordered to wait outside the port. During the evening it was approached by two large boats packed with people. Armed police officers brandished their weapons and tried forcibly to embark Jewish refugees, who were a burden on the local authorities. The leaders of the Pacific, realizing that this was their opportunity to obtain what they needed, demanded that their compass be fixed and that they be provisioned with water and coal in exchange for accepting the refugees, who had been waiting for months to emigrate to Palestine.

After tiresome negotiations, a contract listing the rights of both parties was drawn up and signed. The compass was fixed and the Jewish community paid for the repairs. The ship was requested to approach the pier and embark the people and the supplies. However, before the carloads of coal and vegetables were taken on board, the police forcibly embarked double the number of emigrants that had been agreed upon. Moreover, as the ship was about to sail, it became clear that the amount of coal and provisions delivered was less than what had been promised, but the ship sailed notwithstanding. Among those who had been embarked was a small group of pioneers from Bulgaria from the pioneer youth movement Hashomer Hatzair. There were only twelve of them, but their energetic activity and the fact that they spoke Hebrew among themselves boosted the general morale enormously.

The Pacific passed through the Dardanelles without mishap. In Istanbul a representative of the Chief Rabbinate boarded the ship and presented the heads of the group with a gift that they had tried to get in Rumania: nautical maps without which they would have been unable to continue their journey. The captain then solved the water and coal predicament. As he was thoroughly familiar with the Greek islands and their coasts, he brought the ship to the small hidden port of San Nicola in Crete. The ship dropped anchor and the leaders contacted the "Joint" representatives on the island. After their unhappy experiences in Bulgaria and Rumania, they were doubly comforted by their warm reception at the hands of the Jews and the notables of the Greek community, who came aboard to see how they were and asked how they could be of help. The school children displayed their sympathy in a demonstration: they surrounded the ship in boats and waved flags. An emigrant who was an accordionist greeted them by playing the Greek national anthem, which he had managed to learn from one of the Greek sailors. The "Joint" representative in Athens hurried down to San Nicola and gladly extended aid. They were given water and were provided with all the coal that was to be had in the poor out-of-the-way port. They were also given some sheep to slaughter and a huge supply of vegetables. The emigrants, very grateful, were puzzled by this generosity. This took place in October, 1940, when Mussolini was waging a war of nerves with Greece, repeatedly threatening to invade the country. It seemed that the Greeks looked upon the persecuted refugees as comrades in arms; and indeed, one day after the Pacific left San Nicola, Mussolini invaded Greece.

The ship left San Nicola to the tunes of the Greek and Hebrew national anthems played on the accordion. A party was planned for that night to celebrate the new stage of their journey. Most of the passengers gathered at the extreme end of the deck, and when more people arrived and everyone got up at the same time to make a path for them, the ship became unbalanced, and seemed about to overturn. The captain dashed out of his room, climbed up a mast, and directed traffic as the passengers scattered, and managed to restore the swaying ship's equilibrium.

More trouble lay ahead. After they passed Cyprus, the mechanic informed the heads of the groups that the coal would not last them till Palestine. The work group was given orders to chop up every spare wooden beam. The benches that had served as beds were broken apart. No one went to sleep. Only a few people found space to sit down. At 4:30 A.M., as dawn was breaking, dry land appeared on the horizon: "Eretz Yisrael! Palestine!" the emigrants shouted, as they embraced one another, laughed, and wept.

As the ship approached Haifa it was met by two small boats. Two British officers came on board, and the British flag was run up the mast. The passengers, not realizing the significance of what was taking place, clapped their hands joyfully. Representatives of the immigrant group met with the British officers in the captain's room. Erich Frank, as spokesman, told the British who the passengers were and where they had come from, and added that they sought the help of their brothers in Palestine and the protection of the Mandatory Government.

The immigrants hoped that they would enter the country at once. Many wore white shirts in honor of the occasion. Their hope, however, was a vain one.

On Friday morning, November 1, 1940, a medical committee boarded the ship. Bread and oranges were brought on board, and the immigrants thrilled to see and taste for the first time fruit from Eretz Yisrael. During that entire day they remained on deck, unable to get their fill of looking at the shore. They were puzzled however, as to why representatives of the Jewish Agency or the Histadrut had not yet boarded the ship. Some attributed this to the fact that the Sabbath was approaching. Others were of the opinion that they had not been granted permission. Someone started a rumor to the effect that the ship would not enter the port until Monday since the next day was the Sabbath and on Sunday the English did not work.

As night fell the passengers became aware of a police boat that circled the ship incessantly. What did it mean? During the night it began to rain. Those who were sleeping on the deck tried to find standing room inside the ship. Since all the benches and couches had been dismantled and used as fuel, there was only the floor to sleep on. The steps were filled with women and children and old men trying to sleep standing up.

The Sabbath passed, and then Sunday, but nothing

happened, and the police boat continued to make its steady rounds, day and night.

On Monday word got about that the immigrants were to be transferred to the Patria, that lay at anchor in the port. There they would be kept for three weeks, after which time those who had relatives in Palestine would be released, and the rest would be taken to the internment camp in Atlit. No one knew the source of these rumors but all believed them.

On Wednesday the Milos arrived and anchored across from the Pacific amid a spirited reception. That same morning two small boats approached the Pacific and the transfer began at once. When they arrived at the Patria they formed a chain and passed up the baggage from the boat. Then each person took his own baggage and went to the tables behind which the British officials sat. The latter emptied the suitcases of their contents, threw them together into one jumbled heap, and then ordered the immigrants to pack their belongings, and quickly.

By Friday the transfer of the passengers of the Pacific was completed and on the following day the transfer of the passengers of the Milos commenced. Compared with the conditions they had known for two months aboard the small and shaky ships, the Patria's accommodations were very comfortable. The women and children were put in cabins, and the men in large halls containing wooden double-decker bunks. The pioneers were taken to halls deep in the ship's hold. For the first night they slept on the floor on straw-filled mattresses and slept well, after having spent so many nights on benches and bare wooden floors.

However, it was not long before they realized that their pleasant new quarters were no more than a floating prison. Many British soldiers were on board the ship and armed guards were located in every corner. They would curse the immigrants occasionally, and sometimes hit them with their clubs.

The immigrants on board the Atlantic underwent a similar experience. They were the largest of the three groups, being 1,700 people on board a 1,000-ton ship. Due to a water shortage, the travelers suffered a rash of epidemics, including typhus. In addition, because the ship was overloaded it would occasionally tilt to one side, so a defense watch was maintained on the bridge around the clock. The watches would shout warnings when the need arose and would order the immigrants to shift to the left or right side of the boat. The Atlantic had been undersupplied with fuel and was forced to go to Cyprus after all the available wood inside the ship had been used to feed the engines. At Cyprus they learned of the fate that awaited them in Palestine: deportation. The very word sounded ominous to their ears. Nonetheless they were overjoyed when Mt. Carmel was sighted on November 24. They sang Hatikva so forcefully that they were heard by the immigrants on board the Patria.

By that time it was becoming increasingly clear to the Patria's passengers that there was almost no chance of the Government's changing its mind. No contact was made with the Hagana until two days after they were transferred from the Pacific. The first note delivered to Erich Frank, the recognized leader of the immigrants, clearly stated what most likely lay in store for them. The leaders on the ship then realized that it was to their disadvantage to cooperate with the British in any way. Their principal concern became to foster a feeling of solidarity among the immigrants and make of them a unified group that would fight for its existence. However, not all the groups were of the same color. The passengers on board the Milos included a group of husky members of the "Czech Legion," who did not look upon

Palestine as their destination but wished rather to rejoin the forces of Free Czechoslovakia. They had had no pioneer training background and Zionism held no attraction for them. Their Jewish commander had been a captain in the former Czech Army, and their goal was to attach themselves to that army, wherever it was. Their approaching deportation from Palestine was a matter of indifference to them. For this reason the British officers on board the Patria chose them to carry out their orders.

The members of Hehalutz looked at the situation from an entirely different perspective. They were confronted with one problem: what to do in order to thwart the British scheme. They refrained from acting, however, since they were not sure that they had received their information from a reliable source.

Normal lines of communication with the Hagana had not been set up. British guards were about the ship at all times, and police and secret agents kept watch day and night. With the death of the father of one of the immigrants an opportunity to make contact with the Hagana presented itself. The deceased's son, a citizen of Palestine, obtained permission to bury his father in Palestinian soil. He also obtained permission for his brother, an immigrant, to attend the funeral, on condition that he return to the ship that evening. Upon his return he smuggled aboard a letter written in the same hand as the first note that they had received from the Hagana. Now they knew for a certainty that they would be deported. The Mandatory Government intended to send the ship to the distant island of Mauritius. It was clear that a united effort was required if they were to accomplish anything.

On the evening of November 16, a few days before the official publication of the deportation order, hundreds of immigrants led by the members of Hehalutz gathered on the deck for a protest demonstration. "We don't want Mauritius!" they shouted. "We want Eretz Israel!" They ended the demonstration with the singing of Hatikvah.

Finally the day arrived when the order was read to the immigrants officially. A police officer gathered the leaders of the convoy and told them that since they had requested the protection of the Palestinian Government upon their arrival in the country's coastal waters, the Government was complying and was providing them with that protection in Mauritius. The deportation decree stated that the immigrants would be sent to a British colony as soon as arrangements could be made to assure them safe transfer to their new place of residence and suitable accommodation there. They would remain in the colony until the end of the war, at which time a decision would be made as to where they would be sent. However, the Government did not intend to retain them in the colony to which they were being sent or bring them back to Palestine. The Government promised to take similar actions in the future against any other groups that should succeed in arriving in Palestine illegally.

Two days prior to this the immigrants' leaders had sent a letter to High Commissioner MacMichael, but he did not reply. The immigrants were deeply embittered and on the verge of despair. Every night young men would jump overboard and attempt to swim to shore, but few succeeded, as the British had surrounded the ship with motor boats whose bright searchlights constantly lit up the entire area. Nine would-be escapees were caught in the water, returned to the ship, and locked in the brig, as morale sank lower and lower.

After the deportation was formally announced, a hunger strike was declared on board the ship. The Yishuv, which all this time had been engaged in bitter negotiations with the

Mandatory Government, proclaimed a protest sympathy strike. Prior to this the Constituent Assembly sent a delegation to the High Commissioner, but he refused to receive it. In the course of the negotiations the Secretary General of the British Mandatory Government informed the Yishuv's representatives that the Yishuv had no authority in matters pertaining to Jews outside of Palestine. A protest was lodged by Yizhak Ben-Zvi—later to become Israel's second president—chairman of the National Council, which was the official representative of Palestinian Jewry, having been elected by the Constituent Assembly. The Secretary, however, only replied: "It is the opinion of the Commissioner that you are inciting the public . . . if the country does not calm down we will take all necessary measures. . . ."

The last flicker of hope was extinguished when the leaders of the immigrants were presented with a gift from the Union of Immigrants from Germany, and a parting letter from Henrietta Szold to the children on board the ship.

From then on events moved forward at a dizzying pace. It was Monday morning, November 25, 1940. The 1,800 passengers of the Patria paced back and forth on deck in helpless anger. Some of the men jumped overboard in desperation, in broad daylight, only to be forced back on board by the rifle-wielding British police. Suddenly a muffled explosion resounded from below decks. The ship began to sway and to list to one side. At first it seemed that it was due to an overconcentration of people in one side of the ship. However, it immediately became evident that something far more serious had happened. Screams arose on all sides. People began running around in panic and confusion.

Crews of other ships anchored in the harbor, as well as British soldiers and policemen, rushed to give help. The Red Cross and the Red Magen David worked side by side. The rescue effort continued through the night.

One of those who were rescued had the following story to tell:

That day we had to make some sleeping room available for the passengers of the Atlantic, and all the women whose cabins were in a certain section were ordered to leave. One cabin had been occupied by a woman and her baby, who had been born on the Black Sea. The soldiers entered her room while she was breast-feeding the baby and forced her to go up on deck at once. There was a lot of movement, because at that time of day, between eight and ten in the morning, they would clean the inside of the ship and everyone had to go up on deck. I hung around near the cabin where the fellows who jumped overboard were being kept. A soldier came up to me with a broom in his hand, and ordered me to sweep up the passage-way. I did it willingly, hoping that I would be allowed to sweep the prisoners' cell too. No sooner had the soldier left than I heard a dull blast. At first I paid no attention and went on sweeping. Then I saw people running around and I heard some shouting:

"An accident! Warning! Air raid! Everyone on the back deck—go below!"

People were screaming for help or just screaming. Suddenly I realized that the boat was slowly leaning to one side. I dashed to the prisoners' cabin and found two of them trying to break the door open. I did my best to help, but we couldn't budge the door an inch. A guard appeared. We demanded that he open the door, and after he did, we all rushed up the stairs. The left deck was crowded with hundreds of people, with every-body holding on to the next fellow; the right side of the ship was submerging rapidly. Someone gave the order to put on life belts.

I remembered that I had seen life belts in the men's sleeping hall and I dashed below. I met five people who were lost, including a boy who was crying because he didn't know how to put on his life belt. I put it on him, grabbed as many life belts as I could, and went back up on deck. By that time I had to crawl on all fours: I couldn't stand up. Hands reached down to pull me up to the upper deck. A soldier was holding on to the air vent with one hand and his rifle with the other, still determined not to let anybody jump overboard. Suddenly we heard more explosions and we were showered with beams and chunks of wood. One of the beams fell on the soldier. He slipped and fell into the water with his rifle in his hand. Lots of people jumped in after him. There were only a few left on deck, and they clutched at anything that came to hand. I lost my balance and slipped into the water. As I surfaced, I saw that the ship was only two yards above my head. Fragments of masts, lifeboats, and planks were falling all around. I started swimming away as fast as I could. I saw the anchor chain of an oil boat in front of me, swam for it, and grabbed hold.

Looking back to the Patria I saw that it had turned over completely—the bottom of the ship was above the water. There were some people sitting there, trying to help the less fortunate aboard. Others were still swimming around in the sea trying to save their lives. Twenty yards in front of me a small motorboat stopped and began hauling people out of the water. I left the chain and swam over to the boat. Hands reached down and I was pulled aboard, and the boat made for shore.

Suddenly we heard a horrible scream: a girl who had been swimming towards us from behind had been caught in the big screw and had been crushed. We lifted her body into the boat. Many more boats came out to rescue the swimmers. Only ten minutes had passed since the explosion and many were already standing on the pier; but many had died. "My baby, my baby!" I heard a voice cry cut. I recognized the woman —four days before she had given birth aboard the Patria.

"They saved me at the last minute," she wailed. "My husband took the baby and they both disappeared!"

"I saw him in one of the boats, he was holding something in his arms," I quickly lied to her.

"That's what they all say," she answered, and burst out in tears.

A stretcher was brought in and she was taken outside. No sooner had she left than her husband appeared, with the child. But how different he looked! Then I looked around—and everyone looked different. They looked like ghosts of the people they had been the day before.

The Yishuv was outraged. This had been the first attempt in the history of the illegal immigration effort to oppose the Mandatory Government actively, and the price in human lives had been frightening. In addition to the widespread grief, a question arose: was the deed justified? The country was divided; even the leaders of the Yishuv could not agree. The venture had been executed at the decision of Hagana headquarters and the leaders of the Bureau. They had searched for possible ways of helping the passengers sabotage the ship to delay their deportation as long as possible and demonstrate in the process their bitter opposition to what was being done to them. At first they had hoped to plant a mine on the outside of the ship, but the strict watch maintained by the British made this impossible. Then they decided upon another and more complicated course of action—to sabotage the ship's bottom from within. The main problem was getting the explosives on board. At the time the ship's stoves were in need of repair. The builder, S., chosen by the government's Department of Public Works, was contacted by the works director, A., who suggested that the former take along as his assistant the Hagana member, M., who had volunteered for the task. M. brought the explosives on board in one of the sacks of clay powder used in making cement stones for the stove, and one of the immigrants set the bomb. However, the endeavor failed and the plan was postponed until the morning before the sailing. This time the "builder's assistant" carried the explosives aboard in a leather pouch in his lunchbag. He gave the pouch to one of the pioneer women who, in her capacity as nurse, was free to go from one end of the ship to the other without arousing the suspicion of any of the guards. She gave the pouch to A., the leader of the pioneers on board the ship.

They decided to set the explosion for 9 A.M., when everyone would be on deck while the cabins were being cleaned.

All who were involved in the planning and execution of the ventures were disturbed about it from the very start, knowing the risks involved. Years later, Saul Avigur wrote to a friend who had been involved in the Patria affair:

> As I remember, the situation was such that we could not have acted in any other way, even though it meant all those deaths. . . .
> After all, we tried every other possible approach, and when the British refused to cooperate in any way, we

were forced to take drastic measures. The enemy government and its representatives are responsible for the blood that was shed.

Of course, no one with a conscience will be able to rest easy until his dying day, even if everything I've mentioned is taken into consideration. Yet we couldn't have done anything else without betraying ourselves and our cause. . . .

Three days after the disaster, as the funerals of the victims were being conducted, a declaration signed by "The Yishuv's Guard" was published. It read:

The Yishuv cannot allow that the survivors of the Patria, who saw death face to face, be sentenced to deportation and further wandering. We must not turn our backs on our own flesh and blood. Let every one of us do all that is within his power to ensure that their rescue be genuine, that they might never again be threatened by the same terror from which they were saved. . . .

On December 5 an official proclamation of the Mandatory Government annulled the deportation decree:

It has been decided by His Majesty's Government, as an exceptional act of mercy, after taking all circumstances into consideration and in particular the harassing experience undergone by survivors, not to proceed with the proposal to send these particular persons overseas. They will accordingly be allowed to stay in Palestine subject to existing regulations, and their number will be deducted from the next immigration quota.

This did not mark the end of the struggle. More than a year passed before the Patria's immigrants were finally freed, in February, 1942.

The immigrants on board the Atlantic suffered a worse fate. Upon their arrival in Palestine on November 24, 1941, one day prior to the disaster, the authorities immediately began to transfer them to the deportation ship. Some of those who had been transferred were taking the disinfencting shower when the explosion took place, and were buried by the debris. The Atlantic group was imprisoned in the Atlit camp together with the survivors of the Patria, but they were not affected by the release granted the latter by the Government.

Two days later large groups of British policemen burst into the barracks where the Atlantic immigrants were kept, woke them up and ordered them to get ready for the journey. The day before, armed soldiers sent by High Commissioner MacMichael had surrounded the camp and allowed no one to enter or leave. Nevertheless, the sudden and brutal attack of the armed guards came as a surprise to the prisoners, who did their best to fight back, empty-handed as they were.

At four in the morning soldiers and policemen burst into the barracks and began laying about with their clubs among the half-clad and naked immigrants. Shouts of fear, pain, and anger resounded. Groups of two, three, and four soldiers attacked single immigrants and hauled men off by their hair. One man who refused to get up was dragged across the floor by a blanket tied around his neck. Immigrants wounded and unconscious from the beating administered them were dragged to waiting trucks and were thrown aboard. The soldiers sent to the women's and children's barracks executed their mission in a similar, if milder fashion. Immigrants who had relatives in Palestine or in the Patria groups were especially upset, being faced with the prospect of separation for an unknown period of time. A twelve-year-old girl kept screaming that she had parents in Tel Aviv and had to tell them that she was leaving. A woman whose husband was in Palestine and whose son had died in the Atlit camp lay on the ground screaming and refused to move. Some soldiers and policemen dragged her to the trucks.

The immigrants were not finally subdued until two in the afternoon. The brutality of the soldiers and the police had been appalling. Some of them had been drunk, as their commanding officer had given them all the liquor they wanted, delivered a speech on the importance of the task that they had been assigned, and warned them not to be soft-hearted. The prisoners fought bravely and well. One group of young men barricaded themselves within their barracks and made themselves inaccessible. A special unit of police-men stormed the barracks, broke into it, and attacked the naked prisoners viciously. They beat them relentlessly as they pushed them beyond the barbed-wire fence surrounding their quarters.

By such tactics were 1,645 people forcibly deported from Palestine despite the fact that, in accordance with the White Paper immigration schedules, some tens of thousands of immigration certificates were yet to be distributed.

The prisoners were piled into fifteen covered military trucks so that no one might see them. They were taken under heavy guard to Haifa and were placed on board two Dutch ships that sailed at once.

Twenty-one days later they arrived at the island of Mauritius, located 360 miles from Madagascar and 556 miles from Durban, South Africa. The population of Mauritius at the time was over 500,000, the majority of whom were Catholic Creoles and the rest Hindus. The men were placed in a large internment camp that had been emptied of its Creole prisoners only the day before. The camp consisted of two-story stone buildings with 300 cells in each building. Tin barracks were constructed for the older immigrants, as there were no beds in the cells of the stone buildings. The women's camp consisted of army barracks made of tin. The two camps were separated and guards kept watch to make sure that there would be no traffic between them.

The immigrants underwent much sickness and hardship during the four years and eight months that they spent in Mauritius beginning December 9, 1940. A large Jewish cemetery still stands there as a witness to their stay on the island.

One year after their deportation, a ceremony was held in commemoration of those who had died aboard the Patria. One of the speakers said:

> We have not found a solution to our problem and we will not, until we return to our land. We will return! This is our deepest desire. This is an unquenchable fire within our hearts. Distance exhausts weak love, but strong love only increases. Our love of the Land grows stronger and stronger because it is harder for us to get there than for anyone else. As the Babylonian exiles in their day, we now swear:
>
> "If I forget thee, O Jerusalem,
> May my right hand wither.
> May my tongue cleave to my palate
> If I fail to remember thee;
> If I prefer not Jerusalem
> Above my chief joy."

They did return, despite the official communiqué of the Mandatory Government, broadcast from Jerusalem, which had stated: "The ultimate disposal of the immigrants would be deferred for consideration until the end of the war, but it is not proposed that they shall remain in the same British colony where they are to be sent or go to Palestine."

For years the Jewish Agency carried on negotiations with the Ministry of Colonies concerning the return of the refugees to Palestine. Finally, on August 26, 1945, the Franconia, a British ship with 1,300 immigrants from Mauritius aboard, dropped anchor in the port of Haifa not far from the spot where the Patria had sunk over four years before.

8

The Band of Forty and its Duties

After the Patria disaster, the efforts of the Immigration Bureau came to a halt. Most of its members returned to their homes and kibbutzim disturbed and discouraged. The rigid sea barricade instituted after Italy's entry into the war and the dangers of mines and submarines paralyzed the illegal immigration effort. Nonetheless, on March 18, 1941, a shipload of 800 immigrants, organized and led by the young men of the Bureau arrived in Palestine on board the Dorian II. The Dorian affair, however, was a unique episode and one which led to violent arguments within the group's ranks. The venture was connected with the programs of the British Army's Special Secret Division for combatting the Nazis from behind their lines. From the beginning of the war the Hagana had placed some of its best men at the disposal of the Secret Division. At the outset of 1941, David Hacohen left for Rumania as an emissary of the Political Department of the Jewish Agency, to map out a practical program of work.

One program involved the ship Dorian II, acquired with great difficulty by the young men of the Bureau in 1939. During the temporary cessation of Aliya-Bet due to the war, the ship was acquired by the Special Secret Division for

combat purposes. However, when a last opportunity to save the immigrants situated in Kladovo presented itself, the Immigration Bureau demanded and received the use of the ship for that sole purpose. In the light of the complex political relationship between the British authorities and the people active in the illegal immigration effort, this venture entailed many difficulties and dangers, but the need to save the refugees outweighed all other considerations.

The attempt to save the Kladovo group failed, and even though 800 Jews were brought to Palestine on the Dorian II, the venture had led to bitter conflicts within the Hagana leadership between those in charge of the illegal immigration effort, and those responsible for sabotage activities against the Nazis.

One of the worst disasters to take place in the history of Aliya-Bet occurred on February 24, 1942, when the ship Struma, carrying a group of immigrants organized by a private concern, sank in the Black Sea. Seven hundred and fifty passengers were aboard, and only one survived.

The Struma story began in the fall of 1941. The plight of Rumanian Jewry was growing increasingly serious. Waves of persecution and pogroms were sweeping over the Jewish communities. Every Jew between the ages of eighteen and fifty was obligated to participate in the forced-labor program. The "Winter-Aid" project imposed by the Rumanian Government upon the country's citizens affected the Jews primarily: they were legally robbed of all their clothing. The expulsion of Jews from towns and villages from the Dniester to the Ukraine commenced. The wearing of the yellow badge was strictly enforced. The vast majority of Rumanian Jewry was ready to risk torture and death for a chance to escape.

It was under such circumstances that news of the possibility of sailing to Palestine on the Struma spread throughout the country. The ship had been bought in Bulgaria and a Panamanian flag flew from its mast. The ship's agents gave their word that the Struma was equipped with a new diesel engine and would prove seaworthy, so long as no more than 600 passengers would be taken aboard. They also promised that their representative would obtain immigration certificates to Palestine in Istanbul, as unused certificates from the official schedule were available in that city.

Finally, after the last difficulties were removed and the customs officials had robbed the passengers of their remaining clothing and whatever else they possessed of value—including the ship's provisions—the Struma sailed from the port of Constanta for Istanbul.

The ship was nothing but a ramshackle cattle boat weighing 189 tons in all, originally built as a riverboat for use on the Danube. Living conditions on board the ship were abominable. Not 600, but 769 people were embarked in Istanbul, with children and pregnant women among them. There was only one lavatory, no washing facilities, and no place to put the sick. When the ship arrived in Istanbul its passengers were not allowed to speak with any outsiders. The representative of the company that organized the group informed them that he lacked the means to repair the engine which had broken down in the meantime, and supply them with food. Only after the ship had been in the port eight days were they able to get a small amount of provisions. Wood and coal were also lacking, and hot meals were therefore out of the question. When repairs were begun on the engine it became clear that it would be a complicated job and would not be completed before the end of January. At the same time they learned that there was no chance of their debarking and continuing their journey by land. There was nothing to do but fix the engine.

Still another problem presented itself. The ship flew the Panamanian flag, and in the meantime Germany and Italy had declared war on Panama. Their journey was to take them through the Aegean Sea, past islands occupied by German and Italian troops. The Bulgarian captain informed the Turkish port authorities that since his country was an enemy of Britain he could not take the ship through the Dardanelles, as he might be taken prisoner by the English. The passengers feared that should the Turkish authorities force the Bulgarian captain to stay with the ship, he might take them to one of the German or Italian islands, and turn them over to the enemy. They therefore did their best to get a Turkish captain.

Many of the travelers were workers, and some were artisans. A good number of professional people were on board too, including a large group of doctors. Many of the immigrants had relatives, possessions, and money in Palestine. Some of them had been granted immigration certificates before Rumania had been declared an enemy state. Most of the immigrants had come from Bucovina and Bessarabia, districts wherein Jews were persecuted with more than usual severity. Their hope was that when they would arrive in Istanbul the democratic world would learn of their plight and come to their aid. The Jewish Agency requested that the Struma's passengers be permitted to enter Palestine legally, under the official immigration schedule, and the "Joint" in America expressed its readiness to assist in financing their absorption into the country. However, all efforts were vain. The Mandatory Government did not retreat an inch from its original position: the ship would have to leave Istanbul.

When, after some delay, the ship resumed its journey, disaster struck.

The following report is that of David Stolier, the Struma's sole survivor:

On Sunday, February 2, after weeks of anxious waiting, two telegrams arrived. One was from friends and acquaintances in Palestine, urging the immigrants not to despair, and the other was from Dr. Stephen Wise in New York telling them that two thousand certificates had been set aside and that some of them would be distributed to the Struma's passengers. The immigrants' hopes revived, and in their minds' eye they saw the end of their arduous journey.

The following morning a tugboat approached the ship. The immigrants were worried, but hoped for the best. At 1 P.M. some policemen approached in a boat and said that they had come to unmoor the Struma and move it to a nearby location for disinfection purposes. One policeman casually remarked that they would be returned to the Black Sea, to Burgas in Bulgaria or Constanta in Rumania.

The news spread rapidly throughout the ship, and the whispered conversation between the captain and the head of the police did nothing to alleviate the immigrants' fears. They refused to allow the ship to be unmoored. The few policemen, unable to cope with them, left in the direction that they had come. However, within a short period of time, about eighty more policemen arrived in additional boats and surrounded the ship. The passengers struggled with them for half an hour in an effort to prevent their boarding the Struma, but the police were soon in full control. They lifted the anchor, tied the ship to the tug, and at 4 P.M. the

Struma was pulled out to sea. The captain offered no complaints and the immigrants suspected that he had a hand in the plot. At their insistence, he signed a document stating his obligation to bring them to Palestine.

At 10 P.M. they were in the Black Sea, thirty miles from shore. Here the tug detached itself and its crew shouted to the Struma's passengers, "You're going to Burgas!"

The immigrants knew that very little food remained aboard ship. Over a week had passed since the last shipment, from the council of the Jewish community of Istanbul. They also knew that they had no fuel. No one slept that night and no one spoke. On the morrow it became clear that during the night the ship had drifted almost two miles farther away from shore. According to the captain, the ship was still within Turkey's territorial waters. He was careful not to say anything that might anger the passengers. He claimed that the engine was being repaired and that as soon as it should be in working order he would bring the ship to a Turkish port.

The sea was very calm. The ship did not move from its location. Then, suddenly, shortly before nine in the morning a violent explosion shook the ship, and within minutes it sank into the sea.

I was swept overboard by the force of the blast. When I surfaced I saw scores of people struggling in the waves. Screams of terror rose from the sinking ship. Pieces of wood were floating around in the water, and some, including myself, managed to grab hold of them in an attempt to save themselves. But the water was icy cold and the people grew weaker and weaker. One by one, their grips relaxed and they sank beneath the waves. By the time it was noon, I was alone. . . . My thick leather jacket warmed me a bit. That saved me.

Stolier recalls how he managed to climb onto the platform to which he was clinging and get his body out of the freezing water. Late in the afternoon he spied a bench floating nearby. He got hold of it, dragged it onto the platform, and sat on it, thus removing his chilled body completely from the water. There he sat in the middle of the ocean with no living thing in sight except for the birds that flew about and lighted on the floating corpses and the food scattered over the surface of the water.

At sunset he saw a man rowing towards him with difficulty. He soon made out the weary figure of the first mate. He helped the man onto the bench where he rested a bit. When asked what had happened, the man replied that he had seen a torpedo coming at the ship and had alerted the captain at once, but it had been too late. He also said that he had seen the captain swimming for hours, but that he finally froze and drowned. All but the two of them had perished.

They decided not to fall asleep, fearing that they might freeze. They warmed each other as best they could, even though it was extremely difficult to move their limbs. So the night passed. The first mate grew weaker and weaker, and by sunrise it was evident that he was dying. Toward the end he went insane. During his last moments he began to play with fish, and in the process slipped into the sea and drowned.

Now I was left alone (related Stolier). I saw the shore in the distance, and decided to swim for it. I gathered my strength and swam about two hundred yards, but seeing that I would not be able to make it, I returned to the platform. I feared that I would suffer the same fate as the captain's mate and decided to commit suicide. I barely managed to get my penknife out of my pocket, but my fingers were so stiff, I couldn't slash my wrists.

Suddenly a boat appeared. I shouted with all my might, but even though the boat passed a few yards away from me it did not stop. The people on board the boat pointed at something on the horizon but I did not understand what they meant. Then, when I had given up all hope, I saw a boat approaching.

It was a rescue boat sent from Shilo, a small Turkish village in the vicinity; the boat was manned by Turkish sailors and was equipped with lifesaving apparatus. They removed the mate's body from the water, took Stolier aboard in a stretcher, and administered first aid.

Turkish authorities maintained that the Struma had either run upon a mine or had been attacked by a Russian submarine. Informed persons repudiated both explanations, as the area near Shilo was completely free of both submarines and mines.

The expulsion of Struma from Istanbul was caused, it would seem, by local Nazi pressure. It is known that on February 16 the British consulate in Istanbul was informed that immigration certificates had been authorized for the scores of children on board the ship. However, one week later, on February 23, when the Turkish authorities were asked to take the children ashore, they replied that they had not received instructions to permit this. Representatives of the International Red Cross asked the Turkish authorities to postpone the ship's banishment, and took it upon themselves to look to the ship's provisions. They were promised that in any event the vessel would not be forced to leave before February 26, but the promise was not kept.

Moshe Shertok (Sharett), then head of the Jewish Agency's

Foreign Ministry, summed up the reaction of world Jewry to the Struma disaster in an essay entitled: "Struma—A Declaration of War, A Clarion Call to the Jewish People:"

> This is our common war, the war of the Jewish people. It goes on, though its voice is drowned out by the deafening tumult of the World War. . . .

While the sinking of the Struma came as a terrible blow to world Jewry and the Yishuv, it also marked the beginning of the resumption of the illegal immigration effort. The young men of the Bureau began to ask themselves whether it was at all possible to bring immigrants to Palestine by land routes.

It was not long before the group was fully determined to make up by land immigration from the east what could no longer be accomplished by sea immigration from the west.

So it was that the underground movement was re-established under the leadership of its first active members. They gathered in the old and established agricultural school in Mikveh Israel to discuss ways and means of renewing the illegal immigration effort despite all obstacles. All the activities of the Bureau after that time, all the bold ventures and large shipments of pioneers and refugees were a direct outgrowth of this training program at Mikveh Israel. The forty-day course, undergone by forty men and women, became a symbol of the new vitality of the immigration effort.

Many who took the course had had experience in European countries: Shimon, Levi, Zvi, Agami, and many others. The course constituted a turning point in the lives of its participants and in the lives of their families, for the missions they were sent on determined their future and that of their families for years. To this day the members of the band of forty vividly recall the mysterious and exciting atmosphere in which they trained and lived. To this day many of the graduates of the course always begin relating their experiences with the declaration: "I took the course at Mikveh Israel."

The course was conducted at a time of great danger to the Yishuv, a time when the invasion of the Nazi enemy seemed imminent, whether by way of Egypt, or from Crete, or via Cyprus and Syria. The population was stunned and infuriated by the mass annihilation of European Jewry, reports of which were being smuggled out of Europe's ghettos and death camps. Thousands answered the Jewish Agency's call for volunteers to serve in the Palestinian units of the British Army. Members of the kibbutzim, the Yishuv's most vital pioneer element, took their places among the enlistees provided by every sector of the Yishuv. "Secretly they hoped that in this way they would come in contact with the Diaspora," says Leibel Abramovski, who was then a member of a kibbutz located on the Haifa Bay. Leibel was among the first to volunteer. The members of his kibbutz who were responsible for security insisted that he stay, but when he remained adamant, there was nothing else to do but appoint a committee to determine who among the volunteers would least hurt the kibbutz by their leaving. The committee decided that he should enlist in the illegal immigration effort rather than join the army. This was very acceptable to Leibel, who hoped in that way to work directly and save even more Jews than he would have been able to save by serving in the army. Many were of a similar opinion.

The immediate practical goal of the members of the group was to get through the Iranian border to Soviet Turkestan, wherein were located camps of Polish refugees, with many Jews among them.

One of the immediate goals of the Bureau members was

the immigration into Palestine of the Jews of Syria and Iraq. They also wished to establish Hagana (defense) units among the Jewish communities of Iraq, to ensure that there be no repetition of the June, 1941, pogrom in the Baghdad ghetto.

These and other ideas were considered at Mikveh Israel. Some were discussed publicly and became concrete programs, while other, less likely schemes were whispered about in private. These people had to undergo dangerous and sometimes nerve-racking trials during the difficult years that were to follow, and the forty days spent in Mikveh Israel provided them with standards and criteria for deliberation, decision, and action.

While the course was being conducted, the first three emissaries were sent eastward to the Iranian border. They were Moshe Neta (Misha Notkin), from kibbutz Givat Haim; Yaakov Ben-Yehuda (Yanek Dzebinsky) from kibbutz Usha, and Moshe Agami from Kfar Giladi. All the others were openly jealous. To this day some of them still feel a trace of dissapointment and resentment, recalling that only two of the forty were chosen and that the third was taken from outside. While the course was going on, the emissaries would return to Mikveh Israel to confer about their activities. They were looked upon as heroes returning from the front. For hours and sometimes entire nights they would be surrounded by their comrades, who listened intently to every word they said.

The founder and backbone of the course was Saul Avigur, who worked hand in hand with the pioneers of the immigration effort from the days of the Velos and the Poseidon. Three months before the start of the course, in March of 1942, Saul went to Iraq before anyone else, to feel his way around and look for ways of initiating their program. In

May he set out again and reached Iran. When it came for him to choose and test the candidates for the course, one by one, Saul knew what the mission demanded and what personal traits would be needed.

The commander and practical director of the course, which took on the aspect of a military camp, was Moshe Carmel (Zalitski) from kibbutz Na'an, who had been freed from imprisonment in Acre a year before with the "forty-three"— members of a Hagana unit caught on training maneuvers in Galilee. The director of the agricultural school in Mikveh Israel, Eliahu Krauze, spared no efforts in providing the trainees with good food and accommodations, in spite of the difficult wartime conditions. Students' rooms in the school buildings were emptied and placed at the disposal of the Bureau for the accommodation of the trainees. An isolated building in the botanical garden, somewhat removed from the main buildings and hidden from strangers' eyes, was used for lectures and discussions.

The course of study was quite varied. In addition to basic lectures on the problems of Aliya-Bet, the program included lectures on geography, history, and especially demography, and the mores and regimes of the countries wherein Jewish refugees were massed, and of the countries that they would have to pass through. They were also given field exercises and were taught skills such as driving, use of arms, map reading, finding one's way about an area in daytime and at night, and so on. The course members lived under a military regimen. The long working day began with morning exercises and ended with night expeditions. The participants were called upon to do a good deal of individual work in addition to pursuing the general course of studies. The tension, the effort, and the personal encounters with teachers and lecturers who headed the movement made for an

exhilarating atmosphere. The participants were further inspired by the fact that although they were of different parties
and different settlement associations, they were living and
studying together in a friendly atmosphere in order to serve
a common goal.

Many discussions were devoted to the character and
ethical standards of the emissary. Rigorous standards
typified the Immigration Bureau from its inception. "No
mercy for a commanding officer in battle" was the emissaries' slogan. Such a high level of performance was
demanded of a commander because he was so heavily
burdened with responsibility. On the other hand, a commander could not subject would-be immigrants to trials too
difficult for them to endure.

These topics and others were argued and discussed for
days and nights on end. When the course concluded and all
its participants were not called upon to serve, fifteen of the
group that remained banded together and called themselves
Palmach Bet—the immigration shock troops. They decided
not to disperse or return to their kibbutzim, for fear of
becoming involved with other duties there that might interfere with them when they should be called upon to serve the
immigration effort. They chose as their temporary location
the kibbutz Tel Yosef. There they worked half the day and
spent the other half in continuing their studies, particularly
the study of the languages that they might need for their
missions.

The young men were convinced that illegal immigration
was the Yishuv's most effective weapon in its struggle with
the Mandatory Government, for it accomplished a number
of things simultaneously: while the primary goal of the
effort was simply to save Jews, it also enlarged the Yishuv,
strengthened it, and raised its morale. Above all it helped to

undermine the Mandatory regime and its laws in the most obvious way. The young men who took it upon themselves to realize their slogan of "constructive rebellion" felt that their approach most suited the needs of the Jewish people and the circumstances in which they found themselves, especially since a military conflict with the British was, in their opinion, out of the question.

The realization of the fact that the illegal immigration was one of the most effective, as well as original, measures that the Yishuv was taking came about after long and fierce argument between those who opposed and favored the effort. The arguments came to a halt when the Yishuv was faced with a new situation: masses of hungry and underclothed Jewish refugees who were lost, hiding in forests, and scattered over the steppes of Turkestan on the borders of nearby—yet distant—Iran.

Their practical goal was somehow to become associated with the transfer of American supplies, which arrived in the Persian Gulf and were sent from Khoramshahr, the port adjacent to Abadan, to Russia, America's ally in the war against the Nazi Army. It seemed likely that with free movement in both directions it would be possible for them to function. The principal problem was that of getting into Soviet conquered territory, reaching the refugee camps, and bringing the refugees to Palestine.

The problem proved insoluble. Emissaries left Palestine but did not arrive at their destinations. Some of them reached Pahlevi on the shore of the Caspian Sea, but were unable to proceed further. A Jewish soldier in the American Army who was a member of Habonim, a pioneer Zionist youth organization, tried to help, but lost his life in the process. He got as far as the Caucasus Mountains and was never heard of again.

Nevertheless, the emissaries of the Bureau accomplished much that was of benefit to the Jewish refugees of that region. During that period the Sikorsky-Stalin agreement was being negotiated and Anders' anti-Nazi Polish Army was being formed. The emissaries took advantage of the lines of communication that were established with Russia in the process. They contacted Jewish refugees in Asia through underground letters sent in a variety of ways. They initiated the sending of packages to the refugees. "Joint" took over this project later, expanded it, and saved tens of thousands of Jews from death by starvation. As a result of the communications established by their underground organization, the first emissaries of the Bureau sent to Teheran drew up a huge card catalogue of thousands of addresses of Jewish war refugees in Soviet Asia. In this endeavor too they enlisted the aid of "Joint." Later, it was the Bureau members who smuggled Jewish orphans out of Christian monasteries and sent them to Palestine with the group known as "the children of Teheran."

In the meantime the evacuation had begun. Polish authorities of the Sikorsky Government began bringing their men out of Russia officially. However, while Jews constituted fifty percent of the Polish refugees in Soviet Asia, they constituted no more than six to seven percent of those evacuated. This small percentage included thousands of sick, hungry, and deserted people. The young men of the Bureau joined forces with the Jewish Agency workers to help the refugees in Teheran. Later they organized small groups among Iranian Jewish youth for the study of Hebrew, and in this way brought about the renewal of the immigration into Palestine of Iranian Jews.

At the same time, foundations were being laid for activity in Iraq, Syria, Lebanon, Turkey, Egypt, and North Africa.

By way of Egypt they penetrated to Tunisia, Algeria, and Morocco.

Towards the end of the Second World War, just before the Jewish refugees began streaming to the shores of the Mediterranean to flee Europe, the emissaries arrived in Italy and began to prepare the first ships for the renewal of the immigration effort. They re-established their Istanbul headquarters, which proved very valuable as a center of communication with Jews behind enemy lines, and as a base for rescue efforts and legal and illegal emigration from the Balkan countries after the war.

All these activities and many others were the direct out-growth of the course undergone by the band of forty in Mikveh-Israel.

While the young men were very successful in explaining the principles that underlay their mission, and in winning people over to their endeavor, the fact remained that most of them were still inexperienced in underground work. Since the war was going on and all borders were closed, the problem of leaving Palestine and reaching their destinations was a formidable one. However, it was precisely the wartime conditions and the military control of roads that enabled them to slip through the barriers that had been set up. Most of the emissaries went east either disguised in uniforms of the Jewish units of the British Army, or under the auspices of Solel Boneh, the Histadrut's construction company, which had been granted freedom of movement to engage in large projects for the army and for oil companies in Iraq and Iran. On his first trip to Iran, Saul joined David Hacohen and Hillel Dan of Solel Boneh, who were headed for Abadan and Teheran for a construction job for the Anglo-Iranian Oil Company. For his first trip to Iraq, Saul passed as a private in His Majesty's Army, under the command of Yaakov Trachtenberg (Yashka), the effective sergeant of the Palestinian transport unit that served the British well on the Syrian front.

At the very last moment, prior to his leaving for Iraq, after all the arrangements had been completed and carefully checked, Saul locked himself in a room of the Histadrut Executive building in Tel Aviv with Ben-Zion Israeli, a veteran member of kibbutz Kinneret, and prevailed upon the latter to instruct him in the British Army drill and the proper way of saluting. With deadly serious expressions on their faces the two men marched stiffly about the room, halted, stood at attention, right and left faced, and so forth and so on, while the sergeant was pacing about angrily outside, ready to leave.

After they arrived at the hotel in Damascus, Saul, ascending the steps to the second floor, met a tall British major who was more than slightly puzzled to see a smartly dressed private so clumsy in his movements, and so green, as not to know that a soldier was not required to salute inside a hotel.

Sergeant Trachtenberg began to devise a scheme that would enable them to get from Damascus to Baghdad. He realized that he would have to convince his captain to issue him travel orders. Sergeants know how to deal with their captains. When asked what was his purpose in going to Baghdad, he smiled broadly and replied that he had heard good things about Baghdad girls. The captain understood. They agreed that the official reason for the trip would be to obtain spare parts for the trucks. The order was given. The one problem that remained was how to cross the desert.

At that time there were a few "white" Russians in Damascus who had fled Russia after World War I to escape the Communist regime. Somehow they had reached

Damascus and had established a bus company connecting with Iran. The Palestinian sergeant spoke with them, and learned that they planned to send two trucks over that route shortly. He asked if he could go with them as far as Baghdad, and they agreed.

This was at the beginning of the rainy season. They started out in a pouring rain and a violent windstorm. They managed to cross the *wadi* (ravine) before it filled up with water from the mountains. The sergeant was undisturbed throughout: he knew that the Russians had strong trucks and that they knew the route very well. They were also well supplied with food and drink. They had brought stoves along and at every stop they enjoyed a cooked meal. Saul, whose official role was that of mechanic in charge of inspecting spare parts, was equipped with an identification card, a rifle, and a steel helmet. He felt good.

When they finally arrived in Baghdad and went to the hotel they were met by an assimilated Jew who had come from Rumania and was employed by the British Intelligence. He immediately began sniffing about and asking questions: Who were they? What were they looking for? Yashka, however, was not one to be caught off guard. With a disparaging motion of his hand he said, pointing to Saul:

"Show this guy where a synagogue is and take me where someone like us can have a good time."

They stayed in Baghdad for five days until Saul felt that he had made satisfactory contacts; and then they returned. When safely back in Palestine, Saul removed his military uniform with regret; he had grown attached to it during the two weeks he had been away.

A few months after Saul had laid the groundwork in Baghdad, the first three emissaries were on their way to

Iraq. Their departure marked the renewal of the Bureau's work after the period of inactivity brought on by the war.

The first to set out was Italian-born Enzo Sereni, a doctor of philosophy, a member of kibbutz Givat Brenner, and a father of three children. Later he became a parachutist, was captured jumping into Italy, and killed in Dachau. Shortly before leaving for Iraq he had returned from a difficult mission with the British Army in Egypt. Like many in the Yishuv, he had volunteered to serve under the British. He was given a special job by the British Army—to broadcast and write propaganda aimed at the Italian prisoners. He left for Iraq as a Solel Boneh liaison man. In accordance with the plan arranged by Bureau headquarters, Solel Boneh insisted that the laison man's residence be in Baghdad, which served as a crossroads and a stopover station for the Palestinian employees of the company on their way to and from their places of work. This identity gave an elevated status to the Palestinian doctor who dressed in a European suit and spoke elegant English, and enabled him to accomplish a great deal. In addition, David Hacohen put him in touch with certain officers in the British Army Secret Service, with whom the Hagana worked in the anti-Nazi underground.

The other two emissaries were Shmarya Gutman, one of the founding members of kibbutz Na'an, and a member of the Working Youth movement prior to that; and his friend Ezra Kaduri, a member of kibbutz Maoz, who had emigrated from Iraq in his youth. At that time Shmarya was the chairman of the Working Youth in Tel Aviv. He was chosen to be among the first group of emissaries to go to Iraq not only because he had a Levantine appearance and possessed a British passport, but also because of his intense ardor, the same ardor that he was to exhibit later in the exploration of the Sodom desert and the reconstruction of Massada.

Not only Shmarya, but most of the Yishuv's youth were severely shaken by the reports of what was happening to European Jewry. The barbarous attacks made upon the Baghdad ghetto during the revolt of Rashid Ali only infuriated them further. After the Baghdad riots, a group of twenty young Jews from Iraq assembled in the heart of the desert, on the Iraqi-Transjordanian border, the midway point on the Baghdad-Haifa road, and from there reached Palestine in a truck. The young men stole across the border on foot and came to Ra'anana, a settlement containing a good number of immigrants from Iraq. Ezra Kaduri was very aroused as a result of meeting these people. Kaduri was a member of the Palmach, the shock troops of the Hagana, and one of the workers in the bakery in Ra'anana before he went to settle in Maoz in the Valley of Bet Shean. All his life his sympathy had been with his brothers in the alleys of the ghetto that he had left behind him; whenever he met with his friend Shmarya, that was what they would talk about.

Shmarya was very excited to receive the invitation from Saul Avigur and quickly went to Tel Aviv to the underground headquarters in the Histadrut Executive. When Saul asked if he and his friends Ezra would be willing to undertake the mission to Iraq, he replied, "If you hadn't called us, we just might have gone ahead and done it on our own." However, a long period elapsed between that meeting and the emissaries' departure. In order to work off some tension, Shmarya led a group of young people from the Working Youth and from the immigrant camps to Massada. On their way they split boulders and laid roads leading to Massada.

There, atop the mountain, amid the ruins of the ancient fortress, Shmarya disclosed his secret to his friend:

"They want the two of us to go—what do you say?"

All the way home the two friends walked together in silence.

Months passed before Saul summoned them to headquarters. There he imparted to them the secret information concerning their mission and gave them a detailed account of his impressions of Baghdad. He described in detail the route that they would have to follow in order to arrive at their first destination. At the gates of Baghdad stood a small bridge and there they would meet the first policeman, Saul pointed out. He then moved his finger along the wall and showed them where the second policeman would be standing. Again he moved his finger and stopped, to indicate where they would meet a third policeman after passing through some crooked back alleys.

The two freshman emissaries were given only twenty-five pounds. Saul apologized for giving them such a small sum, but explained that they could not risk the loss of a large amount of public funds should they be captured.

When they asked what their source of funds would be during their work in the underground in Iraq, Saul had no answer for them.

They made a number of necessary purchases for the desert trip, including two pairs of driver's overalls which they promptly dirtied to make them look old. They joined a convoy of Egged buses heading north to pick up Syrian soldiers who were to guard an airstrip in Palestine. The emissaries went along in the capacity of auxiliary drivers. Their true identities were known only to three drivers who were veteran Hagana members, and the commander of the convoy, who saw to it that their names were not included in any list. What with the noise and confusion created by the scores of buses and their drivers, they managed to get past the borders and cross the desert without any identification cards. The emissaries were overwhelmed by the vast desert expanses. The barren sands spread out in a vast circle around them; they were bounded only by sand and sky. They passed piles of brown boulders along their unpaved route. At times the road expanded to a width of fifty to a hundred yards, and for long distances a convoy of fifty to sixty vehicles could travel abreast. When the buses halted, the desert silence was awesome. At times they were attacked by sand-storms: clouds of fine red dust swept down upon them, blotting out sun and sky. After such storms hours would pass before the entire convoy reassembled, as the violent wind would scatter the buses in all directions. By day the members of the convoy suffered from the oppressive desert heat, and by night, from the severe cold.

At last they arrived at the final station, a military center half a day's journey from Baghdad. The British Army patrol stationed there halted the convoy. Even at the preceding station of Ramaday the commander of the Egged convoy had suggested to the emissaries that they leave and continue their journey on their own rather than remain and endanger the entire convoy. They did not take his advice, however, as they had no identification cards.

Now that the convoy had been halted the emissaries feared that they might be forced to return with all the others. Quickly they began considering courses of action that would get them to Baghdad. After they brought up and discarded a few ideas, they asked the convoy's commander whether they could damage the front of one of the vehicles and be sent to Baghdad to have a repair job done.

The commander would not permit it. He asked them who

would pay for the repairs. Ezra suggested that he and Shmarya take one of the buses and go their own way, but this request also was refused. The two emissaries were at a loss for further suggestions. Finally Shmarya came up with an idea. He approached the convoy commander and said:

"Look, why not tell the British patrol that your drivers have just come from a long trip in the desert and they'd like to stop in on those famous Baghdad girls. How can they refuse you permission to go?"

"Good idea!" the commander said, "But if I send two buses there won't be enough room for you, because so many people will jump aboard."

The young man replied:

"You don't have any choice. If you refuse us this time— we'll smash up the front of a bus on our own."

The commander approached the British officer and obtained the required permit. The drivers joyfully clambered aboard two buses; some of them even thanked the emissaries for having thought up the scheme. The buses left—but the two men responsible for the pleasure trip were not on board, as the British guards had counted the passengers as they showed their identification cards. The emissaries therefore got away on foot and boarded the buses only after they started moving. They managed to bring a suitcase and a sleeping bag with them. Underneath their driver's overalls they had on the new suits that they had bought in Palestine. It was the first time that Shmarya had even worn a tie.

9

The First Emissaries to the Baghdad Ghetto

The two buses arrived in Baghdad at noon, and Shmarya and Ezra stopped off at a Jewish garage and checked their bags. The people of Baghdad behaved in a friendly manner toward the Egged drivers who, although they were dressed in uniforms, were clearly not British. Some people thought that they were Russian soldiers, but the Jews recognized them at once as their own people. The British military police could not control them—the spirited group captured the city. The two emissaries of the Bureau, however, were no longer with them. They had left the group and were now on their own.

Their first object was to contact a certain member of the *Shebab al-Inkaz,* or "The Young Liberators," a movement that they had heard of in Palestine. After the attacks upon the Baghdad ghetto, a handful of young people stole across the border and made their way to Palestine, bringing with them proclamations of an underground Jewish youth movement in Iraq and calling for the creation of a self-defense effort. The emissaries naturally wished to contact these people and work with them.

In accordance with Saul's directions they were to deliver a note from him, signed with his pseudonym, "Gabriel," to

173

a Jewish clerk in a certain bank; he, in turn, would put them in contact with the young man through whom they would work. This young man, who was one of the "Liberators," had told Saul that his movement numbered in the thousands, and that it was headed by thirty-seven active members who were waiting for leadership from Palestine.

The emissaries followed the directions that Saul had given them for getting to the bank. They arrived at the bridge, and there saw a policeman, just as he had said they would. When the latter raised his hand they almost panicked, thinking that they had somehow been found out. He, however, was only stopping traffic so that the two pedestrians could cross in safety. When they reached the main streets of the city, they saw another policeman raise his hand—he too was stopping traffic for them. The two men smiled at each other, recalling how Saul, with a deadly serious expression on his face, had warned them of these policemen and had told them exactly where they would meet them.

The bank was closed for the midday siesta. Shmarya said to Ezra:

"Now you can prove to me that you're a Baghdadi."

The latter took him to a Jewish restaurant where they enjoyed a tasty fish dinner. In the restaurant they used a Jewish boy as an interpreter; Ezra did not reveal in any way that he had been born in Baghdad and spoke the local Arabic fluently.

At two o'clock they arrived at the bank, still wearing their Egged uniforms, that gave them a feeling of security. They found Shlomo, the clerk, alone in the room, seated at his table. When they handed him the note from "Gabriel" (Saul), he turned white, then red, and was thoroughly flabbergasted. He quickly offered them coffee, and went to the next room to bring it in. He nearly dropped the tray when he came back:

instead of two Egged drivers in dirty overalls, he found two well-dressed Iraqi gentlemen! The transformation was little less than miraculous in his eyes, and he was the more eager to serve the emissaries from Eretz Israel as best he could.

Two hours had not passed before Shlomo brought them the boy who, according to the information given Saul, was the leader of the "Liberators." The boy had been moved when he heard that the two men had come from "Gabriel." However, when they asked if he would help them get a place where they could stay, he became confused and gave them directions to a nearby hotel.

Shlomo stood listening the while. He would have left the room, so awed was he by the emissaries, but they asked him to stay. They soon realized that the young fellow with whom they were speaking would be of little help to them, so they told him that they would find a place on their own and would get in touch with him in three days' time. As soon as he left, they turned to Shlomo and said:

"We'll go wherever you take us."

He immediately replied:

"Come to my house."

He then led them to his home and sent a boy to bring their bags from the garage.

On the way, Shmarya turned to the young man, put his hand on his shoulder, and said cheerfully, as though he were making a festive proclamation:

"You are the number one halutz of the Jews in Iraq." Shlomo smiled and turned scarlet.

Upon their arrival at Shlomo's house they were given a warm welcome by his family, who at a later date settled in the new city of Beersheba. They sat down with the head of the family and told him who they were and what they wanted to do. They said that they had come to Iraq to set up a defense organization and a pioneer movement, their ultimate goal being the underground emigration of Jews to Palestine, and that by their efforts they hoped to atone for the Yishuv's past neglect of Iraqi Jewry. The father burst into tears and said:

"You are the masters of this house. Here do as you wish."

At that time the family's eldest son was already a member of a kibbutz in Palestine. The emissaries, who knew him personally, gave his regards to the parents, and were the more endeared to them. After a short while they sent the third son, the engineer, to Palestine via the underground. The opportunity for his departure materialized suddenly, and he had to be sent off at once; he had no time to say goodbye to his family. The father, however, was very happy to learn of his son's good fortune, and said:

"Let my sons be foundation stones for building the Land."

Such an attitude was rare in Iraq Jewry at that time. In general, most people stood in fear of the authorities, who were vigorously opposed to Zionism and persecuted anyone who had any contacts with Palestine. It required a great deal of courage on the family's part to take in the emissaries. Moreover, their house was overcrowded to begin with, and it was summer as well, and the weather was hot and oppressive. At night everybody went up on the roof to sleep, but even there it was stifling. Two additional mats were placed on the roof and two more plates were put on the table.

Although they were warmly received, the young men did not wish to overtax the family's hospitality and began looking for a place of their own to live in and work in. They wanted to get away from the center of town, and so went looking for quarters outside the city.

The emissaries realized that two bachelors living alone would most likely look suspicious. They were confronted with the problem of getting someone to live with them, in spite of the risks involved. Once again Shlomo's family came to their aid. They and their relatives moved into a large house in the Jewish ghetto, next to the *"Alliance"** school for girls, whose pupils numbered 2,000, and at times, as many as 3,000. Their new location proved very advantageous to them, for they were able to use the school building when they needed it; they even made a secret hiding place for themselves there. The son of the school's Jewish janitor joined the underground movement and was responsible for the hiding place; except for him, no one knew anything about it. There was also a large cellar in the building, that served as a meeting place. Curtains were put over the windows and were always kept closed, and the members of the family served as a camouflage and as lookouts.

One of the first things that the emissaries did was to try to find out whether the "Young Liberators" movement really existed or whether it was just another tale from "The Arabian Nights." For one month they attempted to track down the movement. As a first step, they tried to set up a meeting with the scores of leaders that they had heard about from Saul. However, they were quickly disillusioned; the movement was non-existent, even though proclamations had been issued. It seemed that after the ghetto had been attacked, three boys put their heads together and decided to get weapons for self-defense. They printed receipts and began collecting funds. In the meanwhile, similar groups sprang up. However, of the few young men who did manage to get pistols, some were dishonest and some were simply

---

* *Alliance Israélite Universelle,* a French-Jewish philanthropic organization responsible for establishing the agricultural school of Mikveh Israel and many schools in Palestine and other countries in the Middle East and North Africa.

adventurers. From time to time Shmarya and Ezra met boys who promised to arrange meetings with fifty, or seventy, or one hundred members of their organization, but in every instance nothing materialized.

The emissaries realized that they would have to start from scratch. Ezra began working with a small group that he organized by himself.

The search for the "Liberators," however, did lead to some positive results. The fact that there were two emissaries from Palestine in Baghdad soon became known among young Jewish circles and some boys wanted to contact them but did not know how to go about it. One such group had huge proclamations printed in large, loud purple letters with the intention of drawing the emissaries' attention. The scheme worked, and a meeting was arranged. When the emissaries asked who the "Young Liberators" were, the boys answered:

"Why look for them? Why not work with us? We have the same goal as they do."

So the effort began.

In every period when Jews lived in Iraq, the longing for Zion was the chief force in the lives of the oppressed Jewish merchants, farmers, peddlers, and artisans, who prayed for the day when the Messiah would come and return them to their land. However, Jewish migration from Iraq to Palestine had always been minute—a family or small groups now and then—and there had never been an open, active Zionist movement in the country.

In the period that preceded the anti-Jewish riots in Baghdad, a band of adults and young people gathered about a distinguished person known as "the Teacher," who founded a Hebrew school in the ghetto which was attended by 300 children. This school turned out a group of dedicated students of the Hebrew language, as well as "The Associ-

12. THE LONGING FOR ZION WAS THE CHIEF FORCE IN THE LIVES OF THE IMPOVERISHED AND OPPRESSED.

ation for the Distribution of Hebrew Books," which ordered inexpensive pamphlets from Palestine and waited for their arrival most eagerly. This group laid the foundation for a Hebrew library and gave rise to the "Ahiever Society," which undertook various Zionist activities.

In the meanwhile, the situation of Iraqi Jewry had deteriorated markedly. As a result of the Yishuv's struggle for the fulfillment of the Zionist dream, a wave of anti-Zionism and anti-Semitism swept over neighboring Iraq. The Iraqi Government began to keep close track of the young people who were members of "Ahiever." The "Teacher's" activities became highly suspect and obstacles were placed in his path. He was finally forced out of Baghdad and went to live in Palestine.

At that time Iraqi Jewry numbered 120,000 people. Of these, about 100,000 lived in Baghdad, constituting one-third of that city's population. Some of them were rich merchants, but most of them were members of the middle class, being small tradesmen, clerks, and artisans. Others were peddlers in the villages and some were unemployed. When Iraq first achieved independence at the end of World War I, and the rulers were not yet in full control of the country, the Jews played an important role in the Iraqi economy and government. The network of *Alliance* schools provided them with a general education and a knowledge of European languages, both of which were necessary for the new status that was theirs. King Faisal I proclaimed officially upon ascending the throne that there would be no discrimination against the various minorities in his country. The Jews were quick to adapt themselves to the new situation: Jewish life and Zionist activity flourished openly. In 1930 there were ten Jewish schools in Baghdad with a total of 7,200 pupils, 2,000 of whom were girls. These pupils were taught Hebrew by teachers from Palestine, who also organized Zionist activities.

This state of affairs changed drastically, however, with the termination of the British Mandate and the entrance of Iraq into the League of Nations and its constitution as a limited monarchy, following the Egyptian pattern of that period. In 1933, the first full year of independence for the Iraq people, not only were great numbers of Assyrians slaughtered, but Kurds and members of the small sect of Yezidis in the mountains along the northern border of Iraq were slaughtered as well. The dream of a peaceful Jewry in the midst of the new Iraqi state quickly dissolved. Laws were passed designed to force the Jews out of the country's economic life. Their freedom of movement was seriously curtailed, and the study of the Hebrew language was out-lawed, along with all Zionist activities. These laws and the Government's policy of incitement against the Jewish community culminated in the attack upon the Baghdad ghetto in the beginning of June, 1941.

The pogrom terrified the peaceful Jewish population of Iraq and led to an immediate wave of emigration to Palestine. Not merely young people, but scores of families packed their possessions and climbed aboard the first train or vehicle that they could find. In this way they reached Rutba, a British military camp not far from the Iraqi-Syrian border. Here they lived in the open, waiting for an opportunity to get into Palestine. However, when the tumult died down, many of them returned to Baghdad.

It was against this background of events that the first band of emissaries from Palestine arrived in the country in the summer of 1942 and began organizing their effort.

They devised a threefold plan of action: Enzo Sereni was to take care of the Zionist movement; Shmarya Gutman—

aliya (immigration); and Ezra Kaduri—Hagana (self-defense organization).

The Jewish population was very fearful, and the emissaries realized that they would first have to educate the people before they could even hope to accomplish anything. They decided to establish a small nucleus of an ideological movement, one that could be counted on in time of danger.

Their first efforts were directed toward teaching Hebrew. Since they had little money to spare and crossing the border illegally was difficult, they did not bring in special teachers from Palestine, but gave lessons themselves, day and night. Every willing person, young or old, who had the slightest knowledge of the Hebrew language was enlisted to teach those who knew nothing. The underground movement for the study of Hebrew burgeoned almost magically—at times its membership numbered in the thousands. The Jewish community of Baghdad began to breathe the air of Palestine. The pupils studied wherever they could, in cellars and attics. The lessons were conducted in utter secrecy, and this led to some humorous situations: some youngsters studied in two or even three groups at the same time and came to know more than their friends and teachers. The emissaries went to great lengths to form a group of older students who knew Hebrew from among those who had studied years before in the Hebrew school under Palestinian teachers. Those teachers, who included Reuven Zaslani (Shiloah) and others, had been expelled from the country by the Iraqi Government.

Because they were so few in number, the emissaries had very long working hours. Once when Shmarya was returning home at two in the morning from giving a Hebrew lesson to a group of movement leaders, he saw two Iraqi policemen following him. He knew that he would be in serious trouble were he to be arrested, for he had a Hebrew book in his hand.

He didn't know what to do. The clack of their boots on the empty street grew louder and louder. "You're in for it now," said Shmarya to himself, as he tilted his feysaliya, the Iraqi hat, to one side to give himself the appearance of a cocky young night-stroller, and looked for a means of escape. Luckily he knew the city well as a result of his trips through its remotest and darkest alleys.

As the policemen drew closer Shmarya overheard one of them say to the other:

"He must be a pimp."

Shmarya heaved a sigh of relief. However, there was still the Hebrew book that he was holding. He had no way of disposing of it, for the policemen were close behind him. The book began to burn his hand and he quickened his pace. He soon reached a dark, narrow alley where one of the city's well-known "houses" was located, with the policemen hot on his heels. He tapped on the door and the madam opened up.

"Let me in," he whispered.

"It's too late," she answered.

"The police are after me," he added quickly as he took a dinar out of his pocket and slipped it into her palm.

Her tender feelings were aroused. Shmarya passed through to the courtyard behind the house, opened the gate that led to another alley, and was on his way. He began his next letter to his wife Sara in kibbutz Na'an by writing: "Cheers for Baghdad's red-light district!"

Ezra, too, had his share of adventures in organizing the defense force in Baghdad. After they obtained maps of the city's districts, the question arose as to where they could hide the weapons that they would smuggle in from Palestine or acquire locally. They also lacked people for the effort and did not know where they would get them. It was clear that

the same people who would be attracted to the defense effort would be attracted to the emigration effort. Therefore Ezra too set everything else aside and concentrated on teaching Hebrew, with the intention of forming pioneer groups to serve as nuclei of the underground. He began recruiting Jewish students from the Iraqi high schools. He succeeded in getting only a few at first, but in short order they were working fervently for the cause. Ezra organized thirteen clubs and he circulated among them, teaching Hebrew. The exhausting summer heat presented a special problem to the emissary, who always wore his heavy suit and tie, which he was unable to get used to; he would not risk wearing khaki, for fear that he might look like an outsider and arouse people's suspicions. Water streamed down him all day long, and at night he would toss about restlessly in his sweat-soaked bed.

The Hebrew study clubs met in the houses of boys and girls who obtained their parents' permission to participate in such a dangerous activity. There were about 100 parents who gave their children permission. In the Baghdad ghetto the houses were generally closed up so securely that no one could see what was going on inside them. The houses were opened to the emissaries only after much hesitation, as most Iraqi Jews were extremely fearful after the trials they had undergone.

A short while after the emissaries began the underground effort, they decided to establish the Hehalutz youth movement in Iraq, during Passover of that year (1943). An impressive opening ceremony was planned. They spent days and nights in the cellar of the house where they lived preparing movement flags, a picture of Herzl, and Hebrew choral selections. They sang Judah Sharet's composition for the Biblical verse from Nehemiah: "With his one hand he labors, and with the other grasps his weapon." When the awaited day arrived, a large table was set up in the cellar and was covered with almonds, pistachios, nuts, and arrack, a liquor popular in the Middle East. They had a victrola and records resting on the window sill, in the event that they would have to pretend that they were having a dance. Lookouts were posted on the roof and in the street, and in the event that the police would come, the celebrants were to put on a record and start cracking nuts, as was customary at such small gatherings. Everyone present had a specific job: one was to hide the flag; another, the motto; and so forth. Those who were invited to the ceremony were allowed in only after they gave the designated password. The participants consisted of two representatives from each Hebrew study group, and by that time there were many of them.

After the successful completion of the ceremony, the emissaries decided to advance one step further and form branches in other cities. To do this they would have to move about Iraq, and within the country's borders one could travel only by train. This meant that the transfer of weapons and books for the study of Hebrew would constitute a problem. They therefore began looking for ways to make a contact with officials in charge of the railroads. Generally speaking, those officials were Jews. The man in charge of the train was referred to by his English title of "guard." He was given a special small compartment at the end of the train and was responsible for everything—the train's departure and arrival, loading and unloading, and so forth. Through the services of a guard who belonged to the family with whom they lived, they succeeded in making useful contacts, and after a short while the Iraqi railroad system was at the service of Hehalutz.

The first branch was established in Kirkuk, in northern

Iraq. There was an oil refinery there and for that reason security measures were more stringent and it was harder to get into the city. They had decided to begin with Kirkuk because of a request by some Jewish groups there who had sent a man down to Baghdad to speak with them. The man had said to them:

"Why aren't you working with us, too? We have a faithful Jewish community and good young people, who want to learn—come and work!"

They then decided that Ezra would go to Kirkuk, for his family lived there. Ezra's family was large and many-branched: it comprised one-third of the Jewish community and included the rabbis. In Kirkuk Ezra was the guest of the young man who had called upon the emissaries to organize activities in the city. A few days after his arrival, the emissary told the young man who he was and to which family he belonged. After that, whenever they would walk in the street, the young man would point out passersby from time to time and whisper in his ear:

"That's your uncle, and there goes a cousin, and there's another cousin . . ."

Ezra would always restrain himself and avoid meeting these people. Nonetheless, one of his uncles recognized him. When they met by chance on the street, the man stopped short and stared intently at the stranger who bore an amazing resemblance to Ezra's father, who had died when the latter was an infant. Ezra was stirred by this meeting. After that, whenever he and his companion would go into a house, he would ask:

"Did you know the sage, Yosef Haim (his paternal grandfather)?"

And the family would reply:

"What sort of a question is that? Who didn't know the sage Yosef Haim?"

After the branch in Kirkuk was established, Ezra returned to Baghdad. One day, as he was seated at the table with Shlomo's father as usual, a friend of the family's from Kirkuk came in—an erect, white-bearded Jew who came to Baghdad from time to time on business. After they talked for a while, Ezra asked him the usual question: Had he known the sage Yosef Haim?

The old man answered:

"We were neighbors, and we shared a window in the front of the house. We kept a water pitcher there and both families drank from it. And you ask me if I knew him?"

Ezra, deeply moved, stood up and said:

"I am Kaduri's son."

The old man sank to his knees, stretched out on the floor and tried to kiss the feet of the young man from the Land of Israel. His eyes streamed tears and he offered up prayers to God.

News of Ezra's identity spread rapidly in Jewish circles. From then on, whenever he would appear on the street, the people would come out on their porches to look at him. In some houses they knew when he would leave and when he would return; they would wait for him, point at him and say: "There he is . . ."

By that time the young men were at home in Baghdad; they had removed their ties and heavy suits and dressed informally.

However, in spite of all their efforts, they did not achieve their main goal at the beginning of their activity. Jews were in no hurry to go to Palestine. One of the principal obstacles that stood in the emissaries' way was the Iraqi Jews' fear that they would have to engage in physical labor in the Homeland. For them, "work" meant trade or peddling, but not physical labor. In addition they were afraid of emigrating to Palestine illegally. Therefore, no sooner did the wounds inflicted by the pogroms of June, 1941, begin to heal over slightly, than the Jews began to sink roots anew in the hostile country. Jews invested large sums of money in the construction of the new Baghdad; they erected a Jewish neighborhood which became the center of the capital. Within two years' time Jewish capital had created an entire city.

It quickly became clear to the emissaries that the Zionist ideology would not be accepted in many, if not most, Jewish circles. Enzo Sereni tried to win converts from among the intellegentsia, but failed. Some of them maintained that the British would destroy the Jews in Palestine anyway, and that therefore there was no use going there.

Such a view was expressed by one well-educated Jew, a very talented intellectual, who had personal contacts with important personages in the government. He had a vast library of books on economics and the social sciences. While he was not a Zionist in his outlook, the Rashid Ali pogroms awoke within him a sense of Jewish self-respect. At that time he broke with his Arab and English friends, whom he held accountable for carrying out the pogroms. Enzo Sereni tried in vain to win him over to Zionism. The emissaries were very anxious to get his help but he avoided them and refused to meet them. Finally they managed to get to him in a roundabout way—Shmarya and Ezra appeared in his office in the company of a friend of theirs who was an Iraqi Jew.

Shmarya, knowing that the man had contributed to the "Young Liberators," began by saying:

"We are setting up cells of a self-defense organization, so

that there will be no more slaughters in the Jewish ghetto. We want the Jews to be able to defend themselves."

The man replied that he thought the idea was a good one and that he would support it.

During the course of the conversation they began to speak of Palestine. He asked them why they were going to such trouble to organize emigration to Palestine. "The British will destroy you on the one hand," he said, "and the Arabs on the other."

"You are absolutely mistaken," they told him. "We are capable of defending ourselves."

He was somewhat taken aback by their response. All his life he had felt that the Zionists were simply deluding themselves, and now he saw that their plans were quite concrete. He shook his head and said:

"All of you will be destroyed, it's really a shame."

After the War of Independence, when he met one of the young men of the underground, he said:

"If you see Shmarya, please give him a message: tell him that in that conversation we had—he was right and I was wrong."

They left his office empty-handed. Nonetheless, the meeting had not been in vain. The mere fact that he had met with them and spoken with them enhanced their status.

One of the first things that the emissaries did at the outset of their mission was to ensure Hebrew instruction for the girls as well as the boys. At first the local youth leaders were shocked at the suggestion. Impossible! Girls didn't set foot out of their houses at night, so how could they come? And who would teach them? It was inconceivable that boys and girls be together unsupervised. Nevertheless, it was not long before this insoluble dilemma was solved. The first girl to be won over to the program was Tikva Shohet (later a teacher in the State of Israel), a bold, spirited girl with a mind of her own. She contributed a great deal in organizing her friends and instilling in them a realization of their own worth.

The program with the girls started when the emissaries gathered together the girls of a family that they knew and taught them the Hebrew alphabet. Two of these, who could scarcely read themselves, shortly became teachers of two other groups. Soon three groups were in existence, comprising 50 girls. When the emissaries told the twelve young leaders of the movement that 50 girls were learning Hebrew, the boys would not believe it until they were taken to the classrooms and saw for themselves.

These seeds took root and flowered into an underground movement consisting of hundreds of girls who gave themselves wholeheartedly to the study of the Hebrew language. All this was done in complete secrecy, and no outsider knew of it.

The activity among the girls assumed large proportions with the arrival of the emissary, Malka Rofe, a member of kibbutz Maoz and a graduate of the Women's Teachers' College in Tel Aviv. Her main task was to instruct her colleagues in underground communications. In the absence of usual means of contact, the emissaries were almost cut off from Palestine, and from the beginning of their work in Iraq they felt a strong need for setting up a secret communications system. Upon returning from one of his trips to Palestine. Shmarya managed to smuggle in a wireless. In this same convoy, explosives too were smuggled in. The men arrived in Baghdad at night and quickly unloaded the shipment at Shmarya's residence. However, the family with whom he was living became so frightened that they had to remove the explosives at once, leaving only the wireless broadcaster in the house, and until Malka's arrival no one knew how to operate it.

Malka, too, was brought to Baghdad in a military truck. The vehicle arrived at an army camp in Transjordan as part of a large convoy, and at that point went its own way to Baghdad. No one except the sergeant and the driver knew that there was any living thing inside the covered truck. The sergeant's dog lay at the rear entrance and guarded the passenger faithfully. They traveled in this manner for four days straight. This was in April, 1943, and Malka, like all soldiers in the British Army, was still wearing the heavy winter uniform. She nearly suffocated from the heat.

They arrived in Baghdad in the middle of the night. Malka had in her possession the address of a young man from Palestine who worked for the British censors and who was to put them in contact with Shmarya. When the sergeant found the young man's residence and woke him up, the latter said that he was afraid to go out in the street in the dead of night. As the saving of Polish refugees was an obligation for which many, if not most, Jews were prepared to risk their lives, the sergeant said to the young man:

"Look, I have Polish 'goods' that I have to get rid of . . ."

He arose at once and went with him. However, they did not find Shmarya's address that night. The truck was parked in the center of the city, and as morning approached their situation became increasingly dangerous. Finally there was nothing to do but take refuge in a parking lot of the Indian Army. The sergeant's daring and sharp tongue stood them in good stead; he cursed and yelled so that the Indian commander became thoroughly confused and ordered some soldiers to guard the truck. During the daytime it was even more difficult to locate Shmarya, who was wandering about

Baghdad's back alleys, and when he was finally contacted, hours passed before he carried out his plan for getting Malka out of the military truck. So the day passed, with policemen snooping about the truck, the driver shaking like a leaf, and Malka sweltering in her heavy uniform inside, waiting for Shmarya to come and free her.

The emissaries had by this time won over a few families and persons in whose neighborhood they lived, having made it a point to develop friendly relations with them. Shmarya approached one of these people, a respected businessman, and said to him:

"It's been a year now that we've lived among you and haven't asked you any favors. Now I've come to ask your help for something urgent and I hope you'll give it immediately without asking any questions. I need your car and I need you to drive it. If you get caught—you'll be in serious trouble, but if you refuse me, a girl we brought here from Palestine might be executed."

The man paled, was silent for a minute, and finally said: "I'll do what you want me to."

They drove past the parking lot, gave the driver a signal, and the military truck pulled out and followed behind them. After they traveled a long and intricate route that took them outside the city, a hand was thrust into the truck and a voice whispered in Hebrew:

"Shalom, Malka, get ready to jump!"

She jumped from the truck and another hand reached out of the car and helped her in. Simha Cohen, a girl from Baghdad (later Ezra Kaduri's wife), gave her a black gown, the traditional dress worn by Muslim women. Malka slipped this over her heavy uniform and the car drove off to the house where she was to stay.

After the operation was completed the excited sergeant

did not know whether to laugh or cry. He jumped up and
down, danced about, grabbed Shmarya and kissed him,
saying over and over again:

"Only in the movies, only in the movies do things like
this happen."

For nine months Malka wore the black gown. At first she
found it very burdensome and constraining, but she soon had
no difficulty with it whatever. In fact, when she finally
removed it, she felt as though she were walking about naked.
During her first days in Baghdad she did not set foot out of
the house alone, but later she would travel even to distant
quarters fully protected by her traditional Muslim dress.

Malka's activities were not confined to communications.
She worked successfully in the educational movement set
up by her colleagues, organized ten groups of young people
for the study of Hebrew, and participated in the first
Hehalutz seminar in Iraq.

After a while when the effort was temporarily discontinued
as a result of the activities of informers and British Intelligence, and it was necessary to return the emissaries to Palestine, a difficult problem arose: how to get Malka back. A
captain who served in a British map-making unit came to
their aid. This officer had earned the title of "the old man"
among the emissaries because of his fatherly attitude toward
them, and was of great service to them in all their activities.
After other schemes were frustrated, he built a trunk in
which Malka was to be smuggled out of the country. For
nights on end he scarcely slept, but carefully planned and
built the trunk, making sure to allow for adequate breathing
space. In the end, however, it was not used, because in the
meanwhile an order had gone out to inspect all trunks in
military vehicles of Palestinian units. Because of Franco-
Syrian tensions, the borders were guarded more closely than

ever. On one occasion Syrians thrust swords through the openings in the sides of a trunk that the emissaries had sent as an experiment. This put an end to the trunk affair and other ideas were considered. They tried to smuggle Malka out of Iraq disguised as a female Polish soldier. Six times she sat for hours in her new uniform, and six times nothing materialized. Finally, they turned to a professional smuggler in Baghdad, who, in exchange for a large sum of money, provided her with a passport and visa of an emigrant to Israel.

She arrived in Tel Aviv wearing a luxurious eastern gown, complete with veil. When she walked into the Immigration Bureau headquarters and asked for Moishele Chervinski, who for years served the Bureau day and night as secretary and communications man, they asked her suspiciously:

"Who is Moishele?"

Only then did she remember that she was supposed to have said upon entering: "I came in a trunk."

That girls took part in the effort indicated more than anything else the revolution brought about by the emissaries in the Iraqi ghetto. Previously Jewish girls had done nothing outside the home, but now many plunged into Hehalutz activities. Some became leaders who "bloomed" as a result of their contact with Palestine. On such was Simha Cohen (Kaduri) of Baghdad.

As a little girl Simha studied in a Jewish elementary school. Her father did not want her to continue her studies, as there was not yet a Jewish high school for girls in Baghdad, and to study in a mixed school would mean overstepping the accepted bounds. The girl was very insistent, however, and was finally permitted to continue her studies in a public high school for girls, where all courses were conducted in Arabic. She became a distinguished student. Not many girls had attended the school previously, but during the period that Simha studied there, there were so many students that the authorities limited the number of Jewish girls who could attend, and accepted only those who excelled in their studies. Simha felt good. She studied alongside daughters of Kurdish *agas* (chieftains) and was not discriminated against in any way. However, during her last year at the school, the skies of the ghetto were overcast with disaster. Jews were aware of what lay in store for them but did nothing. When the blow fell they began to flee the country that had been their home for generations, taking with them only the clothes on their back. After the pogrom Simha returned to the school with final examinations and graduation not far off, and learned that her so-called friends were not bothered in the least by what had happened to her; on the contrary, they were pleased. Simha realized that Iraq was not her home, and that knowledge weighed on her mind from then on. As soon as her examinations were over she bent all her efforts to obtaining a passport in order to emigrate to Palestine.

At that time, one of her Jewish friends approached her and said:

"If you want to go to Palestine so badly, come with me and I'll help you out." So it was, that at the age of twenty, Simha joined Hehalutz. She plunged into her Hebrew studies with a will. She soon met Enzo Sereni, who promised to get her a certificate, but months passed and no certificate arrived. By that time Tikva Shohet was leaving for Palestine, and Simha had to take her place in the movement.

The girls looked upon the effort as a sacred task. They were awed by the emissaries, who worked days and nights on end. This was a period of naive simplicity. Every Jew who was willing to go to the Land of Israel was endowed with a certain holiness. Grapefruits brought into the country by a truck driver from Palestine were fondled lovingly. A bottle of Palestinian Carmel Mizrahi wine was passed from house to house for all to see. Large crowds turned out excitedly to greet a Red Magen David mission that had stopped off in Baghdad on its way to Teheran to assist the Russian Army against the Nazis.

Simha's parents had a difficult time deciding how to react to their daughter's activities. Their oldest girl had been to Palestine previously and had visited some kibbutzim, and thus had an idea of what kibbutz life was like. When their youngest daughter came and told them that she wanted to go to Palestine and live on a kibbutz, the whole family was shocked. On the following Sabbath all her relatives, young and old, came to convince her that she was wrong, but met with no success. After further efforts proved vain, her parents were finally won over.

It was Simha who years later summarized the revival of nationalism among the Jewish youth of Iraq in the following words:

"It was no accident, but the result of generations of longing. When the emissaries came—everything burst into bloom."

10

Through Desert Paths

Shmarya bent his efforts toward finding ways of bringing immigrants into Palestine. The first thing that the emissaries did was to use to good advantage the truck convoys that served for the transport of soldiers from Palestine. As soon as an Egged convoy would arrive in Baghdad, the emissaries would assemble a group of would-be immigrants from among the younger movement members. After a while these groups came to include Jewish deserters from the Polish Army who were fleeing anti-Semitism. They began to trickle into the country by way of the Anders army camps, that stretched from the Persian border to Egypt. The emissaries sent these people to Palestine individually or in groups, as auxiliary drivers.

The emissaries always gave priority to deserters from the Polish Army, who were in danger of being captured, but otherwise there was no discrimination of any kind in the selection of prospective immigrants. On more than one occasion the young men met members of the Revisionist Party and included them in these groups. One such was Michael Ashbel (Mike), who later died in the prison break at Acre on May 4, 1947. When he met Shmarya, the Hagana emissary in Baghdad, he asked him incredulously,

196

"You mean you're going to risk your life to save a political rival like me?"

While imprisoned in Acre he wrote a farewell letter to Shmarya wherein he said that having met the young men of the Bureau in Iraq, and having seen them at work, he was convinced that the future of the Jewish people lay in trustworthy hands.

On another occasion, just as a group was about to leave, an old man appeared and approached Shmarya.

"You have to save me," he insisted, "and I know that you can't refuse!"

When asked why he was so certain, he simply replied that somebody had to save him because he was the only one of his family who was left alive.

He was included with the others.

Whenever an Egged convoy would arrive, Shmarya and Ezra would put on their overalls and their drivers' caps, and openly walk around with the Egged drivers and carry on negotiations with them. In this way they managed to smuggle a few people into Palestine. Even these few people, however, often encountered unexpected and serious difficulties. On one occasion a young fellow who had been given Shmarya's identification card had to chew and swallow it when the group he was traveling with was captured. Another boy was kept imprisoned in Tiberias for weeks and was finally released only because he was so young.

A second means of immigration was afforded by the convoys of the Transport Corps of the Palestine Army. For example, in a 70-vehicle convoy that had brought empty tin containers from Palestine to Iraq, and was returning filled with fuel, 40 immigrants would be smuggled into the country. Sergeant D. did an excellent job of bringing in immigrants, at a great risk to himself. He was sharp-tongued and loved to pose as a hardened cynic who held nothing sacred. He once told Shmarya:

"King George can go to hell; Ben-Gurion can go to hell; you can go to hell. But before you go, tell me what you want done and I'll do it."

Shmarya traveled with him to and from Palestine on more than one occasion. With his help they were able to transport ammunition, bombs, and grenades. During these trips D. would call for military inspections, rollcalls, and the like. Once it happened that Shmarya was last to appear for a rollcall, and he gave him a sharp dressing down. Afterwards he went to the emissary's tent to apologize:

"I have to act that way, you know, otherwise the boys might think that something was fishy."

He looked after the immigrants devotedly, as though they were his own children. It happened that on a return trip from Iraq, a driver who was a member of the Communist Party refused to take any immigrants on his truck, maintaining that such deception was against his principles. The drivers were furious and demanded the right to "take care of him" before he should turn them over to the British authorities. Shmarya calmed them and said:

"Boys, we don't do that sort of thing."

As soon as D. heard of the incident, he ordered the driver out of his cab, sent him to work in the kitchen, and gave him warning:

"If I find out later that a word of this has gotten out to anyone—look out!"

The emissaries also sent immigrants with professional smugglers, both Arab and Jewish. They likewise made agreements with private truck drivers who were transporting merchandise to civilian groups. The emissaries suggested other plans, such as acquiring a truck of their own for immigration purposes, but headquarters in Tel Aviv would not give them permission, as funds were very low.

Another plan involved establishing a new route: Mosul-Kameshli-Damascus-Palestine.

Before such a plan could be put into effect, the emissaries had to familiarize themselves with the country and its roads. With this in mind Shmarya took trips outside of Baghdad. Even during his first stay in Baghdad he had taken a trip to Mosul. His colleagues all opposed the idea because of the close check that was being made on all *jinsiyas* (identification cards) at the time, but Shmarya insisted on going. He left Baghdad dressed like a local young Iraqi, with no papers on his person. He poured oil on his hair and took along some food in a simple wicker basket.

Shmarya was outwardly calm as he sat on the train, but inwardly he was very tense. When he saw the conductor enter the car accompanied by two soldiers carrying rifles, he did not know what to do; he was sure that they had come for him. He calmed down, however, when he saw them approach the passengers one at a time and ask for the pass. He was happy to learn that the "pass" meant the railroad ticket; the soldiers had come along simply to protect the conductor in the event that anyone who did not have a ticket should make trouble—and that had happened in the past on more than one occasion. When the group approached Shmarya he pretended to be napping and stretched out his card groggily as though he had no notion of what was going on around him. At one of the stations near Mosul a traffic policeman in a white uniform boarded the train and asked for identification cards. Shmarya woke up his companion, a member of Hehalutz in Baghdad, who was dozing on the bench opposite him, and prepared to jump out of the car. At the last minute he decided to try his luck with his sleeping routine. When the policeman came over and shook him, he lifted his head, squinted in sleepy confusion, and said with a Levantine inflection:

"Eh?"

"What's your name?" asked the policeman.

Shmarya mumbled an assumed name, turned his back on the man, and resumed snoring. The policeman shook him again and asked:

"Where are you from?"

"Baghdad," he mumbled.

"What do you do?"

"Worker," he answered, and went back to sleep.

Finally the policeman grew disgusted and moved on to question the other people in the car.

When he disappeared, Shmarya's traveling companion could scarcely restrain himself.

"Brother, you were as good as gold!" he whispered excitedly. "Not even an Iraqi could get away with that!"

When they arrived in Mosul his traveling companion went to a hotel while Shmarya went to the *Menzil*—an inn where camel drivers stopped off for rest and relaxation. The poorest elements of the populace would gather there, and it often served as a meeting place for members of the underworld. Here Shmarya learned how he could contact the chairman of the Jewish community, whose name he knew. He met the man, revealed his identity, and told him of his plans. The latter provided him with the papers of one of the local Jews who had recently died but for whom a death certificate had not been issued. Shmarya stayed in Mosul for a while and began to make contacts with smugglers.

During his second stay in Mosul he lived with workers of Solel Boneh to cloak the real purpose of his visit—making contact with the Yezidis, an idolatrous sect of Persian descent. Negotiations eventually broke down because of the high price the Yezidis demanded—thirty dinars for every person they would help to cross the border. They were willing to be paid in weapons instead of cash but Bureau Headquarters opposed the idea on principle.

On his way to the Yezidis Shmarya was joined by another Bureau emissary, Israel Sapir, a member of kibbutz Ramat Hakovesh. He too had participated in the course at Mikveh Israel. A short while after the first group of emissaries had left for Teheran he had been sent alone to Basra on the Iraqi-Iranian border to start work on opening up an exit route for Jewish refugees.

On the dangerous desert route, dotted with police stations for the length of the Haifa-Kirkuk oil line, there was a twenty- to thirty-mile strip strewn with basalt stones. There was no possibility of getting around the police station and no vehicle could get through. The young men racked their brains trying to hit upon a way of getting through that strip despite the difficulties involved. They decided to go north to Mosul, near the Syrian border, and hire a tribesman from the area to help them. Shmarya obtained a car from one of the sheiks and Israel accompanied him on the dangerous trip through the mountains. A Russian Army camp was not far off. Despite agreements made between the allies there was a constant struggle going on between American and Russian forces regarding their influence among these tribes. Rumors were widespread that any American who chanced into the area disappeared as though the earth had swallowed him.

Mosul is inhabited by a conglomeration of nationalities and tribes: Assyrians, Chaldeans, Turks, Circassians, Arabs, Druses, Jews. Among the sheiks with whom they talked were Sabaeans (better known as Mandaeans) and Yezidis. The Sabaeans, known for their striking long beards, proudly assert that their tradition originates with John the Baptist. Their holy books are written in Aramaic. The Yezidis, who speak Kurdish, have long braids, bear their weapons on their persons, and are known as "devil worshippers."

The emissaries traveled in a broken-down jalopy that had no lights, and they often had to get out and push. When the motor would overheat, they would have to stop and wait for it to cool off. The military uniforms they wore proved very useful: soldiers of the Indian divisions camping in the area frequently pushed their car and supplied them with gasoline.

When they arrived at their destination they were informed that the British Military Governor had just been there; they realized that had they come sooner they would have been arrested. They also learned that their journey had been in vain, as the Yezidi sheik had left to spend some time with the governor at the latter's invitation.

On their return trip the car sank into some mud and they could not move it. Suddenly the "weapon bearers" appeared, with plunder in their eyes. The young men offered to pay whatever the sheik would decide. The "braided ones" removed their weapons and began pushing the car forward, but Israel, who sat at the wheel, took care not to start the engine until they were a good distance away from the weapons. Then he quickly turned on the ignition and the car darted off, leaving the cursing Yezidis far behind.

They had only traveled a short distance when darkness fell upon them. Shmarya got out and walked in front of the car and called out directions to Israel. Suddenly he shouted: "Stop! Stop!"

The car stopped four inches away from the edge of a precipice and a 500-foot drop.

A short while after the trip to Mosul Shmarya went to

Basra. After a week's stay there he returned to Baghdad early in the morning, exhausted from a sleepless night spent on the train. Enzo Sereni immediately informed him that he was to lead a group to Palestine in two days. The next day, in the midst of last-minute preparations, Shmarya became involved in unforeseen difficulties. One of the local movement leaders had brought two deserters from the Polish Army along with him in the train. In the station the police halted the man and began searching his belongings. The two deserters panicked, fled, and disappeared. When Shmarya learned of this he went to look for them. After five hours of wandering in and out of back alleys in the far corners of the city where they had disappeared, he came home empty-handed. In the meanwhile, however, the deserters had turned up by themselves. They had come across a fellow in a back alley whom they recognized to be a Jew and had asked him where they could find the "movement." Following his directions, they arrived at their destination.

As a result of this episode, Shmarya had no time left that day to get his own papers in order or to check over the arrangements made for the hazardous journey. His colleague took over his personal affairs for him in his absence. As soon as he received his papers the following morning and opened them, he spotted a serious error: his real name had been written out in full.

The streets of Baghdad were hot and dusty that morning and all the people in the streets were covered with sweat—as usual. The dingy cafes were crowded with men wearing their black "Feisal" hats, and poor farmers wearing kaffiyas, Arab headkerchiefs, sat on the steps. Old black carriages stood about idly as they had for years, and the drowsy teams of horses twitched and flicked their tails incessantly to rid themselves of the swarms of noisy flies. From time to time a boy came out of the coffeehouse and slopped some mucky water into the street to alleviate the heat, but it only served to raise clouds of dust and increase the stench of the open sewers at the feet of the hookah smokers, seated on their low stools.

Life was going on as usual.

What was different, though, was the strange assemblage of 35 British soldiers in front of the office of Rafidein, the Arab bus company that ran a line between Baghdad and Jerusalem. For years, the streets of Baghdad had witnessed many strange scenes. Numerous convoys of soldiers passed through the city from east to west and from west to east. Groups of Palestinian workers and engineers often rode by dressed in British military uniforms. Families of Polish refugees were taken southward under the auspices of the Allied Army.

The particular group of soldiers that were assembled that morning for a long, arduous desert journey looked different, however. They seemed unusually nervous. With tense faces and tightly closed lips, they stood before their short, thin, curly-headed "sergeant," who was busy examining a packet of identification cards in his hand. This was the first time that the young men were taking advantage of Solel Boneh's prerogative of wearing British uniforms. It had required a great deal of effort to convince Enzo Sereni to cooperate in this endeavor, which was liable to endanger the company's status and reputation. He nervously paced back and forth on the pavement on the opposite side of the street, observing the departure as unobtrusively as he could.

The eminent Dr. Enzo Sereni, who lived in the well-known Hotel Semiramis and whose official role was that of representative of Solel Boneh, took pains not to be seen with the young men of the underground, but met with them secretly every day and had a hand in all their activities.

At the outset there was a good deal of debate within the small group over the nature of their program and the means of implementing it. The young men felt that it was necessary to operate completely as an underground organization, but Enzo would not agree. He was not willing to give an inch as far as his Jewish pride was concerned. No sooner had he arrived in Baghdad than he made contacts with some of the city's most respected Jews and with cultured Arabs, and acquired a name for himself among widespread circles. Many Jews avoided meeting him because of his open arguments with members of the Arab intellegentsia over sensitive matters of Arab nationalism.

The young men appreciated his fervor, his broad intellectual background, his colorful personality, and his concern for their welfare. Although he was often reckless where his own health and safety were concerned, he forbade them to engage in any activity that endangered their safety or freedom.

All during his stay in Baghdad, in the midst of feverish activity and a very demanding daily schedule, he did not stop studying. He frequented the library of the University of Baghdad and always walked about with books and magazines that he read whenever he had a minute to spare. Many were the times he took Shmarya to task for not following his example. Often in the middle of an argument over some tedious daily business he would embark upon a lively discussion concerning philosophy, history, or Jewish values.

Only a short while before he was sent to Baghdad, Enzo had undergone a very trying experience in Egypt with the Allied Army. Ever since he had been won over to Zionism while a young student in Rome, his life had become a series of missions, one following another. With his wife and small daughter he left an aristocratic and well-educated family—his father was physician to the King of Italy—and became a farm laborer in the sandy village of Rehovot. There he lived in a small tent colony with the other pioneers who were to found the kibbutz of Givat Brenner, named after the well-known Hebrew writer who was killed in the riots of 1921. Soon after, he embarked upon a series of endless missions inside and outside of Palestine. He went to the United States as an emissary of the Palestine labor movement, and then was sent to bolster the morale of Germany Jewry and save Jewish property and lives under the Nazi regime. In 1940 he was among the first to volunteer for the Palestinian units of the Allied Army. His talents and energy won him the unique role of anti-Fascist propagandist on the radio and in the Italian newspaper "Justice and Freedom." His audience consisted of 200,000 Italian soldiers and civilians who had been captured by the British.

Since Egypt at that time was Mussolini's primary military objective, anti-Fascist propaganda had an important role to fulfill. The Italian prisoners, however, were none too receptive to his message, and his British supervisors found his fiery idealism too left wing for comfort. Their attitude grew increasingly hostile, until he was imprisoned by the Egyptian police on a trumped-up charge of having used a forged British passport.

While in prison Sereni wrote a valuable memorandum for use in the anti-Fascist campaign in Italy. After he obtained his release from the prison, as a result of a twelve-day protest hunger strike, he presented the memorandum to his British military superiors.

He had not recuperated from the rigors of his Egyptian experience when he found himself called upon to undertake still another task. Moishele of the Bureau came to Givat Brenner to recruit him for a mission to save Iraqi Jewry. Without lifting his head from his book Sereni said quietly:

"All right, when do I leave?"

Soon "Ehud," his underground pseudonym, began to appear in the letters received by the Bureau, which now made room in its files for a new country, Iraq. In his very first letter, dated April 13, 1942, "Ehud" asked that five Hebrew grammars be sent to him at once, as well as a few books on Palestine with photographs of the country. Similar requests for textbooks, easy reading material, and information books with photographs were repeated in almost every one of Enzo's letters during his year-and-a-half stay in Iraq. "Nissim," as Saul Avigur was then called, was the one who received the letters with their incessant demands for "books, books, books."

On the day following his first meeting with the two emissaries who had left Palestine shortly after he had, Sereni sent a detailed memorandum to Bureau headquarters in Palestine, analyzing in detail the situation of the Jewish youth in Iraq and proposing a basic plan for the organization of their program. The memorandum emphasized the value of learning "Kaduri lore," (named after Ezra Kaduri, the emissary) as Hagana activities and the use of arms were then called by the young members of the new Hehalutz movement. He then went into further detail regarding the educational program of their first group of people who would band together and undergo training, their ultimate goal being to form their own kibbutz in Palestine, or to join an existing kibbutz. The necessary books were listed. He concluded by stating that they would have to work quickly to exploit the impetus provided by their arrival.

Some months later, "Nissim" received a letter which

showed that its writer was getting satisfaction and results from his work. "We are making rapid strides forward. An interest in Zionism has evidenced itself in the city. Hundreds of people have read the pamphlets that we distributed, and have become very enthusiastic and hopeful. This was the first greeting they received from Eretz Israel after years of silence."

Enzo Sereni paid special attention to two boys who were among the few survivors of Poland's pioneer youth. Both had been active in organizing and teaching children of Jewish refugees in Teheran. Enzo looked upon them as remnants of slaughtered European Jewry and felt that he had to do as much as he could for them, almost as though they were the most important aspect of his mission.

Emissaries of the Bureau had smuggled the boys onto a train in Teheran as deaf-mutes being taken to a doctor in Baghdad. When they arrived at their destination, Sereni sent them to a Jewish family who were willing to risk their lives by taking the boys in. There they spent six weeks in isolation. Sereni came to their room daily for a two-hour study session: one hour for Hebrew and Bible; and one hour for the discussion of personalities in Palestine and the labor movement, and its ideologies.

One day, arriving at the appointed hour as usual, he appeared very upset. When the boys asked him what had happened, he told them that the previous evening a husky Arab had set upon him in a dark alley and robbed him of his wallet, which contained movement funds. He had no means of making up the loss and he was furious. The boys tried to calm him and advised him not to go to the police, for the British and Iraqi authorities suspected him of having connections with the Zionist movement and its underground, and such a step involved the possibility of their discovering

14. EMISSARIES OF THE IMMIGRATION BUREAU HAD SMUGGLED
THE BOYS ONTO A TRAIN IN TEHERAN AS DEAF-MUTES.

his true identity. He nevertheless decided to go to the police and demand that they find the thief. He did so, but the money was not returned.

In the midst of his daily and laborious practical work, he continued to give thought to the Jewish problem in its wider political context. In one of his letters he stated his belief in the need to exert pressure on the Iraqi Government through the United States, "in order to enable the Jews to leave this country," because "it is most certain, that for various reasons, illegal emigration is becoming more and more difficult, and we must discover means of increasing legal emigration, which, in any event, is the only path open to an appreciable segment of the population."

"Ehud's" letters to "Nissim" contained information concerning smugglers and informers, unsuccessful attempts to cross the border, means of camouflaging their activities. He wrote of the need to make the identification papers and documents conform, complained about the lack of support in Palestine, demanded that Headquarters speed up the tempo of the effort and improve communications; he also enclosed an instructive political analysis of goings on in the various sectors of the Arab world. Occasionally his concern for his family crept into his correspondence. He was particularly upset when the bar mitzvah of his only son Daniel drew near and no one had been found as yet to replace him. In the margins of one of his letters to Nissim he wrote: "My conscience will not allow me to leave this country until I am sure that new emissaries have been obtained. . . . Nevertheless, please do understand: I have only one son, and he was very upset when I wrote him that I would not be home for his celebration. If you are good Jews, send the men right away and let a Jewish father fulfill his responsibilities."

His concern over every aspect of the emissaries' activities

expressed itself also on the aforementioned summer morning of 1942, when the first groups of would-be immigrants, disguised as workers of Solel Boneh, were preparing to leave Baghdad.

Shmarya, disguised as a sergeant, stood before the 35 men in front of the Rafidein office, ready to go, while Enzo Sereni, Ezra Kaduri, and the newly arrived emissary, Israel Kopit, nervously walked about on the opposite side of the street. Suddenly two Army Intelligence officers appeared, and at the sight of the unusual gathering, went over to investigate. Under his breath Shmarya whispered a warning to "the boys":

"No one understands English here except me—got it? If I have to, I'll give you a signal and you run for it."

When the officers asked the "soldiers" who they were and where they were headed, they pointed at their sergeant. The officers approached the sergeant and asked where he was going.

"Jerusalem," he answered.

"And where are you from?"

"Excuse me," said Shmarya, coolly, "I've already said too much."

"Can you tell us the purpose of your mission?"

"No I can't."

"Don't you know who we are?"

"Of course I know! You're from Intelligence, but my mission is not under your jurisdiction, and there's nothing for you to investigate here."

His reply constituted an oblique reference to the large oil tanks that had been constructed by Solel Boneh. Due to the secrecy of their project the uniformed workers were permitted to use civilian bus lines rather than the transportation afforded the regular army.

The officers stepped aside to confer. After a few moments they came back and said:

"Excuse us, sergeant, but would it be all right with you if your men show us their identification cards?"

"Certainly," he said, "go right ahead."

The two men were more than a little puzzled by the strange military identification cards that differed markedly from the usual kind. While they did have photographs, no soldier's pay was listed; but in any event the papers did bear orders (falsified) and the signature (forged) of the company commander.

The officers' suspicions were further aroused when the sergeant would not submit his own papers to be examined. He did not want them to see his name. The experienced Intelligence men, however, were not to be put off that easily. They asked that they at least be allowed to look at the names of the soldiers on the lists of the bus company.

The officers finally left without having come up with any-thing conclusive, although Shmarya's story seemed rather dubious to them. As they took leave of the mysterious sergeant, they apologized for not being able to help him in making arrangements for his men's food rations on the journey. This was a last attempt on their part to trap Shmarya: they knew very well that they had nothing to do with providing troops with rations. The sergeant thanked them for their courtesy.

The journey proved to be arduous and dangerous. They passed many convoys of Polish soldiers and they feared that someone might recognize the Polish members of their own convoy. For this reason Shmarya did not stop over at army way stations, nor did he take advantage of other services offered by the military to alleviate the rigors of the long trip. They had to spend the nights in hotels, fearful that the company's Iraqi drivers might turn them over to the authorities. When their signatures were requested on hotel ledgers, the sergeant would sign for all of them. Upon their arrival at the Allenby bridge on the Palestine border, they saw a very long line of vehicles. Shmarya burst into the checking station shouting that his men were on an urgent mission and that he had the right to cross the bridge before anyone else.

Finally, after a five-day journey, they arrived in Jerusalem, via Amman in Transjordan. From there they went to Ramle, and proceeded to Shmarya's kibbutz, Na'an, which lay nearby. There they spent the night in the rooms of the kibbutz members. Shmarya took into his own room one of two young deserters from the Polish Army who had been brought to him in his room in Baghdad in the middle of the night.

One of the two had been particularly quiet and obedient during the trip, and had helped the "sergeant" in every possible way. He stayed close by him all the time, like a student by his teacher, and was eager to carry out any order or request. In reality, he was a British Intelligence agent, and he had gone on the trip to learn all that he could about the workings of the Jewish underground. The "deserter's" true identity was disclosed in a coded telegram sent to Palestine by the emissaries in Iraq, who reported that the fellow had returned to Baghdad and had been seen walking about the city. Shmarya heard the news while he was enjoying a short leave in a sanitarium, recuperating from a state of exhaustion. At once he returned to Baghdad. Upon his arrival he learned that the boy had revealed everything that he had learned and that a house-to-house search had begun. Jews were imprisoned and beaten, but no one turned the emissaries in. Shmarya immediately set to work teaching the refugees how to undergo interrogation. He sat down with every active

15. FINALLY, AFTER A FIVE DAY JOURNEY, THEY ARRIVED IN JERUSALEM.

movement member and rehearsed with him what he would say. Enzo Sereni was forced to leave Iraq. Katling, the chief of the British Police in Palestine and the head of the C.I.D. (Counter Intelligence), was sent from Palestine, and spent three months in Baghdad in an attempt to uncover the Hagana underground. The emissaries in Baghdad were warned in advance of his coming and all of them were re-called to Palestine. Only Shmarya, Ezra, and Malka Rofe remained. The two men looked for a means of smuggling their companion out of the country. Ezra constantly urged Shmarya to return also, for he saw that his friend was tired and sick. Palestine headquarters, thinking that he was in danger, insisted that he return. Shmarya, however, remained in Baghdad until he succeded in getting Ezra out of the country.

Some time prior to this, all the emissaries went into hiding. Shmarya pretended that he was sick, and even Ezra and Malka did not realize that this was a subterfuge on his part. Ezra cooked special food for the "patient" and took care of him like a nurse. Even Shmarya's family in Palestine did not know what had become of him; they thought that he had been taken prisoner.

Shmarya's object at the time was to mislead Katling and in so doing save the underground organization of the Bureau. For weeks he stayed in bed and only once a week did he inform his closest friends that he had to visit the doctor, but he never told them who the doctor was. At those times he would meet with a Jewish soldier who worked under Katling and was the latter's chief source of information on the Jews of Baghdad and the Hagana underground. After a difficult first meeting with the soldier, Shmarya won him over. At first the young man refused, for Katling paid him very well for his services. However, at the time that the emissary approached him, he was lonely and despondent. He could not believe that he was really being asked to work for the Hagana. He asked how they could trust him, seeing that he was in the employ of the British Intelligence. When Shmarya simply replied that he had faith in him and was confident that he would not inform on them, the young man was overwhelmed and agreed to help; and indeed, in the weeks that followed he kept his promise faithfully, without requesting or receiving any payment. Regularly he turned in to Katling the reports written by Shmarya. These reports stated that the Hagana was so powerful and well organized that it would be impossible to destroy it. For days and weeks Shmarya worked on the answers to the questions posed by Katling to the young man and was pleased to see the result of his efforts embodied in the reports prepared by Katling for his superiors.

He did not stop at this, however. He was determined to uncover the whereabouts of the traitorous Pole who was a member of the "Dvoika" (the Polish Army Secret Service), and remove one obstacle from the path of the illegal immigration effort. The principal problem he had to face was how to meet the fellow alone. He disguised himself to look like one of the many Arab peddlers that filled the streets of Baghdad, and began to dog the man's footsteps diligently. Many days passed before he was able to meet him in an alley alone, for the Pole was almost always accompanied by another man, as was customary among the "Dvoika" agents.

Shmarya approached him and said:

"Recognize me?"

The young man was confused and quickly replied:

"No, I don't."

"Not possible!" said Shmarya, "after you spent a night in my room?"

The Pole became frightened and turned to leave, but the "peddler" blocked his path and said quietly:

"Don't move. I see your friend, but you ought to know that I have friends as well behind me in the distance. Pretend that you're looking for something to buy until I've told you what I came to tell you."

The man was so confused that he obeyed the order. Shmarya then said forcefully:

"Leave Baghdad within two weeks, or you're a dead man."

The Pole left.

11

On Eagles' Wings

Of the first group of emissaries that had been sent to Baghdad, Shmarya was the last to leave. Sometime prior to this, before they were forced to disband the organization that they had set up, the emissaries gathered the movement members together from all over Iraq. At this conference they set up a group of leaders who would be able to work on their own when the time should arrive. The autonomous activities of the young group of local leaders continued for months. In spite of the long interval until the arrival of the new group of emissaries, the movement was active in the cities and villages, and underground emigration to Palestine did not cease.

One of the prominent achievements of the first group of emissaries was the revival of Zionism in the provincial towns. News spread secretly from Baghdad to the poor villages in the Kurdistan mountains and gave hope to the Jews in those isolated regions.

Rarely did any emissary from Palestine ever come in contact with these enslaved Jewish communities. In 1936 A. Y. Braver, scholar and author, published impressions of his journey under the title of "Pentecost by the Waters of Babylon." "I enjoyed a peaceful fifty-day journey through

Iran," writes the author. "However, no sooner did I enter Iraq on my way to Palestine, than I was beset with torments and hardships. This was not due to coincidence, but rather to the methods of the Iraqi police, who still follow the example set by the Turkish regime." In a memorandum to Nevil Laski, President of the Council of Representatives of the Jewish Community of London, he described at greater length the saddening and frightening impressions made on him in that corner of the Diaspora. Only a short while before his trip, there had been Jewish slaves in the isolated villages of the Kurdistan mountains. There, entire families were sold to Kurdish masters who did with them as they pleased— worked them, sold them to others, or gave them to friends as gifts on festive occasions. Often children and parents would be cruelly separated, and all this was carried on within the framework of the Turkish laws.

Even prior to this, Dr. Arthur Ruppin and I. Ettinger had brought the situation of Iraqi Jewry to the attention of the Yishuv. In 1934 Ben-Zion Israeli of kibbutz Kinneret took his first trip to Iraq to buy special date saplings for the Jordan Valley. He traveled to the furthermost corners of the Kurdistan mountains where he came upon tiny Jewish communities or families isolated among non-Jews, and after his trip he wrote: "Only after I had met them did I realize the meaning of the phrase 'the far-flung members of Israel!' Their existence there is utterly wretched, and emigration to Palestine is the only solution to their problems." In his note to the Yishuv's official bodies he firmly stated as an opinion what later proved a reality: "Not only do these Jews suffer bitterly now in this Arab Diaspora, but it is most likely that they will be among the first to pay with their lives for our work in Palestine."

And indeed, when the workers of Solel Boneh arrived in

Kirkuk during the Second World War to work for the Anglo-Iranian Oil Company, their first contacts with this Jewry showed them how accurate Israeli's prediction had been. A letter from one of the workers told how the Jews of Kirkuk shut themselves up in their quarter for weeks, not daring to go out. Another letter makes mention of small Jewish communities in the environs of Kirkuk, in Sulaymaniyah, which at the time served as the unofficial capital of Iraqi Kurdistan and the place of residence of the Iraqi Kurdish leader. Very small Jewish settlements were also located in Arbil and Dehuk. Only a few years prior to this, small Jewish communities were to be found in the Kurdish villages, but hostility and oppressive measures eventually forced them out, making impoverished refugees of them.

The Jewish agricultural settlement in the village of Sandur was a unique phenomenon at that period. The visit paid them by twenty-five Jewish young men in British uniforms, who spoke the language of the Torah and took a great interest in their brothers' lot, made a powerful impression on the villagers. The young men toured the vineyards and plots of the Jewish villagers, participated in the evening service in the synagogue, and spent the night there. During the period of the Rashid Ali revolt ten Jewish villagers had been killed in one night, but no investigations were made and no one was punished. "The Jews of Sandur are genuine farmers and are fine human material for a workers' settlement in Palestine. The entire village is very willing to leave this Diaspora. They are even prepared to abandon their lands without selling them, as they realize that no one would buy under the circumstances. They have no future in this village. They are constantly in danger and there is no prospect of a change for the better." So wrote the young men after their visit to the village.

The emissaries of the Bureau took steps to include Sandur in their program. Israel Sapir would arrive in Mosul from Basra every week and would spend two days in the village, going from house to house giving Hebrew lessons. The Solel Boneh workers also lent a hand; when a company of Palestinian soldiers of the Engineer Corps arrived in the village, they too came to the emissaries' aid. A movement of boys and girls sprung up, and became strong enough to function autonomously.

A short while after the departure of the first group of emissaries from Baghdad, a new group arrived, which included Leibel Abramov. The first thing they did was to re-establish the emigration bases along the border. They made connections with Kameshli, the Syrian border town, and began to re-examine the possibilities of taking the route through the dangerous Syria-Iraq-Jordan triangle. This route, in addition to passing through three countries, ran the length of the Iraq-Haifa pipeline. One of the local residents was assigned the task of finding out whether the British consulate had any immigration certificates for Iraqi Jews and until when would they be valid. He was also to determine whether there was any movement of tourists from the country and to make connections with local and foreign transportation companies. Another, who spoke fluent Arabic and was not recognizable as a Jew, was sent to frequent the places where tribal chiefs, Bedouin sheiks, and men of the desert gathered, and to learn who among them would be willing to smuggle Jews out of the country. A third took it upon himself to meet with high police officers and members of the Ministry of the Interior, in hopes of arranging for the semi-legal emigration of large families with many children.

All these activities were carried out with the help of the handful of young members of the defense organization of the Iraqi Jews. The emissaries from Palestine had trained them well for the difficult and dangerous tasks that they were given.

After weeks of general groping about in all directions, it became clear that in the British consulate there were indeed a number of immigration certificates whose owners did not intend to use them. The young men decided to get Iraqi passports, make them conform to the data given in the certificates, and prepare them for use in emergencies, or use them shortly before they were to expire. Some experienced smugglers were found among the Bedouins. After many investigations they finally decided to use the smugglers to get the first group of pioneers to Palestine.

The route that they mapped out was: Mosul—Kameshli—Deir ez Zor—Damascus. Before they left, all the emissaries in Iraq gathered in conference and worked out the final version of the plan. Leibel met the Bedouins on a moonlit night on the Tigris River and a detailed agreement was concluded to the satisfaction of both parties. One of the conditions of the agreement was that the smuggler would not be paid in advance. Rather, he would be given a token; upon the group's arrival at the Syrian base, if the immigrants were all right with no complaints regarding his behavior along the way, he would receive another token in exchange for the first. Upon his return he would present his token to the emissaries and would get his wage plus a bonus. If he continued to prove reliable he would get occasional advance payments. The second token was given to one of the immigrants without the knowledge of the others. He concealed it on his person in such a fashion that it would not be seen even if his clothes should rip, or would not be lost in going through water. He was instructed not to give the impression of being one of the leaders of the group, but rather to limit himself to his role as an observer and submit a faithful account of the smuggler's behavior upon his arrival in Palestine.

The first group started out. The trip proved difficult and many obstacles were encountered; the smuggler returned without the token. Nevertheless he received his wage after he gave a detailed explanation of what had happened. A second group set out and arrived safely. The third group, however, was caught. Some of its members returned to Baghdad at once and told what had happened to them. They had been robbed of everything, including the clothing that they had worn. Some were sent to prison, but thanks to the emissaries' connections in Mosul, they were quickly released. The smuggler too had been caught, and in exchange for a promise of a lighter punishment, revealed who his employers were. From then on greater care was exercised.

At about the same time, a comfortable and safe route was opened for families and children. With the help of local tourist agencies the emissary made connections with police officers and was able to purchase from them trunks full of Iraqi passports and emigration permits. The transfer of the money and the passports would be effected in one of the synagogues outside the ghetto. The Iraqi officer would arrive with his "merchandise" and sit down on one side of the street, and the emissaries would sit on the other. A member of the local Hagana group, a quiet, shy young man, was the go-between. He would take the passports over to Leibel, and then bring the money over to the officer.

Hehalutz expanded, and the number of emigrants to Palestine increased with each passing month. The emissaries in Baghdad were joined by Ezra Kaduri, who had been a member of the first mission sent to that city. Together they worked and planned for the eventual transfer of all of

Iraqi Jewry and its wealth to Palestine. However, they were in for a grave disappointment. A pack of letters was discovered in an oil truck and was sent directly to Central Intelligence in Baghdad. The letters, written by Jewish boys and girls of Baghdad to their friends who had already emigrated illegally to Palestine, disclosed secrets of the underground movement and called down the wrath of the authorities.

The first step taken by the police was to activate the members of the Jewish Community Council, starting with the rabbi, against the underground organization. The emissaries did their utmost to prevent the arrest of any movement members, and decided to smuggle the letter writers out of their homes and hide them, without letting their families know where they were being kept, and send them to Palestine at the first opportunity. This plan was especially difficult to execute, as most of the parties concerned were girls. The parents felt that bribery would afford their daughters full protection upon their return home. The emissaries, however, feared that the girls would not stand up under the brutal interrogations of the Iraqi police, and would reveal everything. Leibel met with all the parents and tried to win their cooperation. He assured them that the girls were being kept in safe hiding places and that absolutely no harm would come to them. He urged them not to inform on the emissaries, but rather to wait patiently until the tumult should die down, and tell the police in the meanwhile that the girls had run away on their own, and that they, too, were looking for them.

The parents had no choice but to cooperate. The emissaries used the immigration certificates that they had obtained from the British consulate to send the three "couples" who were most wanted by the British directly to Palestine by plane.

However, the Jewish Community Council had been roused to action. It spread panic, maintaining that the activities of the Zionist underground movement would lead to a renewal of outbursts against the Jewish population, and that it would be best to turn the guilty parties over to the authorities. There was nothing left to do but meet with the President of the Council face to face.

Leibel informed the President that he represented thousands of organized, armed young Jews; that he was not afraid of anti-Jewish riots; and that he knew what he had to do and would continue to do it.

The meeting served its purpose. Not one of the movement members was caught. The police learned no more than had been revealed to them in the letters.

However, the emissaries soon discovered that they could accomplish nothing, forced as they were to remain hidden in cellars. For the second time then, everything had to be suspended, and once again the emissaries had to be smuggled out of the country and back to Palestine.

In spite of the forced suspension of effort brought on by mishaps and the activities of informers, the work continued, with each new group of emissaries benefitting from the experience of their predecessors. The Bureau enlisted its best people and drew upon all its resources to train emissaries for the "Iraqi front." No sooner would one group leave than another would take its place. As time went on, a special headquarters was set up to coordinate all underground activities in the Middle East and land immigration into Palestine. This task was given to the Hagana member Munia Mardor, who was accordingly freed of his other Hagana duties and took to scouting about on desert roads.

The hundreds and thousands of letters, memoranda, and reports that poured into the Bureau were now signed with new aliases, but the problems, general approach, and goals were the same.

There was one change, and that was in the nature of the pioneer movement in Iraq, which had become firmly established. Like the pioneer movements in Poland, Germany, Austria, and other European countries, it too grew out of the wretched existence of the Jews in the Diaspora.

One of the letters found in the oil truck read:

> Before our movement was founded, we were groping about in the dark, not knowing where we were going. When the first emissaries arrived, they lit up the path for a few of us, and from that day on we began to change our way of life and prepare ourselves for the future. And that little light continued to grow; and empty, dead houses became hiding places full of life, where pioneers met and trained for their new life in the Homeland. . . .

In a newsletter entitled Nevatim ("Buds"), Tikva Shohet, the first girl pioneer to emigrate to Palestine from Iraq, wrote:

> A few of us from Iraq are located in the kibbutz Bet Hashitta and we intend to form the nucleus of a new kibbutz. We are running into the usual difficulties that confront pioneers, but we are stubborn and are bearing up. We are the first. In Baghdad we knew very little about Zionism. Our physical and psychological training were far from sufficient. In Eretz Israel we have taken upon ourselves many tasks: to unite, to pull ourselves together, and to overcome the difficulties of everyday work: in Baghdad we did not know what physical labor meant. We have also taken it upon ourselves to absorb new immigrants, and by this we mean to understand the new immigrant, to help him and to

forgive him his mistakes and be willing to overlook a great deal.

Every one of us is responsible for all immigrants who come from Iraq. We have to give them a warm home atmosphere, stand by them when they take their first steps, and take part in their happiness and in their sorrow. We are learning how to do this in Bet Hashitta; the people here are very patient and very kind.

We must build the Land with the same dedication that the first pioneers had. True, we have come late. We do not have to drain swamps or pave roads. But there is still much to be done. . . .

On December 2, 1942, one and a half years after the first conference of Hehalutz in Baghdad, the second conference began. This conference was attended not only by members from the capital, but also from Basra and Mosul, which possessed almost autonomous chapters. The speeches and work sessions revealed that the first stage of Hehalutz development had passed and that the movement no longer depended solely upon the enthusiasm of its members, but was well organized and had gained a good deal of working experience. A girl named Aliza welcomed the delegates and pointed out with pride how their organization had grown since the first conference:

We worked under difficult conditions, but we have results to show for it, both here and in Palestine. . . . Our main task, however, still lies before us. We cannot be satisfied with the small number of people our movement embraces. We are responsible for all Jews. So long as there are Jews in the Diaspora, we have to worry about them and educate them. We cannot turn our backs on them. This conference must sum up past activities, point out achievements, but principally concern itself with the future. . . . It is true that we are few, but we are not alone. We are part of the camp of Hehalutz that is spread throughout the world, even if we are an underground movement. . . .

It was no coincidence that two of the last emissaries to serve in Iraq, Shlomo Hillel and Yerahmiel Assa, and one of the first to serve in Syria, Avraham Abbas, during the period of the establishment of the State of Israel were elected to the Knesset (Parliament). The people were very grateful towards the young men and women whose dedicated efforts had contributed so much to the creation of the Jewish State.

Yerahmiel Assa, a member of kibbutz Hulata, arrived in Baghdad in the beginning of 1947, hidden in a truck carrying sacks of goods from Palestine. Emigration to Palestine had been discontinued for some time, and the movement members waited restlessly for the arrival of some emissaries and a revival of the effort.

Younger boys and girls pleaded to be taken to Palestine. The girls insisted that at least one of them be sent, so that the other girls would not give up hope. The emissaries did their best to comply but met with a serious setback in March of 1947. At that time a large group was sent out under the joint leadership of Sheik Abdullah, from the vicinity of Rutba, and the Emir Shaalan from Syria, who controlled the area bordering on Iraq. The two sheiks, however, proved unreliable. The pioneers camped in the desert for eight days, having almost no food and water with them, and finally returned to Iraq, very shaken. On their return trip the truck overturned, injuring many and killing two of their number. The two were buried by the pioneers in the desert.

The accident did not lead to the termination of the program, however, and on the eve of the United Nation's declaration on the State of Israel, headquarters in Palestine received a letter from an emissary in Iraq concerning one of the largest groups of emigrants ever sent from that country.

> There are times (he wrote) when one has to assume large responsibilities, even when one is aware of the many dangers involved. Such was the case when I sent those young people—children some of them—with professional smugglers. Do I have to tell you how I spent sleepless nights waiting to hear from them? Or how torn I was with doubts as to whether I had the right to send them in the first place? Or how overjoyed I was to get the wire telling me that they had all arrived safely?

On a return trip from Palestine, where this emissary had gone to confer about certain aspects of the program, he passed a convoy of twenty trucks decorated with flags and proclamations, loaded with Armenians returning to their homeland. "They stood proud and tall as they rode by. And we, unaided, try to return to our homeland like thieves. . . ."

The situation of Iraqi Jewry grew even worse as the United Nations decision on Palestine drew nearer. It had been a drought year, the people were hungry, and the Government used the Palestine issue and Zionism as a scapegoat. Jews were fired for no reason whatever from their posts in the government and the management of the railroad. Angry Iraqi youth called for a *Jihad,* a holy war against Palestine. The rabbis of Baghdad announced a day of fasting and prayer in the wake of the drought, but every Jew knew that this was simply a pretext to assemble and pray for the fate of the Land of Israel on the eve of the U.N. decision. Young Jews in the capital and in the provinces listened to the radio broadcasts, which reported ominous news from Palestine. On the night of the vote in the General Assembly they stayed up until dawn, and the next day blessings of gratitude were offered up in silence by thousands. The frightened leaders of the Jewish community ordered the teachers of the Jewish school to stifle any spontaneous outbursts on the part of the children, and even urged them to participate in the mass demonstrations protesting the U.N. decision. Many, however, refused to comply. The head of the Jewish Community Council wrote a servile declaration for the authorities. However, the educational efforts of the young men of the underground had their effect: some representatives of the Jewish community opposed the declaration and left the Council meeting as a sign of protest. A number of community leaders headed the list of contributors to the fund for the volunteers for the holy war in Palestine, but at the same time, the movement members, drawn from the younger element of the community, announced the creation of a fund for the defense of the Hebrew State, and despite the danger to themselves, donated of their own money and solicited contributions from others.

On the eve of the declaration of Israel's statehood, the Jews shut themselves up in their houses and did not venture out into the street. Members of the movement and the defense force were ready to answer any calls for help.

As night fell on May 15, 1948, the young men went out to their posts. "Not a soul could be seen on the street, except for our patrols and those of the police," wrote the emissary. "The 'boys' were ready and waiting. I saw worried Jewish mothers peer fearfully from behind window shutters, and heard them sigh in relief at the sight of the young Jewish defenders."

Shlomo Hillel went to Iraq three times to serve the immigration effort. He first went there in the summer of 1946, a period wherein many arduous attempts were made to get Jews to Palestine illegally with the help of Arab smugglers.

Shlomo found it necessary to engage in a great deal of haggling and to make weighty decision quickly. There were serious and disheartening setbacks. Once, six young people, after having journeyed for one month on foot, arrived at the kibbutz Bet Ha'arava on the north shore of the Dead Sea, barefoot and naked. Shortly before they had reached the border, the smugglers had robbed them of everything. Then there was the episode of two young men who left Iraq and were never heard from again. Others died also; not many, but enough to have a demoralizing effect upon the entire movement.

The young emissary did not find it easy to stand up under such rigors, even though years of struggle against the British had hardened him considerably. Shlomo had disguised himself as an Iraqi to get into the country. For years he had used all kinds of forged papers. He had no set residence and occasionally changed his name. Time and again he was confronted with complex and vexing problems, but in the end his labors were rewarded. By the end of his first mission, the shipments of emigrants had reached relatively large proportions. He was proud to have arranged the departure of 73 people in three trucks, no mean achievement for that period, and one that bolstered the morale of the movement.

On his second mission he took part in "Operation Mikelberg," the illegal immigration airlift. It all began in September of 1947, just prior to the U.N. decision on the establishment of the State of Israel. A short while before that Hillel had returned from Baghdad to kibbutz Hatzofim Aleph in Rehovot, very upset over the state of affairs in the underground in Iraq and embittered by the unwillingness of the Yishuv's official bodies and the Immigration Bureau to do more. One morning he was approached unexpectedly by

Moshe Carmel, who told him that two pilots had been obtained. The next day Shlomo left for Baghdad in a large, two-engined American plane, and after two weeks returned on the same plane in the company of 50 immigrants. A landing strip had been prepared near the village of Yavniel in Galilee. All rocks had been removed and fires were lit to guide the plane in. In addition, armed Palmach units were stationed around the area. The same plane brought two more groups to Palestine: one from Italy and another from Iraq.

After the outbreak of the War of Liberation in 1948, Shlomo returned to Iraq. It was obvious that groups of prospective immigrants could no longer be taken through the desert, as a large army was located in Transjordan; as a result, Iraq was isolated. During the first truce Shlomo left for Iraq via Paris, equipped with a forged Iraqi passport. In France he met a priest by the name of Glassberg, who had made the plight of the Jewish refugees his own after the Jews started to stream from Europe in 1947. The priest had a plan that no one had much faith in. He envisioned smuggling Jews from Iraq to Iran and keeping them there in a camp until such time as they could be brought to Palestine. While a similar program had been carried out in Europe towards the end of World War II, the priest's plan did not seem feasible to most people, as Iran was surrounded by mountains and no one knew what they concealed. Shlomo was the only one to share the priest's enthusiasm for the plan. They worked it out together in greater detail and decided to go to Iran, there to meet with experts on the Middle East and organize the venture.

While he was in France, Shlomo managed to exchange his own papers with those of a Frenchman from Morocco. Two weeks later he arrived in Iran and was joined shortly by the priest. The two of them lived in a monastery and met with members of the Chaldean faith and Catholics who had suffered persecution under Islamic rule, but soon despaired of receiving any help from them. Shlomo then met with influential Jews and tried to win their support for the project.

In the end he decided that there was no reason for him to return to Baghdad, and that it would be best for him to remain in Iran and set up the underground emigration network there. The project was very dangerous; death was the punishment for anyone caught smuggling people across the border.

The emissaries then in France were not enthusiastic about the idea. It was difficult enough keeping in touch with headquarters in Palestine, and communications between Iran and Baghdad would be possible only via France and Israel. Shlomo requested a wireless to enable him to communicate directly with his colleagues in Baghdad, but a long time passed before he got it. Moreover, he lacked funds, and every message he received came through garbled and only after many delays.

In the end the project met with success. Within the space of a year and a half, approximately 10,000 people were sent to Palestine in this manner; and the airlift immigration into Palestine, "Operation 'On Eagles' Wings,' " followed shortly after. At first the Iraqi Government steadfastly refused to allow the Jews to leave. In spite of the shootings and jailings, however, about 2,000 people were smuggled out of the country each month.

The emissary was confronted with difficult problems. Iraqi Jews were not used to a cold climate, and the first group of immigrants had to remain in Iran for four months during the winter in 28-below-zero weather. At first they were housed in a cemetery in the room in which the corpses were washed. Later a building was erected there, and in certain seasons it accommodated up to 2,000 people. When finally a route was opened to Baghdad and contact was made at the borders, one of the two wirelesses that were in the Iraqi capital was sent to Iran, greatly facilitating communication. Also, money no longer presented a problem, as well-to-do immigrants from Baghdad contributed generously to the general fund for immigration into Palestine.

Eventually the Government changed its policy. The authorities, seeing that Jews were leaving the country anyway, decided to confiscate their wealth.

12

From Syria via the Northern Border

Underground immigration from Syria via the northern border went on as long as laws forbidding Jewish entry into Palestine were in effect. These laws were first promulgated by the Turkish regime and later by the Mandatory powers.

When the first limitations upon immigration into Palestine were instituted, only a few years after the Balfour Declaration, Jews who wished to enter the Homeland set their hopes on slipping through the hilly and mountainous border area in the north. As early as the beginning of the British Mandate, Jewish immigrants, with groups of Hehalutz members among them, came from Turkey to Beirut by land and sea. The few Hebrew settlements along the northern border were an indispenable help to them, these being: Safed and Rosh Pina during the Ottoman rule; the veteran kibbutzim of Kfar Giladi and Ayelet Hashahar at the beginning of the Mandate period; and Hulata, Dafna, Dan, Hanita, and others later. Thousands of immigrants would not have reached their destination had it not been for the help provided by these settlements, often at the cost of human life. In the period 1922 to 1935, kibbutz Kfar Giladi served as a shelter and way station for 8,000 immigrants.

At the beginning of 1921, when the Zionist Executive

commenced its struggle with the Mandatory Government's Immigration Department over the allocation of each certificate, self-seeking tourist agencies sprang up in Warsaw, where pressures for emigration to Palestine were greatest. The agents of these companies would pocket the money of those Jews who dared emigrate to Palestine and would send their victims in a ship to Beirut as tourists, after assuring them that in Beirut they would get immigration certificates for the Homeland. Only upon their arrival in Beirut would the travelers learn that they had been duped. At that point they had no choice but to contact Arab smugglers, whose fees were exhorbitant and who often enough robbed the immigrants of their possessions in the process of smuggling them across the border. Most of the time the destitute victims were brought to the vicinity of a Jewish settlement and there were left to fend for themselves.

The Mandatory Government gave its immediate attention to the problem of illegal immigration. Bands of Arab guards were posted along the northern borders. These guards were given a meager monthly wage and an additional English shilling for each illegal immigrant they caught. Later on, for a period of years, this task was carried out by the Arab Border Patrol, which was stationed in the vicinity of Rosh Pina. Most of the immigrants captured by these patrols were imprisoned, mistreated, and in the end, returned to the countries they had come from. Those who crossed the border safely found refuge in kibbutz Kfar Giladi. The kibbutz members would hide the new arrivals about the farm and then disguise them in order to smuggle them into the interior of the country. This entailed getting them through the customs (police) station in Rosh Pina, where inspections were very rigorous. Frequently, surprise searches, quite thoroughgoing in nature, were made inside

16. MOST OF THE IMMIGRANTS CAPTURED BY THESE PATROLS WERE IMPRISONED AND MISTREATED.

the kibbutzim near the border, and the concealed immigrants were found on more than one occasion in spite of all the ingenious schemes employed to camouflage them, and were subsequently imprisoned along with the *mukhtar,* the headman of the kibbutz.

Sometimes, honest and experienced Arab smugglers would bring the illegal immigrants openly and directly to the courtyard in Kfar Giladi. The tiny handful of kibbutz members were hard put to take care of these people, as they did not have enough food for themselves. At times the smugglers brought in one group after another—including families with many children—and the kibbutz had to maintain them for long periods of time, until it was possible to send them into the country's interior. On occasion some guests demanded that they be put up at the Kfar Giladi "Hotel" in elegant rooms, as they had been promised by the agents of the tourist bureau in Beirut, whom they had paid handsomely for the accommodations. The total population of Kfar Giladi at the time was less than 100 people. At a later period, when the flow of immigration through the northern border increased, there were days when the number of guests exceeded the number of kibbutz members.

The Zionist Executive did not look favorably upon this "wild," uncontrolled immigration, and for that reason did not grant the kibbutz's request for funds to defray its expenses. The kibbutz members argued among themselves over the advisability of continuing to play host to so many people, and if they were to continue how best to go about it, since they lacked sufficient money and time. Finally, at one of the general meetings, Haya Krol rose and volunteered to take personal responsibility for looking after the immigrants in addition to fulfilling her regular workday duties. If laurels were to be awarded to the stalwarts of the illegal immigration effort, one of the first would surely go to the members of tiny Kfar Giladi.

After hiding the immigrants and housing them, there was the problem of getting them past the Rosh Pina police station. Once, three illegal immigrants from Russia, two men and a woman, the remnant of a group of fifteen, arrived in Kfar Giladi after a journey of eight months. The woman was completely exhausted and had to be taken to a doctor in Tiberias immediately. On that day a wealthy couple from the United States happened to be passing through the kibbutz in the course of a tour of Upper Galilee. As soon as they got out of their large and elegant automobile to see the kibbutz, Manya Shohet, one of the veteran settlers of Kfar Giladi and one of the founders of Hashomer ("The Guard," the first group of Jewish watchmen in Palestine), approached their chauffeur and sought his help. He agreed to put the sick woman in the trunk of the car without telling the tourists anything. The trunk was narrow, but the woman was short and thin, and they somehow managed to lay her inside. Just as the tourists were about to leave, Manya asked that they take her with them as far as Tiberias, and they gladly agreed. All during the ride she spoke to them of the immigrants who had to enter Palestine illegally, and of their problems. After they had put the customs stations in Rosh Pinna a safe distance behind them, Manya told the tourists what she had done and asked the chauffeur to stop and open the trunk before their sick passenger should suffocate. The woman was unconscious and they extricated her with difficulty, while Manya kept apologizing to the shocked and furious tourists.

On another occasion, at a later date, friendly Arabs told the *mukhtar* of Kfar Giladi that an Arab band planned to attack the kibbutz during the night. They also told him

where the attack would come from, and Hagana patrols were
sent to that area at once. The night was dark and stormy.
Suddenly the commander discerned tall, strange shapes
approaching the kibbutz. He called out in Arabic, ordering
them to halt, but they continued to advance. He then fired
three shots in the air—a signal for his men to get ready to
attack. But suddenly, above the wail of the storm he heard
a voice cry out *Shma Yisrael!*—"Hear, O Israel!"—the
declaration of faith recited by pious Jews when death is
imminent. He saw that the tall shadows were stretched out
on the ground. Confused, he told his men not to shoot, and
he himself approached the figures that were crawling towards
him, whispering incessantly *Shma Yisrael*. Advancing a
little further he discovered who they were: a group of
illegal immigrants from Bukhara, families with children.
Some of the adults had died en route from a contagious
disease, and the fifteen who remained bore their own
children and the orphans on their backs, and it was for this
reason they had presented tall, weird silhouettes in the darkness. They were skeletally thin and covered with sores, and
had to spend three weeks in Kfar Giladi recuperating before
they could be sent to their relatives in Jerusalem.

Incidents such as these took place in every settlement in
Upper Galilee, even before the illegal immigration became
an organized effort.

From the start the Jewish youth of Syria took a more
active role in assisting the emissaries of the Bureau than did
the young Jews of Iraq. In Syria, the first small group of
Hehalutz was formed as early as 1929, in the alleys of the
Damascus ghetto, and was directly influenced by the
example of the labor movement in Palestine. Two years
later the movement provided from its midst leaders for
groups of *Hehalutz Hatzair* ("The Young Pioneer"), an

organization that included hundreds of children and youth, some of whom attended school and some of whom worked as coppersmiths' helpers, putting in sixteen hours of hard work a day for wretchedly poor wages. This movement sprang up almost by itself, and was the first of the Hehalutz movements that arose in Jewish centers in Middle Eastern countries. It was the Hehalutz youth movement in Damascus that educated its members toward *aliya*—emigration to Palestine—and a life of labor in the Homeland, and took upon itself the responsibility for organizing underground emigration even before the coming of the emissaries of the Bureau. The initiative of these pioneer youths and the help they gave the emissaries made possible the emigration of the majority of Syrian and Lebanese Jewry into Palestine in the period between the two World Wars.

It was Syria's proximity to Palestine that was largely responsible for the above-mentioned developments. Palestinians who became refugees and deportees during the First World War established the first Hebrew pioneer group in the Damascus ghetto. The flickering flame blazed up at a meeting between a group of ardent youngsters and Yehuda Kopilevitz (Almog), who at that time was a member of kibbutz Ramat Rahel; he was then returning from a mission to the Jews of Iran. This was the first live contact that the eager young people had with an emissary who preached the goals of Hehalutz and the Hebrew labor movement. In his talk he dwelt on the necessity of settling the Hauran area. He told them that prior to World War I there had been a plan for establishing Jewish settlements in the Golan, Bashan, and Hauran districts to the east of the Jordan and the Sea of Galilee, but the few halfhearted attempts that were made did not succeed; the colony of B'nei Yehuda founded east of the Sea of Galilee, was destroyed by Arabs in

1920. Baron Rothschild had bought tens of thousands of acres of land in Hauran and there founded a colony, but the Turkish authorities forced the settlers to leave in 1899. Since that time the lands had been left untenanted.

"You who are near this area," he said, "could very well play a serious role in settling those abandoned tracts."

As a result of this discussion, thirteen youngsters banded together and laid the foundations for the federation of Hehalutz in Damascus.

The founders, realizing that by their act they were embarking upon a new path, and that the creation of such a movement would meet with strong opposition from the general Jewish population, decided to carry out their activities secretly. They met by night in a field outside the city. One evening the thirteen gathered in the house of one of the members, sat in a dark room, and spoke in whispers so that no one would be aware of their presence. One of the young people took a rope out of his pocket and all of them took hold of it and swore to maintain secrecy; to remain loyal to Eretz Israel, to aliya, and to agricultural labor, and to work toward the establishment of a kibbutz in the Hauran area. The rope was cut into pieces to symbolize the fate that would befall anyone who betrayed the oath.

That night marked the beginning of serious and intense activity on the part of the boys, who came from widely different social strata. From the very start they set out to imitate the pioneers of Palestine as best they could. They stopped wearing ties, and when that time of year came when it was customary for well-to-do parents to have two new suits made for their sons, they decided that from then on they would all wear simple clothing. In so doing they were setting themselves apart somewhat from the general Jewish population, though not conspicuously enough to disclose their secret association. One of the incidents that convinced them of the power of Eretz Israel occurred with the visit of Rahel Yannait (Ben-Zvi) to Damascus, for the purpose of selling young saplings grown in training farms for girls in Palestine. This visit took place just after the boys had started out on their new path, when their intentions had not yet been revealed to even their closest relatives. Rahel met with the group at night and saw by the intense expressions on their faces how great their longing was. "We will help you," she told them. Immediately they made their first request of her: to arrange for the emigration of a blind, ten-year-old Jewish boy who wandered about the streets, and was constantly ridiculed by the Arab children. After some brief negotiations, the boy was sent to a school for the blind in Jerusalem, where he studied and subsequently taught for many years.

On Purim, 1929, Menahem Luzia was sent to Palestine as the group's envoy. His first step upon arriving in the country was to head for the building of the Histadrut Executive, then located on the Jaffa-Tel Aviv road. Upon entering the building he met a man wearing a black Russian shirt with a string that tied around the waist. They ascended the steps together. The elder man asked the younger what he was looking for.

"I want to see the chairman of the Histadrut, David Ben-Gurion," he replied.

"I am Ben-Gurion," the man said.

They sat in the chairman's room and talked for hours. The chairman was astounded to learn that a Hehalutz movement, whose members longed to come to Palestine, had arisen on its own in Damascus. He sent the boy to the treasurer, where he was given eighteen pounds, three years' rental money for the Hehalutz headquarters in Damascus— a ruined building that the boys had renovated themselves.

Moved and hopeful, Menahem left for the small room of Berl Katznelson in the "Workers Apartments" on Maze Street in Tel Aviv. He found the latter sick in bed, but with his door open to all who wished to see him—as it always was. After a while Berl obtained from the Jewish National Fund, of which he was a director, a monthly allotment of six pounds to help support that kibbutz member who would serve as Hehalutz emissary in Damascus.

When Menahem returned, the band of thirteen decided that they would spend their training period in kibbutz Kfar Giladi, which was near the border, and whose soil was similar to the soil of the Hauran area, their ultimate destination. They agreed that at first only six of them would go to Palestine, and there was some competition among them as to who those six should be.

A few days after Passover the boys who were to emigrate set out in the morning for Ein Kenya, a Syrian village, and arrived there in the evening. They spent the evening in the house of an uncle of one of the members of their group. Through him they met the sheik of the village, who led them across the border himself. After walking all night they arrived at Kfar Giladi. The kibbutz members were few, and lived in wooden barracks, but they greeted the newcomers warmly, and after two days of rest, put them to work in the barn, the field, and the pasture.

This marked the start of pioneer immigration from eastern countries. Thus were the first seeds planted that gave rise to a flourishing, deep-rooted movement.

One of the band's most daring and loyal members was Eliahu Cohen. When all the founders of Hehalutz had emigrated to Palestine, he alone stayed behind to lead the movement, as well as to care for his widowed mother, whom he supported. He received an allowance of four pounds from

Palestine, and Berl Katznelson added another two pounds, enabling him to continue his work.

When Hitler came to power in 1933, Jewish refugees arrived from Turkey in Beirut and Damascus with transit visas that allowed them to stay in Syria for twenty-four hours. The members of Hehalutz took it upon themselves to smuggle these people into Palestine. In so doing they saved the lives of scores of refugees but used up the small sum that they had accumulated in their treasury, thirty gold pounds in all.

Once Eliahu had to lead a group of refugees across the border because the Arab smuggler refused to go at the last minute. Since Eliahu did not know the route, he sketched a map from the description given him by one of the smugglers, and so led the men to Tiberias. A truck took them close to the border, and after they reached El Quneitra they turned southward to the Sea of Galilee. The group included, among others, an old man and an old woman. The old woman found it difficult to walk. Eliahu hired a mule from a Bedouin they met along the way and the woman rode on the mule. However, after an hour had elapsed, the Bedouin insisted that his animal be returned. Journeying onward, they arrived at the bank of a river. There they removed their clothing and carried the old woman across on their shoulders. Once again they chanced upon an Arab riding on his horse, which Eliahu promptly hired, but that Arab too shortly demanded his animal back. He then showed them the way to the house of the Arab *beg* (notable), and as soon as they left, he went to the police and informed on them. The group arrived at the *beg's* house near the Syrian-Palestinian border, and he received them hospitably. Eliahu told him that he was heading for Palestine in order to join his relatives there. The *beg* replied that he understood everything, and he had a dinner prepared for Eliahu and the group, as befitted a proper host. Then Eliahu told him of the Bedouin whom they had met on his territory who had deceived and cheated them. The *beg* called some of his men and ordered them to bring the Bedouin before him. They brought in two Bedouin but neither was the culprit. Once more he summoned his men and told them to get boats for ferrying the people across the river. As they were sitting about waiting, an Arab policeman entered the room. The refugees were terrified, and one by one they slipped out to the porch. Eliahu turned his head so that the policeman should not recognize him. The host, however, did not get excited. He ordered his personal servant to bring in some beer, and after the policeman had drunk, the *beg* asked what it was that he wished. The latter replied that suspicious people were hiding in the house. The *beg* replied:

"Do you think that you are going to harm my guests, who have come under my roof?"

They sat for a while and talked until the servants brought a small boat. It was a moonlit night. The *beg* himself rolled up his trousers and carried the old woman to the boat on his back.

Eliahu continued to be active in the immigration effort even after he settled in Palestine. In 1941, during the Second World War, the Political Department of the Jewish Agency requested that he go on a special mission to Syria. Some graduates of Hehalutz in Syria and Tuvia Arazi, a Hagana member who had been working in that country for Allied Intelligence, had been imprisoned by the Vichy Government on charges of collaborating with the Free French underground. Eliahu was sent to free Tuvia. To this end he had to speak with a certain judge in Beirut. He left from Hulata, accompanied by an Arab smuggler. After they crossed Lake

Hula the Arab turned back and Eliahu had to go on alone. Vichy's men ruled El Quneitra, and Eliahu had to take care to avoid them. However, he was at home in the area and was thoroughly familiar with every path in it. When he arrived in Beirut, the Jewish community there demanded of him that he leave at once and go back where he had come from, as his life was in danger. He, however, refused to return before carrying out his mission.

He made his way back alone also. While in the mountains near El Quneitra he spied a group of Circassian border guards headed in his direction. All he had with him were some olives, dates, and a *pita,* a flat, round loaf of Bedouin bread. He crammed the *pita* into his mouth, as Bedouin are accustomed to do, spat out an olive pit, and turned to greet the approaching soldiers. His rude manner of eating and the *kaffiya* (Arab headdress) that he wore confused them, and after they hesitated for a moment, they let him continue his journey undisturbed.

From the very outset of its work in Syria the Bureau took advantage of Eliahu's experience and daring. After the Border Patrol erected a barbed-wire fence across the north road next to Nebi Yusha and placed an Arab patrol there to inspect the identification card of every person who wished to cross, the Bureau put Leibel Abramovski and his men in charge of receiving the illegal immigrants at the border from the hands of the Syrian smugglers sent by Eliahu, and bring them into the country's interior.

Such a venture was carried out in the course of two nights. On the first night Leibel and his men would lead the immigrants through swamps and rocky terrain in the vicinity of Nebi Yusha; on the second night they would take them through the mountains surrounding Rosh Pina, and at daybreak would lead them to one of the kibbutzim in the vicinity of Haifa. A major difficulty was presented by groups that included old people and children. In addition to groping through thorns and over rocks in the dark, it was often necessary for a guide or immigrant to carry a child on his back for miles. Most of the children felt the gravity of the situation and behaved themselves very well. Sometimes groups were caught by the border patrol and got away only by quick thinking or by handing over a good-sized bribe. At times they were forced to leave a hostage in the hands of the border guards overnight and bring ransom money in the morning. The guards were invariably disappointed when they learned on the following morning that their "hostage" was none other than a Palestinian citizen, one of the group's guides and often a native of Rosh Pina, and therefore one who could not be held for ransom. Often border guards would steal away from their companions and lie in wait alongside the road in hopes of catching some illegal immigrants and supplementing their scant income thereby.

As the effort expanded and a pattern was established, more and more Palmach men and native members of Rosh Pina were recruited to guide the groups. The mountain route that they covered at night was not long, being about ten miles in all. However, it was strewn with rocks and with man-made fortifications from the period of the invasion of Syria. In addition, there was always the danger of running into border patrols, who were on the lookout for hashish smugglers as well as illegal immigrants, with the identical purpose in mind: obtaining ransom money. On more than one occasion the immigrants witnessed exchanges of fire and real battles between border patrols and smugglers who were unable to divide up the loot amicably.

Insofar as possible, the young men avoided encounters

with such smugglers. Every trip was carried out as a military venture, well-planned and organized, with prior inspection of the route to discover if any obstacles would be encountered. Every so often they would choose new routes. The journey was conducted in silence and group discipline was rigorous. The guides were constantly in touch with men of the Information Service, who kept close track of the police and the border patrols. Security precautions were also taken on the Palestinian side of the border, particularly in the area surrounding the settlement that was their destination.

The immigrants' baggage presented a difficult problem. Even though the few articles they had with them were almost worthless, their owners would not part with them for a minute. Often the guides had to carry the bags on their shoulders.

Sometimes undesirables infiltrated the groups. Once a Nazi who had not managed to escape from Syria after its conquest by the Free French was detained in an internment camp. He escaped from there with a young Muslim from Kurdistan and the two of them reached Kfar Giladi. The Nazi introduced himself as Mr. Kalman, a Jewish refugee from Germany. The kibbutz members, suspicious at once, investigated the two men, revealed their identities, and handed them over to the police.

The members of kibbutz Hulata, and especially Moshe Yavo from Damascus, took an active part in the illegal immigration ventures. Yavo knew the immigrants' language and customs, was familiar with the area, and was ready to serve at a moment's notice. No small part was played by Rabbi Moshe Zilber of Safed, who zealously fulfilled the religious obligation of redeeming prisoners. Once, two boys, twelve and thirteen years of age, were captured on the way to Rosh Pina and were returned to Syrian territory in order to be sent back to Damascus. Leibel contacted Rabbi Zilber and asked for his help; the latter immediately purchased large, choice fish as a gift for the guards and dashed in a taxi to the Syrian border. He brought the children back with him in the taxi's trunk.

On another occasion twenty-eight young men from Damascus were captured and turned over to the Safed police. Again Rabbi Zilber was called upon to act as the prisoners' guarantee so that they could go free until the trial. As a result of the high esteem in which he was held, the Rabbi's request was granted. When it came time for him to sign the guarantee document, the police officer, noticing how large the required sum was, said to him:

"All you own is a little paint store worth a few pennies. How will you ever pay if these men don't show up for the trial?"

Zilber replied at once:

"If you open your records you will see that I have already guaranteed tens of thousands of pounds. Have I ever owed you a penny?"

The men were subsequently released and remained in Palestine.

One Sabbath morning Leibel was walking around the streets of Safed engaged in a venture of smuggling thirty people. Rabbi Zilber, who was always on the alert for such affairs, even when he was told nothing, came on his own to the bus terminal, instead of going to synagogue. Leibel, who stood smoking a cigarette—a violation of the Sabbath—did not see him approaching. When suddenly the eminent rabbi appeared before him, Leibel embarassedly tried to hide the cigarette in his hand. The rabbi, however, clapped him on the shoulder and said:

"You needn't worry about going to hell, my good friend;

because of what you are doing for the immigrants you'll go straight to heaven."

The rabbi would go to the jail wearing his tallit (prayer shawl) and tefillin (phylacteries) to pray with the prisoners, and during the prayers he would give them instructions. He also provided them with food and helped them in many other ways.

Second to him in Safed was Yossel the driver. Everyone in northern Palestine knew Yossel. There wasn't an Arab child who did not know him. He made an impressive figure, being a very tall, broad-shouldered fellow. He was a warm-hearted person and was always ready to endanger himself for the sake of the illegal immigration. One night he was sitting together with some other drivers in Ayelet Hashahar; they had brought large numbers of people to that kibbutz from settlements in Upper Galilee for a theatrical presentation. Seated in the audience were Leibel and forty-five immigrants from Kurdistan, families with children and baggage; Leibel did not know how he would get them into the country's interior. When he spied Yossel, he asked his advice. The latter furrowed his brows and replied with the Arabic oath:

"By my head and by my eyes!"

When the performance was over, and the vehicles began to depart, Yossel left behind the passengers that he had taken with him, filled the bus with the illegal immigrants and started on his way. When they arrived in Rosh Pina and the policemen saw their friend Yossel at the wheel, the barrier was opened, and a policeman approached to make a routine check. Yossel did not turn on the light, but laughed and said:

"They sure guzzled it down there; everybody's out like a light."

Ditches and fortifications were scattered all along the route. The area between Kfar Giladi and Ayelet Hashahar was very rigorously patroled and no one was allowed to pass without having his papers checked. In effect, the illegal immigrants had to cross three borders: the Palestinian-Lebanese border, the checking station at Nebi Yusha, and the checking station at Rosh Pina. In addition, there were few people available to serve as guides. As time went on, the settlers of Hulata could no longer do all the work by themselves. They felt the need for full military protection, and this was provided by a Palmach unit that was stationed in the area. At first only a small group of soldiers were incorporated in the program, but eventually an entire company, which included young women, was placed at the disposal of the illegal immigration effort. The project was dangerous and required responsible leadership; much labor went into planning and organizing it. Preparations were made, and groups were sent in accordance with fixed schedules.

When the flow of immigrants increased, a tent camp was set up for them in Ayelet Hashahar, where they were provided with sheets and blankets. Their meals were brought inside their tents so that they should not be seen by any strangers.

The guides were often confronted with very difficult situations. At times teenagers would have to make decisions upon which human lives depended.

The following story, concerning one group of boys and girls, was told by Amalia Ben-Ari, a Palmach girl who was their guide: "We enjoyed leading groups like that one. Walking with them was easy. There were two of us to lead the group—one to feel out the path in front, and the other—myself—to stay behind with the group. The night was dark. Every tree looked like a moving patrol. We were passing close by a patrol—it was safer that way! Suddenly we heard a scream and one of the boys fainted. I was so frightened that I hardly knew what to do. We sprinkled some water on him. He opened his eyes and stammered that he would not move another inch. In the meantime I had lost sight of the guide in front. It was a tight situation. I didn't speak the language of the boy who had fainted, and we didn't dare remain there. A few slaps across the face changed his mind: he got up and went along quietly."

Then there was the incident of the woman who arrived at Ayelet Hashahar at night and gave birth the next morning. Amalia was given one more job: taking care of the new mother and the baby.

Once, when a group of thirty people set out, the entire network of guides, lookouts, and Palmach members went out at night to bring them through safely. The mothers found it difficult to carry their babies and the guides helped them. The group moved forward slowly. When the time came for them to cross the road, one of the babies began to cry very loudly. In the distance the bright lights of an automobile appeared. The group hurried across the road, and only Amalia with the baby in her arms remained behind. She flattened herself out on the ground and stuffed her hat into the baby's mouth. After the car passed and drove out of sight, she sprang to her feet and ran to catch up with the others.

For a while they tried to smuggle children into the country in military vehicles. One Saturday it happened that two groups of youngsters were stranded on the road, some distance before the customs station at Rosh Pina. After all other schemes for getting them farther inside the country proved ineffectual, the children of kibbutz Ayelet Hashahar were taken on a hike to Biria, a religious settlement, and the immigrant children, who had been brought from Kfar Giladi, were included among them. Yossel the driver was already waiting for them in Biria. Some of the "hikers" were very young and the day was hot; all were thirsty. The guides asked the settlers of Biria if they could give them some drinking water. The latter, afraid that they might violate the Sabbath in so doing, were reluctant to grant their request. However, when they were told that some of the children were illegal immigrants, they complied at once.

One of the factors that contributed to the success of the illegal immigration project was wireless communications with Palestine. With the help of the wireless, the people on the Palestinian side of the border knew when the various groups set out, and so were able to coordinate activities.

One of the first emissaries sent to Syria was Naftali Golomb, a member of kibbutz Tel Amal. His inclusion in the effort took place at a time when the emissaries of the Bureau were already located in three central bases: Damascus, Aleppo, and Zahle, Lebanon. As the British Secret Service was putting more pressure to bear on the illegal effort, the emissaries found it necessary to avoid any contacts with local Jews; instead they placed one of their own men in each of the three cities. For these assignments they chose for the most part people who had been born in Syria and had settled in Palestine, but who had not forgotten local customs and were indistinguishable from Syrian Arabs in every way. The first three emissaries were chosen from among those who had previously worked in Syria or had been sent there by the Hagana as members of the special unit in the British Secret Service. One of these was Akiba Feinstein, born in Rosh Pina, who had served in a military camp disguised as an Arab; he set up residence in the Lebanon Valley. Akiba blended in thoroughly with his surroundings. He managed to get Lebanese papers identifying him as a Greek Orthodox Christian. He bought a house for himself and lived there as though he were among his own people.

The emissaries lived in a disguised dwelling in the Damascus ghetto. Their center of communications was located in the Damascus market in a small souvenir shop run by a young local pioneer, who years later became a member of a kibbutz in Palestine. Emissaries from Iraq would come to the store pretending to buy souvenirs, and would give the young man the password and wait for any message, or hand him a note. The pioneer who owned the store worked devotedly and at great risk to himself. He kept in touch with the emissaries by means of daring Hehalutz members of Damascus, who would deliver notes by bicycle— just as the Hagana boys did in Palestine during the War of Liberation. They also did some detective work in the streets and market place and passed on valuable information to the emissaries, who were set about by dangers.

One of the first things that Naftali attempted was to find a new way of bringing the immigrants from Iraq to Syria through the desert. A great part of the 500-mile Baghdad-Damascus route lay in Syria. Along this road, about eighteen miles from Damascus, there lived the large, powerful, and wealthy Rwala tribe. The Damascenes were sensitive to anything that went on in the tents of the Rwala, as the tribe was well armed and was feared by the city. After the death of their powerful sheik, the desert region was ruled by two brothers, one a cultured man, a member of the Syrian Parliament, and the other a strong, armed Bedouin who in effect controlled the entire area from Damascus to the Iraqi border. The members of the Rwala tribe supplemented their livelihood by smuggling goods to Syria. In that region immunity was granted to the vehicles of the tribal sheiks who engaged in smuggling nylon stockings, opium, and the like. The young men tried for a long time to get in touch with the tribe, and the Rwala, on the other hand, were anxious to make contact with the illegal immigration movement. In their search after the "Zionists" they managed to arrive at the souvenir shop in Damascus that served as the emissaries' meeting place. The Rwala said:

"We live in a very large area that we can't cultivate. We know what Jaffa used to look like before the Jews came to Palestine, and we know what the Jews have done. We want to sell you land—come and settle it."

After this meeting they set another meeting for the purpose of visiting the area. There was of course, no plan for settling Jews there, but the emissaries were interested in looking around and hearing what these people had to say. A Bedouin liaison man accompanied by African bodyguards came to pick them up. En route, their host pointed to the scenery around them and said:

"See what an ancient civilization used to be here in this area, and now everything is barren and desolate."

Their car—the gift of King Ibn Saud, the sheik's father-in-law—was an elegant red Packard that could travel any road. The African bodyguards sat in the car too, and at the checking station no one dared to inspect them or ask them anything. They sat down to eat inside an elegant and richly carpeted tent. After a regal meal had been consumed, they got into the car again and traveled a distance of 190 miles. Ancient walls testified to the former existence of an agricultural society in the area. The Bedouin sped after a flock of gazelles that appeared in the distance. The car overtook an exhausted gazelle and another feast was prepared. Later, when they saw a herd of camels in the distance, the Bedouin called to the shepherds and they brought over a gourd of milk. En route they saw some of the tractors that had been distributed in the area by the British.

However, no further meetings took place, probably as a result of British intervention.

After a while the boys set up a "hostel" in the Jewish cemetery outside Damascus, a city resembling an oasis in the desert surrounded by thousands of acres of flourishing plots of fruit and olive trees. The grave of a holy man was located in the cemetery and there the young men met to avoid detection. At times they slept over in the house of the Jewish watchman. The Jewish cemetery inside the city was used as a parking lot.

When they decided not to endanger the effort further by entrusting it to foreign smugglers, they discovered what a brilliant talent they possessed in Akiba Feinstein. When he first joined the effort in Syria, the local members looked down on him—what could such a youngster accomplish? They soon changed their outlook, however. He first asked permission to accompany the Arab smuggler so that he could learn the latter's methods, the route, and so forth. It was agreed that Akiba would go along with a group as an immigrant.

At that time the borders were very closely guarded. British Intelligence had its eyes and ears open for all movement. It was necessary to improve the coordination between the Arab smugglers and Palestine, but efforts toward that end did not meet with success. Then Akiba made a few trips, became familiar with the area, and began to work with amazing coordination with Palestine. No matter what the circumstances, he passed as a native Christian Lebanese. He knew all the appropriate prayers and blessings and could reel off generations of false ancestry. He soon became the central figure in the expanding program. Everything went off smoothly, for the young men's cherished goal had been realized: they had a "smuggler" of their own, thoroughly competent and familiar with the route.

A total of 1,350 children and young people were smuggled across the border, thanks to Akiba and thanks to Yani Avinadav of Nahalal, who was responsible for initiating the program. It had not been an easy task for Yani to convince the Bureau to agree to the project. In addition to the hazards involved in smuggling the children into the country, there was the problem of their absorption: they had neither parents nor relatives. The Youth Aliya Office was still occupied with the difficult problem of dealing with hundreds of "Teheran children"—war refugees. Workers' settlements were not keen on the idea of taking responsibility for young children who could not look after themselves, without a budget to cover the expenditures that would have to be made. In addition, some of the children had been neglected or were sick, and would require special attention. After engaging in nerve-racking negotiations by coded correspondence, Yani saw that he would have to return to Palestine in order to get results. He slipped across the border and carried on a fiery and successful one-man campaign to combat the reservations of the people and institutions concerned. After the Bureau agreed in principle to his plan, he managed to convince the Youth Aliya Office to include in its budget the expenses for the upkeep and education of forty children from Syria. After he visited many kibbutzim and moshavim (smallholders' settlements), and met with no success, he turned to his own moshav, Nahalal, and with the help of his wife Nesya, a member of the village council at the time, the moshav decided to accept the forty children who were to be brought in illegally from Syria.

Shaula Pines of kibbutz Ma'oz played a large role in the immigration of the children of Syria. Her friends called her "the princess." Shaula went to Syria openly, with official papers and a legal visa, to work in an *Alliance* school which had obtained permission to employ Hebrew teachers from Palestine. Shortly after her arrival she was joined by Rivka Kuzviner of Rosh Pina, who, like Shaula, had graduated from the Levinsky Teachers' College in Tel Aviv. In their room in the Beirut ghetto, the two young teachers did much to transform Yani's dream of the children's immigration into reality. The backbone of the *Alliance* school in Damascus was the Bureau's emissary, Menashe Babayoff (Harel), another teacher who volunteered to help organize the emigration of children to Palestine.

Shaula served in Syria and in Lebanon for two years and eight months and returned to Palestine in February of 1946, after she had undergone imprisonment and interrogation. Years later, she had this to say concerning Akiba Feinstein and other emissaries of the Immigration Bureau: "Actually, the people involved in Aliya Bet were no braver than others. Like everyone else, they knew what it meant to be afraid, but the cause that they served gave them the courage that they needed to carry out their missions."

Shaula taught Hebrew to all the grades, and so came in contact with hundreds of Jewish children. The first prospective illegal immigrants, whom she chose from among her students, were three girls who had established a particularly close relationship with her. They were sisters whose father was always drunk and whose mother was unable to support them. Their older brothers agreed to their going to Palestine. However, after some weeks passed and nothing was heard of the girls, the father began coming to the school every day to ask questions. Finally, when it looked like the father's patience was running out and it seemed likely that he might tell the police the circumstances of the girls' departure, a special emissary was sent to Palestine to find out what had happened; when the latter returned with good news, the father burst into the class and kissed the teachers' hands.

In addition to her other duties, Shaula took on the job of librarian in the Palestinian Soldiers' Club; there, at a great risk to herself, she served as a liaison with the soldiers who helped the illegal immigration effort. There was a sergeant in the Transport Division, Y. G. from moshav Merhavia, who every night drove soldiers to the movies from the army camp outside the city. While the film was being shown he would take immigrants to the border, return, and continue with his usual work as if nothing had happened. His army truck transported over 1,000 children. Sergeant D. B. worked hand in hand with him. The two willingly sacrificed all their free time to engage in their anonymous and dangerous task. Every night, upon returning to Beirut from their venture they would stop off at Shaula's and tap on her window—her apartment was on the ground floor. If they did not tap, then she knew that something had gone wrong.

In the end Shaula was imprisoned as a result of the capture of one of the Jewish smugglers who worked with them, a Turkish Jew. He had never even met Shaula. In an effort to protect himself, he said to his interrogators:

"Who am I compared with 'the princess'?"

The police came to the school and arrested her as she was conducting a class. She remained in prison for two weeks, was examined by a special court for aliens, and released after substantial bail was provided. Prior to this hearing her passport had been taken away from her. The Bureau was not sure that she should remain in Damascus. She, however, fought for her right to stay on and continue her work. She maintained that she was waiting for the Government to return her passport, but actually she did not want to leave her post after she had invested so much effort in the job. She also did not want to weaken, by leaving, the atmosphere of aliya that had grown up around the school, or to endanger the privilege of learning Hebrew or the situation of the other teachers.

A month after her release she was again imprisoned by the British on a pretext: they maintained that they wished to protect her as a citizen of a British Mandate and that it was therefore their duty to establish her identity. Shaula understood that the time had come for her to leave. She had to escape four police forces at one and the same time, these being the Syrian, Lebanese, French, and British police. In the morning she left her apartment at the usual time, headed in the direction of the school, got into a truck, and went straight to the border.

During her stay in jail she was cross-examined every morning. She requested the protection of the British consul. At first the examination was perfunctory and leisurely, and it was not difficult for her to avoid saying anything; but later, when the English became involved in the investigation, the situation changed. At this period a few of the local leaders of the illegal immigration movement were in prison and the interrogators wished to learn their names and pseudonyms. They also sought information concerning illegal sea immigration from Beirut. It seemed that a group of young leaders from the local movement had gone to Palestine to take a course—designed especially for them—in the use of arms, and returned to their work in the underground movement.

The wireless set gave "the princess" some difficulty. At first Saul Avigur was opposed to the use of the apparatus in an Arab country during the war, fearing complications should it be discovered. Nevertheless he decided to give Shaula a chance to learn how to operate the apparatus when she returned to Tel Aviv for a vacation during the days when a curfew was in effect. A long time passed before the wireless got to Beirut, and when it finally did arrive, it was decided that Rivka, and not Shaula, should operate it. A male wireless operator was sent from Palestine, and they all sat in Shaula's room and practiced. After a while they moved the wireless to a special two-room apartment in the center of the city. Rivka lived in one room and in the other lived the mistress of a French officer.

One morning, at dawn, Rivka was awakened by the sound of rapid hammering and before she was fully aware of what was happening, the door was smashed open. Four gendarmes burst into the room and began to conduct a search. They turned the room upside down, even looked in the mattress, but found nothing, as the wireless was hidden in a special compartment in the record player. Later Rivka learned that they had not been looking for a wireless or an emissary of the Bureau, but for the French officer, who had absconded with funds.

After this incident they again returned the apparatus to its prior lodgings. However, owing to the noise of the trolley car line that passed nearby, the Bureau in Palestine could not receive the broadcasts. The wireless was sent back to Palestine for repairs in a coffin. It was finally returned to Damascus and set up in Akiba's apartment.

After a while Rivka was summoned by the police and was ordered to leave the country within forty-eight hours. Once again the wireless remained unused. After a week had passed, Akiba was captured and put in prison, where he remained for three years.

13

First Mission to North Africa

The search for new bases for the illegal immigration effort was an unending one. Step by step the young men of the Bureau combed every Jewish center of population that was accessible to them by land. As a result, in the thick of the Second World War, they hit upon the idea of expanding the effort to include North Africa.

The Jews of North Africa, and particularly of French North Africa, were scarcely known to the Yishuv until the Second World War. Soldiers in the Palestinian units of the British army stationed in Egypt advanced across the western desert as far as Libya. The territory beyond that point was occupied by the German Army and the forces of the Vichy Government. Over a half million Jews lived in Morocco, Algeria, and Tunisia at that time and the Yishuv knew almost nothing about them. It was to this unknown and distant Jewry that the Bureau turned in 1943 in its search for new bases of operation.

The first three emissaries sent to Tunisia were Efraim Friedman and Yigael Cohen, members of kibbutz Bet Oren, and Naftali Bar Giyora, a member of kibbutz Sde Eliahu.

As late as the night prior to their departure they were still not clear as to what they were to do or how they would operate. During Efraim's last meeting with Eliahu Golomb, the latter told him that he did not feel that their mission would produce any tangible result in the near future. Nevertheless, preparations were made and the three were provided with military identification cards. One day the emissaries were given an urgent order to come to Tel Aviv at once. Upon their arrival, Enzo Sereni told them that they would have to leave for Egypt by train on the following day. In spite of the fact that they had prepared themselves for their mission and were anxious to begin, the sudden order took them by surprise and baffled them: they saw no reason for such haste. However, when they went to see Saul Avigur to clarify the matter, he confirmed the order. Within a few hours' time they acquired the necessary military equipment, and exchanged their civilian clothes for uniforms in the house of Efraim's parents in Tel Aviv. Prior to their departure Efraim went to take leave of Saul. The latter grasped his hand warmly and said:

"Remember, Efraim—being careful isn't the same as being a coward."

They left on the train, accompanied by a Jewish soldier who had been assigned to stay with them until they should reach Cairo.

They hid a few addresses in an empty shaving-cream tube and put their money, four hundred Palestinian pounds in all, in their shirt pockets. A few moments after they boarded the train their identification cards were inspected by the police, but all went well and they breathed easy.

The soldier who had acompanied them left them in Cairo and the three emissaries stood alone on the platform of the railroad station with no prior arrangements having been made for them, and with an inadequate knowledge of how they should behave as soldiers. Their first goal was to reach

Benghazi and find a sergeant major C., whose address they had. The question was, how to reach Benghazi. Suddenly Efraim saw a sergeant whom he recognized to be a kibbutz member. He spoke to the man, and after learning that he was headed in the direction of Derna, Libya, told him a little of the purpose of their trip. The sergeant agreed to travel with them to Tobruk and from there to Derna. However, no sooner had they boarded the train than he disappeared, and when they saw him later he deliberately avoided their company.

Seated opposite them in the train was a member of the FSS, the Field Security Service, and they felt sure that he was trailing them. As soon as they arrived in Tobruk they got off the train, walked around the military camp, went to the NAAFI, and kept their ears open in an attempt to learn from the conversations of the soldiers where the road to Derna lay. They finally were picked up by a truck that was headed for that city. There they contacted sergeant E. S., whom they knew from Haifa, and he put them up overnight and helped them get transportation to Benghazi, at that time a bustling military base and the location of a lively Jewish colony that centered about a Solel Boneh engineering unit in the British Army.

They found sergeant major C., who looked after their every need, and warned them to avoid certain Jewish officers and soldiers who would not look favorably upon their mission, whether because of principles of military allegiance or because they might assume that the unusual group with its strange Hagana missions would interfere with them. Some would look upon the entire matter as an unwarranted adventure, C. assured them. For this reason the young men told no one of their mission, and avoided meeting even their closest friends. Whenever they were questioned they said that they were members of the 178th Battalion, located in Tripoli, and that they were returning there from home leave in Palestine.

They remained in Benghazi for ten days, waiting for a convoy to Tripoli. Although this meant a loss of time, they benefited from their stay in the army camp by familiarizing themselves with army life. From then on they looked and acted like soldiers in every respect.

One morning C. told them that a convoy was leaving. However, no sooner were they on their way than Efraim discovered that in their hurried departure C. had failed to return forty pounds of the money that they had entrusted him with upon their arrival in Benghazi. An argument broke out among the three as to whether they should return or not. Efraim, who felt responsible for not having noticed the error at once, impulsively jumped out of the moving truck and called to his companions to wait for him at the Marble Arch, 220 miles away.

He returned to Benghazi, and C., who in the meantime had discovered the error and had taken steps to remedy it, rebuked him for his rashness and told him that no convoy was scheduled to leave the base for a few days. Not wishing to be separated from his companions and sit around idly for weeks, Efraim decided to get to the Marble Arch on his own.

The distance from Benghazi to Tripoli was 625 miles. Efraim left Benghazi on foot in the afternoon and covered 31 miles that day. He lay down in a ditch beside the road and went to sleep on an empty stomach, as his friends had taken all the provisions. On the following day he stood at the crossroads of the main highway from the morning on. Only at nightfall did three trucks appear heading westward. Although the drivers, who were Zulus from South Africa,

did not share a common language with the emissary, they
agreed to give him a lift. For two days and nights they
crawled along at a rate of fifteen miles per hour, making
long stopovers. Efraim did not eat or drink until they came
to a water station of the 405th Battalion. There he met some
Palestinian boys from the Water Supply Battalion, and
after they provided him with a shower and a meal, he continued his journey with them and somehow arrived at his
destination.

The Marble Arch, erected by Mussolini in the heart of the
desert, served as the official boundary line between Cyrenaica
and Tripolitania. A regiment of the Australian Army that
included some Jewish soldiers was encamped out there in
the lonely waste. When he arrived in the camp, Efraim
learned that his friends had left the day before, as they had
been offered a car ride straight to Tripoli.

Once more Efraim was stranded and did not know how
to continue his journey. The following morning he went out
to the road. A sandstorm arose and buffeted him about so
that he made almost no headway. This was during September, when the sun was at its hottest. He stood on the road all
day with nothing to drink. When night came, he was forced
to return to the camp. He was determined, however, to
continue his journey, even if it meant taking great risks.
He asked one of the Jewish privates if there was a chance of
flying to Tripoli. The private sent him to a corporal. The
corporal sent him to a sergeant; the sergeant sent him to a
captain. Finally Efraim came before the camp's commanding
officer, a kind-hearted Australian major. Efraim told the
major that he had been granted leave from his company, and
that should he return late, the entire company would be
punished by having their leaves cancelled. The major
believed him and said that he would try to help. That day a

two-seater plane arrived, and the gunner's cockpit was un-
occupied. Efraim was given the empty seat. The plane took
off, and that night they arrived at the Kastel Benito airfield
near Tripoli.

As soon as the plane landed and came to a stop, Efraim
jumped out and ran past the MP whose job it was to inspect
identification cards. The MP stopped him, however, told
him that there were no more buses going to Tripoli that
evening, and that he would have to spend the night in the
military camp located within the airport. Efraim took advantage of the fact that it was the eve of Yom Kippur, the
Day of Atonement, and explained to the non-Jewish guard
that he was in a desperate hurry to get to synagogue and
could not wait even an hour. The guard was convinced by
this line of argument, and allowed Efraim to leave the airfield
and start out on foot for Tripoli. A passing military vehicle
picked him up and took him into the city.

He had a few addresses in his possession, and he walked
along the dark, winding, main street searching in vain for
one of them. As he was walking about, he was approached
by a British MP who had been following him. The MP
suggested that he sleep in the police station. Efraim could
neither refuse nor escape without arousing the man's
suspicion, so he went along and listened despairingly as the
MP said that in the morning they would call his company
and ask them to come and pick him up. He realized that as
soon as the police would call that company and learn that
no soldier with his assumed name existed, that would be
the end of his mission. He desperately sought a way out. A
soldier appeared in the distance. Efraim did not know
whether the man was a Jew or not, or what language he
spoke, but in his desperation he called to him aloud in
Hebrew:

"Fellow, give a positive answer to all my questions."

The soldier stopped, and when Efraim asked him in English whether he knew the location of the 178th Battalion, he replied that he did. Only after the Palestinian soldier took it upon himself to lead the lost private to his destination did the suspicious MP agree to part with his charge.

Efraim's deliverer did not know how to locate the desired address. He led the emissary to an open door leading into a pitch-black room. Efraim groped his way through the darkness and bumped into a table, on which he immediately stretched out. Within minutes he was asleep. When morning came he learned that he had arrived at the right address and that he had slept on the battalion's dining room table; and he was more than pleasantly surprised when, after a short while, the door to the room opened and his two fellow emissaries walked in.

The three men were in for a bitter disappointment in Tripoli. Eliahu Ben-Hur of the Hagana had gone to Italy with his company a few days prior to their arrival, and had left an order stating that immediately upon their arrival they were to return to Palestine, as the road from Tripoli to Tunisia had been cut off. The army in Tripoli was under the Mediterranean Command while the army in Tunisia was under the North African Command, which did not include Palestinian units, and there was no contact between the two armies. However, the emissaries would not agree to return after they had undergone so many dangers and hardships in order to reach Tripoli. They wandered around the city for a few days and took in the scenery, but gave no rest to the sergeant who had taken Ben-Hur's place; they kept insisting that he help them continue their journey. The sergeant, who had been handed an explicit, written order, at first would not comply. However, when he realized that there was no chance of the stubborn emissaries' obeying him, he began looking for transportation for them. Finally, after providing them with special passes, he sent them off in a military mail truck that was to travel the route between Tripoli and Sfax in Tunisia. Their passes, authorizing them to cross the border, were unique and without precedent in that region.

They started out early in the morning. Not far from the border, on the Tripolitanian side, they passed an MP riding a bicycle. When he saw soldiers riding in a mail truck, which was not allowed to give anyone rides, he chased after them, halted the truck and shouted:

"You're Italian war prisoners trying to escape!"

They yelled back angrily that they were legitimate Palestinians and at the same time whipped out their identification cards and waved them angrily in his face. The MP, dumbfounded by their reaction, begged their pardon and left without even looking at the cards, and they continued on their way. However, their troubles were not yet over. From the start the driver had not liked the idea of their traveling in his truck illegally. Therefore, as soon as they entered the Tunisian border city he took them straight to the city's commanding officer. After a few moments the latter came out and asked to see their papers. He glanced at what was written on them and said angrily:

"Don't try to make a monkey out of me. There is no such pass!"

They started to explain but quickly realized that it was futile. Switching to a different tack, they said to the officer:

"We'll tell you the truth. We're Jews from Palestine serving in the British Army and our camp is in Tripoli. We were told that relatives of ours escaped the Nazi concentration camps and arrived in Tunisia. We're not sure that this is true, but we won't know any peace until we've gone and seen for ourselves."

The story made an impression on the officer. He hesitated for a moment and said:

"All right, I haven't seen you. On your way!"

The driver was furious in failing to rid himself of his passengers. When they arrived in Sfax, his destination, he drove the truck up to the gates of the military transit camp, parked, and waited to see what would happen. The young men did not want to enter the camp, fearing that their papers would be inspected. However, seeing that the driver would not leave, they decided to enter notwithstanding. They were barraged with questions at once. Who were they, where were they headed, what were they doing, and so forth. This was a new British unit and a rather isolated one. Not too long before they had been visited by a Palestinian soldier who had spent his leave in England. He won the hearts of his listeners with stories of what had happened to him there during his leave. Because of this, when the three emissaries presented themselves as Palestinians they were welcomed enthusiastically. They were given a meal and provided with quarters to spend the night. The emissaries, emboldened by their good fortune, turned to the officers in charge of the camp and asked if they would help them get to Tunis. Their request was granted:

"A train leaves tomorrow and you'll be able to board it."

That night they met Jews in Sfax. Walking about the streets they made friends with some Jewish children, who brought them to their parents' homes, where they were warmly received. They ate their fill and spoke about Palestine, and their hosts drank in their words thirstily. The next morning they went to the railroad station. Since they knew that there would be a great many MPs there examining passengers' papers, they waited until the last minute, and when the train started moving, burst into the station and jumped aboard one of the jam-packed cars.

They arrived in Tunis, a city filled with soldiers, after midnight. They went from one hotel to another but could not get a room. They were afraid to wander around the streets too long and risk capture, so having no choice, they payed an exhorbitant price for a room in one of the brothels.

There were over 80,000 Jews in Tunisia at that time, scattered in communities throughout the country. Some Jewish communities had long histories and prided themselves in a distinguished Jewish tradition. To all intents and purposes, the Jews constituted the link between the people of the country and the French rulers. They controlled the cooking-oil and spice trades, and they were the big land owners. They constituted the greater part of the Tunisian intelligentsia also—they were the doctors, the pharmacists, the lawyers, and so forth. The vast majority of them were subjects of the Bey, the native head of Tunisia, and only 6,000 were French citizens. The Jewish community from Italy, who had migrated to the country in the nineteenth century, was in a class by itself.

The Jews of Tunisia were organized into Jewish communities, or kehillot, headed by semi-elected leaders, or parnasim. Three outstanding personalities headed Tunisian Jewry: Albert Basis, Paul Gaz, and Dr. Katan. Albert Basis was a famous lawyer born of an aristocratic family, and was a member of the Tunisian Parliament and chairman of its Financial Committee. He served as counsel to the French regarding Arab affairs, and was a liaison of sorts between the French and the Government of the Bey. He was also a professor of maritime law, and an observant Jew and an ardent Zionist. Paul Gaz, also a Zionist, was a proud French

Jew who had served as a captain during the two World Wars; he was the Jews' representative to the French Government. Dr. Katan was a veteran Zionist, and the chairman of the Zionist Federation.

These three men, despite differences in outlook and status, worked together in matters pertaining to Tunisian Jewry and constituted the unofficial high-level leadership of the Jewish population.

The emissaries of the Bureau arrived in Tunisia four months after its liberation from the Nazis, who ruled the country from November, 1942, to May, 1943. During that period the Nazis had managed to set up work camps to which young Jewish men were sent, and some of them were killed in Anglo-American bombings. A *Judenrat,* or Jewish Council, was set up. It was headed by Paul Gaz, who carried out his role honorably.

The Vichy regime was no better than that of the Germans. Like their predecessors, they handed Tunisian Jews over to the Arabs, to do with as they pleased. That almost no harm resulted to the Jews despite these circumstances was due to the Bey, who looked upon the Jews as his subjects. He invited the parnasim of the Jewish communities to his residence, and there, in the presence of his court, he declared his loyalty to the Jews—and he stood by his word. However, after the Germans withdrew, the French deposed the Bey and replaced him with one of his weak-willed relatives, who obeyed them in everything.

One of the strange phenomena which the emissaries came across shortly after their arrival in Tunisia was the fact that the Jews did not hate the Germans, who had not killed many people during the short time that they controlled the country. The Germans did succeed, however, in creating a split in Tunisian Jewry by bestowing special privileges upon a cer-

17. **They refused to believe what the emissaries told them about the mass murder of European Jewry.**

tain segment of the community. After the Germans left, the Jews wanted to forget everything. They wanted to consider the Nazi conquest and occupation as a passing episode and were anxious to return to their old routine. In addition, they refused to believe what the emissaries told them about the mass murder of European Jewry. Those who conceded that their story was true maintained that the Germans might do such a thing to the "insolent" Jews of Poland, but not to obedient Jews like themselves.

During the months of September and October, 1943, when the emissaries had just arrived in Tunisia, the country was in an anarchic state. Factories were empty, as the Germans had taken everything of value. Food was rationed out—less than half a pound daily for each adult. The emissaries arrived empty-handed and did not possess food coupons. In addition, they had to change their military uniforms for civilian dress immediately. They went to the market place and bought some second-hand clothing which, when put on, gave them the appearance of beggars.

They spent their first night as civilians in the house of a Jewish boy whom they had met by chance in the street. Their talks with him marked the beginning of their efforts. With their first contact with the isolated Jewry of Tunisia, the emissaries felt that they were not only responsible for the specific task that had been assigned them, but for all the needs and problems of the Tunisian Jewish community.

The first small group of young Jews that they met were educated youngsters who had formerly looked upon themselves as French patriots in every respect. When their illusions were shattered, about ten of them, the oldest of whom was twenty-one, banded together and formed the society of Zeirei Zion ("The Young of Zion"), and some of them studied Hebrew in the *Alliance* School. Now that their

Jewish consciousness had been aroused, they wanted to do something, but did not know what.

When the emissaries met with these restless young people, they saw at once that they were ripe for activity. Deciding to get down to business without delay, they picked three members of the group and spoke with each one privately. They told them what their goal was and suggested the formation of a tight and loyal nucleus that would be able to stand up under duress. They wanted to establish such a group along the lines of a secret Hagana cell in Palestine, in order to mold the young people and strengthen their resolve for the obstacles that they would encounter while serving the illegal immigration effort. They explained the principles of the Hagana and the rigid tests that had to be met by those who wished to join its ranks.

The swearing in of young Tunisian Jews into the Hagana constituted an impressive and moving ceremony. Initiates were led into a dark, candle-lit room. Upon the table lay a pistol and a Bible. The oath administered to them had been written by the emissaries. With this oath of loyalty to the Hagana (the Jewish defense effort in Tunisia) taken by a handful of loyal young people, the foundation was laid for the great revival of North African Jewry and its mass migration to Palestine.

At the outset of their work among the young people, the emissaries learned that, with the exception of a feeble Revisionist movement, there was no Zionist organization among the Jewish population of Tunisia. The Zionist Federation existed on paper only. Dr. Katan, the head of the Zionist movement, died about one month after the emissaries met him. He had become active in the movement prior to the First World War. At that time he was a very wealthy man, known inside and outside his country. He served as a mediator in the Bosnia-Herzegovina dispute, as an expert in Arab affairs. Mussolini appointed him as a mediator in Libya, and in 1939, at the request of Dr. Chaim Weizmann, he participated in the Round Table Conference in London. In spite of his mortal illness he greeted the emissaries warmly. They told him the purpose of their mission: to get Tunisian Jews to Palestine. He approved of their program and asked only one thing of them:

"Don't get mixed up in Arab politics: that's one thing you know nothing about."

The emissaries were aided greatly by Dr. Bartos, a Jewish physician who had escaped from Hungary and had become a professor of medicine in Palermo. When Mussolini came to power he emigrated to Tunisia. Efraim met him by chance —he went to him as a patient during his first few days in Tunis. The doctor, seeing how shabbily his patient was dressed, refused to charge him for the visit. After that they became fast friends. Bartos dedicated himself wholeheartedly to the Zionist cause. He contributed generously of his own funds, put aside his own affairs, and worked day and night for the Zionist underground at a great risk to himself.

To disguise their true identities from the local Jewry, the emissaries, when pressed, said that they were refugees from Europe who had gotten into the country by chance, illegally, and for that reason did not want non-Jews to know of their presence.

All three of them lived an austere existence in a small room adjoining that of one of the young members of the movement. They were unsuccessful in obtaining identification papers, and so were in constant danger.

In mid-1943 Tunisia served as the base for the Allied invasion of Italy, and Tunis was full of spies and counter-spies. Everyone had to carry identification papers, and often the police would stop people in the streets and search them. Once, two of the emissaries were sitting on a bench in a public park and talking; in the course of their discussion, Efraim took out a notebook from his pocket and wrote down the titles of some books that they needed for the movement. Suddenly they found themselves surrounded by Tunisian soldiers, who were eyeing them suspiciously. They rose to leave, but the soldiers would not let them go. They said that there was a military camp in the vicinity and that since the two were sitting there and taking notes they had to be German spies, and they were going to take them to their sergeant who would examine their papers. The young men knew that they were in a tight spot. People had already been killed because they were suspected of being spies. Thinking quickly, Efraim whipped the notebook out of his pocket, thrust it at the soldier who had addressed him, and said:

"Here, look at what we wrote!"

"But I can't read!" replied the soldier.

At that moment a French sailor was passing by. Efraim asked him if he would read for them. Fortunately, the first line was written in French. The sailor read off the name of a book and the Tunisian soldiers were satisfied. The emissaries had feared that the sailor would go on to read the second line, which was written in German, but fortunately he was in a hurry and promptly went on his way.

One of their first activities for the benefit of the general Jewish population of Tunisia was the re-establishment of the Zionist Federation. They had a serious conversation with Dr. Bartos, and his house became their center of operation. With his help they enlisted the aid of a number of other people, including some of the wealthiest and most respected members of Tunis' Jewish community. They chose a national council, with Bartos as its head. They also won the support of Mrs. Nelly Bokara, of Italian descent, who later became one of the mainstays of their effort. Through her help they established a chapter of WIZO, the Women's International Zionist Organization, in Tunis, which she headed as chairman. She won over the women of Tunis to the Zionist program and founded "Young WIZO." All these activities were carried out secretly, as Zionist activities and institutions were outlawed by the Government.

The emissaries were mainly concerned with the youth movement. At first they worked with the small group that they had gathered about them. They taught them Hebrew, history, geography, socialism, the history of the Yishuv, and similar subjects. As the movement grew, they began to send emissaries from the group of original members to other Jewish communities, in order to form pioneer groups there.

After a while, the emissaries felt that the time for concrete action had arrived. They decided to have some of the members undergo agricultural training. They found a farm owned by a Jew who was willing to give work to a few Jewish boys. They sent him some young people, among them leaders of the movement. This was a bold step. Although up to that time the Jewish community had reacted favorably to the activities of the pioneer youth in the city—their performing at celebrations and holiday gatherings, the Palestinian folk dances, the Hebrew songs, and the fine spirit—no one had imagined that this was a movement in earnest, one whose members took its goals seriously. Who had ever heard of young Jews in that part of the world becoming farm laborers of their own accord? The parents of the leaders of the movement and its first members were of the bourgeoisie who had left the confines of the ghetto. The youth knew nothing about its residents and were not even familiar with its streets; only through the emissaries did they come in contact with the ghetto and its problems. Inspired by the young men from Palestine, they began to organize the movement there and a new world opened before them; and due to their efforts, the movement struck roots in the ghetto and flourished. Still, who would have believed that boys from respected families would go to a village and engage in grueling physical labor side by side with local Arab workers?

This act brought about a revolution in the Jewish way of thinking. The people were all the more astounded when, after a few months had passed, the emissaries and movement leaders decided to try to send some of the members across the Tripolitanian border and get them to Palestine overland. They chose two of the movement's stalwarts and sent them to pave the way. They tried twice, but met with no success.

The emissaries had had no contact with Palestine since their departure for their mission. After a while they learned that all sorts of rumors had spread about them. Once their families were told that they had been killed. When by chance they met a Jewish soldier of the French Foreign Legion who told them he was about to go on leave in Palestine, they asked him to give their regards to their relatives. When the legionnaire arrived in Palestine, he spread a rumor that the emissaries had been captured and that he himself had seen them in prison. On the basis of his report he received a certain sum of money from the Bureau and their families to deliver to them. Not only did he pocket the money, but he also said that the young men had disclosed all the secrets of the underground movement to their French captors.

The emissaries, in the meanwhile, were using up the meager funds that they had been given in Palestine in order to provide themselves with the barest necessities and to buy what was needed for the movement and for the agricultural training program. At that time one of their acquaintances was a Jewish member of the British Air Force, a kind-hearted fellow by the name of Komrad. He had been born in Poland and spoke Yiddish, but was not at all Zionist in outlook. His principal occupation in the air force was tailoring officers' uniforms. He had accumulated two hundred pounds sterling in the service—all the money he had in the world. One day he came to the young men and told them that he was being transferred to Cairo and was going to visit Palestine. When, on the day before he was to leave, he came to say good-by to the men whom he knew as refugees, they said to him:

"We don't have a cent. Give us your 200 pounds and you'll get it back in Palestine."

He looked at them as if they had gone mad. They offered to give him an address in Palestine where he could get the money immediately upon his arrival. He did not agree, said good-by and left. After two hours had passed, he returned. He started stammering apologetically, explained that that sum represented his life's savings and asked that they at least give him a receipt for the money and the address of "someone" in Palestine. For security reasons, they refused. He implored, pleaded with them, but they stood firm. He got up and with tears in his eyes asked their pardon, and left. In the middle of the night there was a knock on the door. It was Komrad again. He came in, put the 200 pounds on the table, wished the young men well, and disappeared.

Months later, when the emissaries happened to visit the soldiers' club in Cairo, someone approached them from behind, seized them, and kissed them. It was Komrad. He took them aside and told them his story:

"When I got to Palestine I went to the address that you gave me—Eliahu Dobkin, the Jewish Agency, Jerusalem. I walked into the building and asked to see him. They told me that he was too busy, but I kept insisting until I finally got an appointment. I walked into a large room and found him sitting behind a big table. I told him that I had given 200 pounds sterling to two young fellows in Tunis and they had told me that I should come to him and he would repay me. He asked if I had a receipt. I told him no. He asked what your names were. I told him I didn't know. He thought I was crazy and said so politely. I went over my story again and I demanded my money. He repeated his questions and said that he couldn't give money to a stranger who didn't have a receipt and didn't even know who he had lent the money to. Well, I was as stubborn as a mule and so was he. But the hotter I got, the quieter he got. Finally I just flew off the handle. I pounded on his desk and yelled: 'Here you sit nice and easy behind your desk while they're starving there, and risking their necks! I don't need you or your money. They'll pay me back!' I got up and walked out boiling mad. I was outside when he caught up with me. He brought me back to his office with a broad grin on his face. And believe it or not—he gave me the 200 pounds. . . ."

The movement continued to grow, and branched out into other sectors of the Jewish community. Its membership consisted of 300 boys and girls of all ages, organized into clubs and interest groups and headed by an elected council and a band of leaders. Finally the time came for the first of those who had undergone farm training to go to Palestine, where they were to lay the foundation for the first kibbutz of immigrants from North Africa, one which would serve to draw their comrades. When the emissaries finally received two certificates, they decided to send Yizhak Avrahami, who had worked and studied for the movement in Algeria; A. Z.; and R. C. as the latter's wife. R. C.'s parents had been the first to open their house to the emissaries, at a time when all other doors were shut to them. However, in spite of their feelings of gratitude toward this family, they felt obligated to act contrary to the parents' wishes. A. Z. tried to convince R. C.'s parents to agree to the wedding so that she could go to Palestine with him, but the parents refused, shut their daughter in her room, and put a padlock on the door. The emissaries decided that they could not retreat, and that the future of the movement and the emigration to Palestine depended upon the outcome of this, their first struggle.

They drew up a plan of action and set to work. Outwardly the girl gave up her plans of emigrating to Palestine and obeyed her parents in everything. After a week the parents decided to let her resume her teaching lessons and that the mother would accompany her to the class and back. In the meantime the emissaries studied the country's laws and learned that a Jewish girl above the age of twelve and a half could be legally married in accordance with Jewish tradition, in the presence of any Jew, and on these grounds would be given a notarized marriage certificate. One day, after the mother had accompanied her daughter to class, the girl slipped out of the building for a few moments, signed the requisite forms in a notary's office, returned to the class, and went home with her mother as usual. After all the preparations had been made, she left the class one day, and after a traditional wedding ceremony—disappeared. In the meantime, however, the emissaries had learned that even a married woman could not get a visa without her parents' consent. The girl remained in hiding for seven days and tempers became white hot. The parents threatened to inform the police of all they knew concerning the movement, but the girl and her companions stood firm. In the end the parents capitulated, on condition that they be allowed to see their daughter before her departure.

So the emigration of the first halutza (girl pioneer) to Palestine was effected.

14

Between France and North Africa

Almost a year went by. Vague reports of a Jewish underground in France began seeping into North Africa and the emissaries began to dream of parachuting into that country, or of getting there some other way. At that time a soldier in a Palestinian unit that had been sent from Tripoli to Tunis came to the emissaries with an order that they were to return to Palestine. The uniforms were taken out of their hiding place and the emissaries forged the necessary papers. At last, when everything was ready, they sat down with the Tunisian leaders of the movement, outlined the work for the near future and sadly took leave of the friends they had made and the members of the movement that they had established.

The program that they presented to Saul Avigur for direct penetration of France from North Africa was not acceptable to headquarters. After the emissaries enjoyed a leave at home the Bureau decided to return them to North Africa in the uniforms of officers of the French Information Service, with the help of some members of the French underground who worked jointly with the Hagana. To this end a group of five was formed that included Bertha, Efraim's wife, who had been born in France. It was decided that the group would contact David Shaltiel, who was about to go to France via

Lisbon on a mission of the Bureau. This was not Efraim's first meeting with David Shaltiel; as a child, he knew him in Antwerp, where David had been active in acquiring arms for the Hagana. On the day that he was arrested by the Gestapo on a train passing through Germany he had stayed at the house of Efraim's father. For a time he remained the Nazis' prisoner and underwent torture. Years had passed since that time, and once more his and Efraim's paths crossed.

They had not been in Cairo one day before a mishap occurred that immediately upset all their plans. Efraim and Bertha had taken a cab in the noisy city, swarming with soldiers at the time, and Bertha, who was a member of a kibbutz and was not used to carrying a handbag, left it in the cab. It contained her falsified military papers. It so happened that on the next day Lord Moyne was murdered. The handbag came into the possession of the military police at the same time that they learned of the mysterious murder, and in the murky political atmosphere that then prevailed in the city, Cairo authorities sought to connect the owner of the handbag with the killing. A search was instituted throughout all the military camps for an Israeli female soldier whose name corresponded with that written on the identification papers in the handbag. Yaakov Chernovitz (Zur), the representative of the Jewish Agency in Cairo, informed Efraim and Bertha that they would have to return to Palestine. They, however, were in no mood to obey the order. With the help of one of the local Jews, an old friend of his father's, a room was obtained for Efraim and they went into hiding there. While in hiding they managed to win over Chernovitz and he agreed not to send them back. After things had cooled down, he arranged a meeting between them and a representative of the French underground in the Middle East.

The young French engineer had a genuine desire to help the Hagana underground, but as a result of the murder of Lord Moyne he was wary of dealing with them and insisted that under no condition would he get anyone besides Efraim into North Africa. Efraim asked to be given some time to familiarize himself more thoroughly with French Army regulations, but the underground officer replied:

"*Mon ami,* if you want to go, this is your opportunity. And remember—if the English capture you, I don't know you . . ."

He left in a lieutenant's uniform that was slightly too large for him, and he carried identification papers of the Gaullist underground. He was conveyed to Heliopolis, that section of Cairo which during the war was occupied completely by the Allied forces. He was taken to a military hotel and shown into a room with two beds. The other lodger was not in the room. Immediately Efraim was confronted with a problem: how would he know the rank of his roommate, and whether it was higher or lower than his own? As he was pondering the problem, there was a knock on the door. At once he sat down on the bed in a position that enabled him to see the door but made it appear as though he were looking in another direction. An officer came in, snapped to attention, and stated his name and rank. Efraim saw that he himself was the ranking officer of the two, and asked him some questions in order to learn as much as he could about accepted procedures in the Free French Army.

Next day, when they boarded the military plane, they were seated according to rank. There were four other officers aboard—a colonel, a major, and a captain, and a female officer who was a general's daughter. Efraim, known to them as "Lieutenant Emile Perbel," completed the party. During the flight an informal conversation ensued. Efraim was asked where he was from, and replied: "From Syria." At once the captain remarked that he had just come from that country. To Efraim's delight the man then proceeded to give a detailed account of his impressions of Syria. Since the captain was of a higher rank than he, and in order not to give himself away, the young lieutenant laughed whenever the captain laughed, became incensed whenever the latter did, and agreed with everything that he said.

The flight took two days. Efraim was introduced to a new world as the professional officers, thinking he was one of them, freely discussed confidential intrigues and complained about the mission upon which they were being sent.

At the airport in Algiers they were met by an officer, who took them to French Intelligence Headquarters in the city. There Efraim was introduced to Commandant Caro, head of the Intelligence Bureau in Algeria and Tunisia. After a friendly conversation during the afternoon meal, Efraim was shown to his room. He then went out to the street to look for his friend Yigal, who had arrived in the city before him. By chance he met the daughter of Dr. Bartos, an acquaintance of his from his first mission; the girl was then studying in Algiers. She took him to the Sharki residence.

This was in the spring of 1945. The Sharki residence in Algiers was always open to Jews and was always overflowing with guests. The head of the household, a father of ten children, was a long-bearded, pious Jew, and a devoted Zionist. He was a well-educated man with a keen sense of humor, a pillar of the Jewish community. There was not a Jewish soldier who set foot in Algiers during the war who did not eat at his table. His wife was a Jewish mother in the full sense of the word, not only to her own children, but also to anyone who came under their roof. It was as though the house existed only for the sake of the guests, and everyone served them warmly. It was here that Efraim and Yigal lived during their stay in Algiers.

The emissaries divided up their field of operations. They decided that Yigal would work in Algiers and Efraim would take a trip through Tunisia. Afterwards the two of them would do their best to get to Morocco, in spite of the fact that they had been strictly forbidden to do so by the representative of the French underground.

Efraim left for Tunis. He presented himself to the representative of the French underground, was accorded a friendly reception, and was given into the care of a French naval officer.

Efraim's meeting with the movement members and his friends in Tunis was very emotional. Everyone was astounded at the miraculous transformation that had taken place—the same young man who had walked among them months before in clothes that were falling apart, suddenly reappeared as a French officer in a smart new outfit that contrasted sharply with the shabby old uniforms worn by local officers.

After a period of vigorous, renewed activity in Tunis, he left to tour the country with the permission of the French underground authorities.

In Sfax, the city where he had had his first meeting with Tunisian Jews, he met with a few boys who years later founded an agricultural settlement of Sfax immigrants in Israel. At that meeting the foundations were laid for a branch of the Hebrew underground, and an educational program for the local youth was planned. He then continued his journey, traveling from village to village and from one Jewish community to the next. In Gabès a branch of *Zeirei Zion* was founded. From Gabès he went to the island of Djerba. He traveled for six hours on a bus, and then transferred to a small boat crammed with passengers and freight. A storm arose and the passengers filled the hold with wailing and prayers. They finally arrived on the island, and Efraim took a bus to the Jewish district.

The Jews of Djerba had retained their dress, names, and language for many generations. According to their traditions, one of their two Jewish communities was composed of kohanim, descendants of the ancient priesthood. Unlike other Jewish communities in North Africa, they had refused to establish an *Alliance* school for fear of assimilation. The Jewish community of Djerba was strongly nationalistic and religious.

At the time of Efraim's visit to Djerba there were two Hebrew printing houses on the island that put out prayer books and religious "questions and answers." The study of the Torah and the practice of traditional Judaism were flourishing. Efraim went to the house of a young tailor, the only member of the community who dressed like a European. He was welcomed politely but somewhat reservedly; a French officer, who claimed that he was a Jew, and, what is more, a Jew from the Land of Israel, was a bit suspect. Almost immediately two young Jewish men in traditional dress entered the house. Efraim was invited to join them all in a meal, and noticing the disbelief in their eyes, knew that he was being tested. That he had been raised in an observant household and had studied in a school of Agudath Yisrael, a world organization of ultra-orthodox Jews, now stood him in good stead. He put to good use his knowledge of Jewish practices. When the food was served, he asked if he could first wash his hands, and when the water was brought, he said the appropriate blessing in a loud voice. Then he made the blessing over the bread. He saw by the look in his hosts' eyes that they were beginning to trust him. As he was a vegetarian, he refused to touch any meat dish, and he immediately rose in the esteem of the Djerbans, who thought that his refusal was due to a stringent observance of the dietary laws. And when, after the meal was concluded, he said grace, there was no doubt that he had met the test successfully and had won the confidence of all who were present. They took him into the heart of the city, to the house of Rabbi Yose Hacohen, the founder and leader of Ateret Zion ("The Crown of Zion"), the local Zionist organization. He spent two full days with Rabbi Yose and his students, and they drank up his words thirstily. For the students and the rabbi, this meeting with a Jew from Eretz Israel was an overwhelming experience. The emissary, too, was stirred and felt himself privileged to be sitting with Jews on the lonely island, hundreds of miles away from home, telling them in Hebrew of The Land and its upbuilding, and encouraging them to return to Zion. He became very attached to them.

One week after Efraim left, a number of young men formed a group to undergo agricultural training, and in 1947 they were among the first to emigrate to Palestine. The entire Jewish community of Djerba was not long in following after. They struck roots in Israel and settled all over the country as workers and people of the soil.

After having spent five days on the island, Efraim returned to Tunis in a small two-passenger plane. The flight was a difficult one. When they were over the desert a storm arose and the plane bounced up and down ceaselessly. Finally something went wrong with the motor and they were forced to land in the desert. After the pilot spent hours attempting to make the necessary repairs, he told Efraim that he was not sure whether the plane would be able to get them to their destination. He absolved himself of all responsibility and said they had to choose whether or not to continue on foot or stay where they were in the middle of the desert. They chose to continue. After a long and tiring trek Efraim arrived in Tunis and at once met with Yigal to make plans for their trip to Morocco.

Morocco was then divided into three parts—the French, the Spanish, and the International Zone of Tangiers. Theoretically, the Sultan and his court ruled French Morocco, but to all intents and purposes, the French controlled the country. The Spanish Zone and Tangiers were ruled by a council of representatives of different countries, headed by an appointed commissioner.

At that time there were 280,000 to 290,000 Jews in Morocco: 250,000 in French Morocco, 20,000 in Spanish Morocco, and 10,000 to 20,000 in Tangiers. The Jews were considered "subjects of the Sultan," as in the Middle Ages in Europe, and possessed no rights whatever. Scores of Jewish communities were scattered throughout the country, most of them in the cities and a few of them in small towns and villages, from the Atlantic coast to the Algerian border, and from the shores of the Mediterranean to the outskirts of the Sahara; some were even to be found in the Atlas mountains.

Moroccan Jewry, like all other Jewish communities, was organized into kehillot, headed by "elected" parnasim. In the Casablanca kehilla, comprising 80,000 members, fewer than 1,000 were eligible to vote, and the parnasim were actually chosen by no more than 200; and even these elections required the certification of the Sultan's appointee. The Jews were entirely at the mercy of the Sultan and his governmental machinery. In addition, the attitude of the French authorities of Casablanca was none too friendly toward the Jews.

The Zionist movement was organized in an illegal federation that functioned secretly. At that time there was a branch of HIAS, the Hebrew Immigrants Aid Society, in Morocco; it was headed by a Polish Jew. The emissaries knew that they could not stay long in Morocco, and so decided to work quickly. The contacted the head of the HIAS, told him who they were, and asked him to introduce them to the leaders of the Jewish community. He contacted three representatives of the kehilla, and the president of the Zionist Federation.

At the meeting, the young men came right to the point: "We are emissaries of the emerging State of Israel, and we have come here to teach the young people to defend themselves and to emigrate to Eretz Israel. We ask your help."

The president of the Zionist Federation rose and replied: "Command, and we will obey."

Jewish life was well organized in Casablanca. The Carl Netter Association and the alumni of the *Alliance* school owned a large building that served as a center where the Jewish youth of the city met, primarily for sport and recreational activities. The emissaries' suggestion that they run a seminar in the building for one month was willingly accepted. Each night young people would gather to listen to lectures, engage in group discussions, and answer questions. They would pass the time this way until after midnight. After they left the building they would continue the discussions, sometimes even till dawn. In this manner the emissaries discovered several outstanding young people, and put them in contact with a group in Palestine who were preparing themselves to found a kibbutz; some of the young people from Djerba joined that group after a while.

During this trip Efraim had his first contact with the Casablanca ghetto in all its filth and degradation. Never before had he seen such poverty. He came across a family of ten living in a hole in the middle of the street. Fifty-five thousand people had lived within the confines of the Casablanca ghetto before the war. When the war broke out, 30,000 more were added, and with no new structures being built, the people lived almost literally on top of each other.

The scenery outside of the ghetto was magnificent. The city spread over a considerable area, and as its name Casablanca ("White House") indicated, was entirely white. One of the most important districts of the city was located in the vicinity of a square called *Place de France*. On one side of the square were lovely cafés, and across from them, concealed behind the tall, stately pillars, lay the filth and the wretchedness of the ghetto. Holes, alleys, courtyards, tiny rooms and cubicles massed together—such was the ghetto. Sanitary measures were non-existent. Thousands of diseased, maimed, and blind people lived there. Against this background, crime flourished. Thousands of youngsters in the ghetto were crying out for care and education. Despite everything, the strong, unassimilated Jewish community believed devoutly and faithfully in the eventual coming of the Messiah, who would take them back to the Land of Israel.

Only a few hundred yards separated the majority of Casablanca Jewry, living in the ghetto, from the minority— that included some very wealthy Jews—living outside; yet it seemed that nothing could bridge the gap between these two disparate worlds. Even the Zionists on the "outside" felt no responsibility for the greater part of their people, and claimed that as Zionists they negated Diaspora existence, symbolized by the ghetto, and that it would be futile to waste their efforts on the ghetto residents.

Moroccan Jewry had a national "Council" for communal affairs, which was founded during the Vichy regime. Among other things, the Council published a book, a copy of which was presented to President Roosevelt, concerning the history

18. THE PEOPLE LIVED ALMOST LITERALLY ON TOP OF EACH OTHER.

of the Jews under the Vichy regime and documenting instances of anti-Semitism, which were not lacking. Jews were
attacked and were subject to terrorism, particularly in the
Atlas Mountains. Some Jews from that region traveled to
Casablanca on foot, a journey that took months to accomplish, in order to complain to the authorities. There were
instances of official discrimination: in various places, when
milk was distributed for infants, Jews were given smaller
quantities than others or none at all.

All during this period, the young men never gave up the
idea of parachuting into France. News reached them of an
American airfield near Marrakech. They heard that a Jew
from Palestine lived there and was in charge of the Baron
Rothschild farm in that vicinity. They set out for Marrakech.
When they arrived at their destination, at the foot of the
Atlas Mountains and surrounded by desert, they were struck
with wonder—the city seemed submerged in a sea of tall and
flourishing palm trees. The two emissaries soon found the
house they were looking for, and knocked on the door. Two
women appeared in the doorway, and the men, dressed in
the uniforms of French officers, asked where the director of
the farm was. They were told that he was not home, and, to
the "officers' " amazement, one of the women turned to the
other and said in fluent Hebrew: "What do these fellows
want?"
When the strangers replied in Hebrew, it was the women's
turn to be astonished. The emissaries were invited in and
spent a pleasant evening. They met two American pilots,
played some Hebrew records on the phonograph, and
learned that there was a possibility of their flying to France
within two days.
Next day they were taken on a tour by their host. As they

neared the Atlas Mountains they saw a figure seated on a donkey approaching them. The farm director recognized by the rider's dress that he was a Jew. He spoke to the man in French, but the latter did not understand him. However, as soon as the director began to speak in Hebrew, the rider's eyes lit up. He was a member of the tribe of tall, blue-eyed cave-dwelling Jews of southern Morocco, who numbered about 7,000.

When the man heard that they were from Jerusalem, he got off his donkey and rushed to embrace them and kiss their hands. There they stood at the foot of the Atlas Mountains, Jews from the Land of Israel and a Jew "from beyond the dark mountains," centuries and continents apart, yet brothers by virtue of the Hebrew language and Jerusalem.

After this encounter, they made their way into the mountains. The journey was impressive. The mountains were as high as the Alps and many valleys lay between them. In the midst of these mountains they came upon a Jewish village of cave dwellers. When the villagers learned that their visitors were from the Land of Israel, they were overjoyed. They quickly brought out a Jew who understood Hebrew, and he invited them to his home. They followed him, bent their heads, and entered the cave. It was spotlessly clean. They were served refreshments and ate their fill. When they left the cave, they found all the villagers assembled with bundles on their shoulders and staffs in their hands. They were told that these Jews, who thirsted for redemption, had come to the obvious conclusion: the emissaries from the Land of Israel had come to take them to Jerusalem; and they were prepared to leave at once. The young men were deeply moved, and promised the villagers that they would not forget them; and indeed, after some years had passed, their promise was kept, and the Jews of the Atlas Mountains were enabled to settle in Israel.

From Marrakech they returned to Tunisia, still planning to parachute into France. They decided, however, not to take such a step without first obtaining the consent of Saul. In the meantime they grew so deeply attached to North Africa's Jews, that they began to question whether a mission to France would be more important than the work in which they were then engaged. They expanded the scope of their activities. They began secretly to distribute reading material which they had printed in the printing shop of a Jew with whom they had dealings. Among other things, they translated and printed the letters of the first three movement members who had emigrated from Algiers and settled in Palestine in Bet Oren, the kibbutz of the two emissaries. These letters were circulated in Algiers as well.

The lion's share of the work of the pioneer underground movement in Tunisia fell to Nadia, who came from a well-to-do family. During the first mission of the young men of the Bureau, Nadia, then a university student in Algiers, wished to emigrate to Palestine. Her parents were opposed, and she was forced to return to Tunisia. Nadia was a strong-willed and talented girl, modest and unaffected, a gifted speaker who always held her audience captive, and the life breath of the movement in Tunisia. Before the emissaries told anyone of the possibility of their leaving for France, they broached the matter to Nadia.

In the discussion which ensued, the girl insisted that their place was in North Africa, and not elsewhere. She spoke of the half-million Jews of the Maghreb, who, although rooted in the Jewish past, had somehow remained outside the stream of Jewish history. Yet in spite of everything, they had not assimilated but had remained faithful, ever yearning to return to Zion. These Jews would make excellent human material for the upbuilding of the Land, and were only waiting to be roused, organized, and given proper leadership. Nadia herself was, in the emissaries' eyes, a symbol of the Jewry on whose behalf she spoke. She persuaded them to remain.

In the meantime, Germany surrendered, and the world was intoxicated: peace had come at last. On Victory Day and during the night that followed the two Palestinians rubbed elbows with tens of thousands of Jews and with the rest of the population in the streets of Tunis. Together with the crowds they stood in the courtyard of the French High Commissioner, sang the "Marseillaise," and stood at attention as the Bey's anthem was played. In their hearts they felt that although the termination of the war had not brought freedom to all humanity, at any rate a new period of great possibilities was opening up to the Jews of the world and to the Yishuv in Palestine.

The emissaries began to reap the rewards of their labors. A new farm was obtained, and the agricultural training program expanded, this time to include new members of the movement as well as the founders. New branches sprung up in other cities, and a group of prospective kibbutz members in Palestine was formed.

The emissaries' accomplishment was symbolized, in their own eyes, by a girl from the island of Djerba. When Efraim first met her she was a bashful little girl who wore the traditional Djerban dress and sat on the floor in the corner of the room, not used to sitting on a bench and unaccustomed to the company of men. It was not long before the same girl became one of the most active and devoted members of the movement. The emissaries looked upon her as their most significant achievement—first as a member of the movement, and later as a worker and builder in Israel.

However, ominous shadows soon fell across their path. The activities of the emissaries in Tunisia had aroused hostility in certain Jewish circles. One day the young men were summoned before the authorities and were shown letters informing upon them. Most of the letters were from assimilated Jews who were opposed to the emissaries from Palestine and were only too willing to be rid of them. The emissaries were ordered to leave Tunisia, and they returned to Palestine.

15

Istanbul—Base of the Rescue Effort

Istanbul, the former capital of Turkey—neutral almost until the end of World War II—was, from 1940 to 1945, a turbulent center of international activity. Foreign diplomats abounded in the city, and as it was so close to the Balkan front, it served as a center for underground networks and spy rings of many nations. International relief societies and various philanthropic organizations set up their headquarters there to prepare for times of crisis. In the wake of the calamity of European Jewry, representatives of the Jewish Agency, the Zionist Federation, the "Joint," and other groups were sent to Istanbul distraught at the reports of the mass slaughter and helpless to rescue its victims.

One of these groups was the small band of Immigration Bureau men, who lived in modest quarters at 48 Istiklal Street. The group had not yet recovered from the blow dealt the immigration effort by the outbreak of the war. The emissaries who were sent to Istanbul were anxious to recoup the losses they had suffered elsewhere. The desperate straits of the Jewish populations of Greece, Bulgaria, and Rumania under the Nazi occupation, as well as the moral support and occasional criticisms of the Yishuv, spurred them on to ever mass slaughter and helpless to rescue its victims.

Zvi Yehieli was the first emissary to go to Istanbul after the Bureau decided to renew its activities there for the first time since the sailing of the Dorian II (1940-1941). Working on his own, Zvi acquired a small pleasure boat called the Lilly and sought other boats that could serve the effort. At the end of 1942, when news of the Nazi genocide of Polish Jewry first began to reach the outside world, four more members of the Bureau took up residence in Istanbul: Zeev Shind (Danny), Ehud Avriel, Moshe Agami, and Saul Avigur. All four were among the pioneers of the illegal immigration effort.

Actually, the members of the Bureau had never stopped trying to get Jews to Palestine via Turkey. In the autumn of 1941, immediately after the Germans sealed all roads leading out of Rumania and Bulgaria, Danny was sent on a mission to Istanbul. At that time Palestine headquarters had not worked out a specific plan of action, but they realized that they had to send emissaries of the underground to live in Istanbul, build up contacts, and try to rescue Jews from the Nazi inferno. So Danny remained in Istanbul and did what he could.

At the beginning of 1942, Danny began to probe for ways of getting Jews out of Bulgaria and Rumania with the help of certain departments of the British and American armed forces. He was aided in his first efforts by Eliahu Epstein (Elath), who was, at the time, the representative of the Jewish Agency's Political Department in Istanbul. With Epstein's help, Danny met with the heads of the British naval agencies and the American consul general in Istanbul. The emissary hoped that through those two people he would be able to win the Turkish Government's support of his program, and make contacts with shipowners in Bulgaria. Danny returned to Palestine and brought his plan before headquarters, where it was officially authorized. It was also decided that Teddy Kolak should help him establish contacts with the Americans and the British.

The plan originally called for bringing the ships to Mersin, Turkey, debarking there, and continuing the "illegal" journey to Palestine by land. While the emissaries of the Bureau were busy obtaining a vessel, the picture brightened somewhat. British authorities, pressured by the Jewish Agency, agreed that under certain conditions Jewish refugees who had escaped from enemy countries would be permitted to enter Palestine. However, the problem of getting Jews out from behind enemy lines still remained unsolved.

After the sinking of the Struma and the loss of other small Rumanian vessels, the Bureau had strictly forbidden its emissaries to send any ships from Rumania. The underground workers in that country did all that was in their power to have the order rescinded, but to no avail. For months they negotiated for the purchase of two Greek ships that would fly the Greek flag, but nothing came of it. Simultaneously they tried to acquire a Turkish ship, but there, too, negotiations proved unsuccessful.

Danny made a special effort to obtain a Bulgarian ship. Bulgaria was then an ally of Germany, but was not at war with Russia, and for this reason a Bulgarian ship was one of the safest in which to cross the Black Sea, which was swarming with destroyers and submarines at the time.

After the Dorian II episode in the fall and winter of 1940-1941, the immigration effort came to a temporary halt. Zvi Yehieli, prior to leaving Istanbul for Palestine, made contact with an Italian agent who was willing to undertake a mission to Bulgaria for the Aliya-Bet underground. The agent had suggested that Yehieli contact a Bulgarian by the name of Spassov who, as far as he knew, would be willing to help them obtain a boat and have it registered in his name. No sooner did Danny arrive in Istanbul in the autumn of 1941 than he renewed these contacts. The Italian left for Bulgaria and after a while wrote to Danny recommending a boat called the Mariza.

The young men wanted to charter the boat for the one mission they had in mind rather than buy it and have it registered in Spassov's name and thus endanger themselves through joint activity with Bulgarian owners on the other side of the Black Sea. However, after a short while it became clear that they would have to get a boat of their own. In order that they might fully understand the conditions of the prospective agreement, and have a first-hand acquaintance of the man with whom they were dealing, Teddy Kolak and Danny decided to invite Spassov to Istanbul. For ten days they negotiated with him and explained to him the workings of the illegal immigration movement. Spassov had lived in Greece for many years, and when the war broke out, he returned to his native Bulgaria. He knew a great deal about seamanship and was looking for a way to get rich, but in a "decent" manner. He explained to the emissaries that all his money was in Greece, and that he would only be able to give them a promissory note in exchange for having the ship registered under his name.

Communication with Palestine was very difficult at that time, especially when a delicate and top-secret matter was at stake, so the emissaries had to decide on their own whether or not to enter into a transaction wherein they would have to invest a great deal of money without even being certain that the boat would be placed at their disposal or that Jews would be allowed to leave Bulgaria and Rumania. However, the emissaries, feeling confident that they would be able to overcome all obstacles if they would only make some beginning, decided to buy the Mariza and work with Spassov.

The agreement was signed in the middle of May, 1943. The young men took pains to "educate" Spassov. Until he left for Bulgaria, they incessantly drummed their message into his ears.

Despite their reservations, the emissaries felt that they had no alternative, for the efforts of the Jewish Agency to assure immigration through legal channels had bogged down in a morass of papers and fruitless meetings with representatives of various governments. The British did everything in their power to ensure that no progress was made; they employed endless red tape to slow down procedures and nip any promising plan in the bud. They explained to the representatives of the Jewish Agency and to the entire world that Jews could not be rescued because they were not being permitted to leave the occupied countries and because there was no transportation to remove them from there.

In the middle of June, the Bulgarian Government issued Spassov a permit allowing him to take 1,000 Jews to Palestine by sea. This permit, which was to be valid only until August 30, was obtained after the Mariza was purchased with the help of Spassov's relative and associate, one of the generals in the Bulgarian High Command. In order to take advantage of the permit promptly, the emissaries sought to use the Jewish Agency's list of candidates who were waiting to emigrate to Palestine. These lists, that included over 1,800 adults and children, were forwarded to Spassov. However, complications arose, and official authorization was not granted.

The expulsion of Jews from Sofia took place at that time, and the center of Zionist activity shifted to Plovdiv. The representative of the Palestine Office could do no work whatever for several months. The emissaries lost contact with him completely and received no replies to their questions and requests. They sent Spassov to Plovdiv with all the lists that had been forwarded to him from Istanbul, and directed him to Dr. Romano who, like most other Jewish public figures, put no faith in the plan. Everyone maintained that the proposed project was impossible. They refused to believe that the Mariza existed, that it was seaworthy, or that it could be acquired. On top of everything else, most of Bulgarian Jewry stood in fear of sea travel, for the sinking of the Salvador in the Black Sea in 1941 with 320 people aboard was still fresh in their memories; nor was the Struma disaster forgotten. They therefore rationalized, maintaining that "things weren't really too bad after all," and pointed out in a variety of ways, how very difficult it would be to get Jews together after the expulsion from Sofia.

The project almost came to a standstill. For months the wearisome negotiations dragged on. Romano and others disclaimed any responsibility for the affair, which was looked upon by the Jews as the private business venture of a non-Jew. Finally, in the beginning of October, the Bulgarian Government replied to the request that the people on the lists be allowed to emigrate. Their reply was that the special permit had expired.

This was one of the most trying periods for the members of the Bureau. The greater the success of the Nazis in liquidating the Jews, the greater the young men's despair over their inability to help their people escape. Their feelings of helplessness were only increased with the publication of the letter of the British Colonial Secretary, Lord Cranborne, to the British consul in Istanbul. The Secretary, submitting to the pressures of Jewish institutions and British and world opinion stated that while the British would not encourage the smuggling of Jews out of the Balkan countries, any Jews who did manage to get across the border and reach Turkey were to be granted the right to enter Palestine. To this end the British Government set aside the 30,000 certificates that were remaining, according to the White Paper, for the immigration of children and a small number of adults. Prior to that time, refugees from Nazi-occupied countries had been denied entry to Palestine, on the pretext that they might include foreign agents and "undesirable" elements.

As soon as the British change of policy was announced, the Bureau members plunged into the task of obtaining boats. Weeks and months of fatiguing, nerve-racking effort went by, but none were acquired.

Only in the beginning of 1944, almost a year and a half after the feverish renewal of activities in Istanbul, did the group's labors begin to bear fruit. They were finally able to report to headquarters, Palestine, and the entire world:

> We were privileged to see with our own eyes the Milka enter the Bosporus, bearing refugees from Chernovtsy. It seemed that we were in a dream, watching the boat nearing the shore, and the passengers crowding together and shouting for joy. . . . Our feelings were mixed: we were overjoyed, yet fearful of what lay ahead, and we were thoroughly disgusted with our "well-wishers" who have left the remnants of our people to fend for themselves. We will never forget the proud entry of a boat filled with Jews saved by the efforts of Jews after our "sympathizers" had announced that all possible steps had been taken to advance the rescue effort. Let the Milka bear witness to the sin of neglect on the part of the "enlightened" world. . . .

Among the tens of thousands of letters and documents in the archives of the Bureau there is a note signed by Danny expressing his and his colleagues' great joy:

We are writing this note one hour after the second arrival of the Milka with emigrants aboard. Although we have often met with setbacks, our work has not been in vain. We only hope that we will have enough time to save greater and greater numbers. . . .

The reply from underground headquarters, of May 3, 1944, reads:

Congratulations to you and to us! As we see it, it is quite possible that the exodus will continue. We feel certain that you, as well as we, can draw only one conclusion: to take the fullest possible advantage of the slight opening that now exists. . . .

The letter concludes with specific instruction:

Rent any boat that can be used to carry people. . . . It seems that the authorities there are not standing in your way. Therefore—forward!

The Milka was the first of eight small wooden vessels (weighing 300 to 400 tons each) from the Balkan countries that, in spite of the sea blockade, brought Jews to Istanbul, thus saving them from banishment and death. Within ten months' time (March—December, 1944) 7,790 people were rescued in this fashion. The names of the boats were Milka, Mariza, Kazbak, Marina, Bulbul, Mafkura, Salah-ad-Din, and Taurus. The first two boats made two trips apiece.

Eight thousand is a very small number when weighed against the multitudes who were exterminated. However, it is impossible to describe what their rescue meant to the handful of people who had labored so diligently to bring it about. And they were not alone in their rejoicing. Unofficial reports of the rescue boats circulated on both sides of the fighting front. The Yishuv was overjoyed. Eliezer Kaplan, then treasurer of the Jewish Agency, visited Istanbul and author-

ized the young men to spend whatever amounts they deemed
to be necessary. The principal representatives of the "Joint,"
who were also summoned to Istanbul to engage in rescue
activities, at first refrained from working with the Bureau,
and instead supported the efforts of their local representatives to come to agreements with Turkish shipping companies. However, after they witnessed the arrival of the
Kazbak, with 735 passengers packed aboard, they too lent
their support to the effort. The emissaries were also aided
by President Roosevelt's personal ambassador for rescue
efforts, A. Hirschman, who arrived in Istanbul in the
summer of 1944, with a great deal of authority and having at
his disposal the machinery of the American deputation. At
the start, he tried to arrange for the Red Cross to sponsor a
ship. However, he quickly learned that such a plan was im-
practicable and that the only realistic program was the one
being carried out by "the boys."

In a letter sent from Istanbul to the Histadrut Executive,
during the darkest hours of the Yishuv and European Jewry,
the young men wrote:

"We have had only two rays of light: the boats that we
were able to get from Rumania." The rest of the letter
speaks of their attempts to re-establish contact with Hungary
and Slovakia.

The emissaries' activities at the time were not confined
strictly to emigration matters. Being so close to what was
happening in the Balkans, they tried to interest Palestinian
headquarters in the problem of the Jews in Russian-
conquered areas. There were Jews stranded in Trans-
Dniestria and its environs, in Chernovtsy, in Bucovina, and
in Bessarabia, many of them Zionists and pioneers with
whom the emissaries in Istanbul kept in contact. Some of
them had immigration certificates. The emissaries felt that

if negotiations could be carried out between international institutions and the Russian authorities, these people might be allowed to emigrate to Palestine.

The base in Istanbul was also important, therefore, in that it enabled the Yishuv, to the degree that war conditions permitted, to obtain accurate information about what was going on in the Balkan countries.

The group in Istanbul came to feel that they had to keep trying to organize the exodus of Jews via the sea. Although all the ports in Bulgaria were under Nazi control, the situation in Rumania was not quite so bad. The program that they devised entailed getting permission to sail in neutral Turkish ships to Istanbul. While Turkey did not permit her ships to leave her territorial waters, there was a chance that she would change her policy if the United States would guarantee to replace any ships lost in such an undertaking. There was no hope of utilizing Rumanian ships at that time, since the entire Rumanian fleet was being used by the Nazis to evacuate the Crimea.

The group made efforts to obtain Swedish and Portuguese ships. Neutral Swedish ships then sailed the seas, bringing food to hungry Greece. However, these were cargo ships, and the Red Cross would not allow them to be used to transport people. Another thing that created difficulties for the effort was the Red Cross regulation that no vessel weighing less than 1,000 tons would be sponsored by that body. At that time every available boat was small and did not measure up to these requirements. The emissaries were finally forced to buy old wooden Bulgarian boats, and at exhorbitant prices too.

Again, mishaps occurred that made it more difficult for the emissaries to operate. On June 2, 1944, Reuters reported the sinking of the Mariza after it had left Istanbul and was heading back to Constanta in order to take on another group of refugees. Even though the boat was old and very small, its loss constituted a heavy blow to the effort.

The greatest disaster was the sinking of the Mafkura on August 5, 1944, with 359 Jewish refugees on board, as it was making its way from Constanta to Istanbul in the company of two other ships, the Bulbul and the Marina. The entire convoy comprised 1,079 people.

The story behind the sinking of the Mafkura has not been wholly verified to this day, and perhaps it never will be. The only witnesses, five passengers who survived the disaster, told of two or three German submarines that had appeared in front of the ship suddenly and sunk it with automatic cannon fire. One of the survivors, Amalia Lederer, said in her account:

> . . . Everyone went berserk. No one knew what was happening. The ship was lit up with searchlights. I was standing on the deck, next to the railing. . . . Not far from our ship I saw a German submarine, which was shining the light that was blinding our eyes. Suddenly a terrible, deafening noise and a blinding flash blotted out everything, and the ship fell apart at once. . . .
>
> I was thrown a great distance into the water by the force of the blast. As I began swimming I hit a board— a fragment of the ship—and held on to it. Voices were crying out for help all around me, but they were soon silenced. Heads sank beneath the surface. Burning fragments of the ship floated about on the waves. In the distance I saw the Bulbul, whole and sound. The waves swept me toward the undamaged vessel. . . .
>
> I suddenly became aware of barking dogs approaching from the direction of the German submarine. At

first I thought that they had been sent to help us, but I became terrified when I saw that they were blood-hounds who had been lowered for one purpose: to attack us and prevent the rescue of all who had not drowned.

The waves swept over me as my hands clutched at a rope thrown from the Bulbul. At that same moment, one of the dogs which swam toward me caught up with me. The people holding on to the rope on the ship's deck began to pull me up as the dog sank his sharp teeth into my heel. In another minute I was hauled up on deck where I collapsed, unconscious. . . .

The young men in Istanbul were stunned. This was the worst sea disaster that had directly involved one of their vessels. Not since the days of the Patria had they known such distress and painful soul searching. On top of every-thing else the Bulbul was damaged by a storm and found refuge in a bay along the Turkish coast. The passengers, panic-stricken by what they had seen, refused to put to sea again. They were finally brought to Istanbul at great diffi-culty in truck and wagon convoys.

A few days after the disaster, a rescue commission arrived in Istanbul and appointed a committee, whose job it was to investigate the details of the disaster and its causes in order to squelch false rumors and prevent further complications, as there were various elements who wished to use the incident to discredit the entire rescue effort and those active in it. The committee did what it could and enlisted the aid of an independent maritime expert, but they were unable to add anything substantial to the reports of the survivors. The committee report established that the captain had been thoroughly incapable of protecting the ship and had been the first to leave; he and four other crew members had saved

themselves in the lifeboat. Scores of people jumped overboard but were shot in the water by Nazi rifles and submachine guns. All the others were either burned to death or
sank with the ship.

In the Mafkura file in the archives of the Immigration
Bureau there is a document translated from Rumanian
(August 8, 1944) stamped "Top Secret." It contains a coded
message of the Rumanian-German Communications Bureau
which could possibly shed some light on the circumstances
that led to the disaster. The message intimates that the group
on board the ship contained revolutionary partisan forces—
Poles and Serbo-Croatians—whom "the Jews, through their
emigration network, are continuing to send to the Allies in
the Near East." The document lists six names and says of
them: "We have established that the persons listed below
are on board the Mafkura, leaving Constanta, and were
taken on board with papers forged for them by Jewish
partisan movements camouflaged as emigration organizations. . . . In accordance with the orders we have been
given, we will let them sail, in order not to alert the
suspected parties. However, we have informed the appropriate counterespionage department of the coast guard, so that
they might do what is necessary. . . ."

The emissaries relied upon this document in demanding
an international investigation of this tragic episode. In a
letter to "Artzi" ("my country," the pseudonym for headquarters in Palestine) from "Meir" (the band of emissaries
in Istanbul), dated August 12, the disheartened and shaken
young men wrote:

> It is not necessary to tell you what impels us to keep
> on working as vigorously as ever in spite of the terrible
> catastrophe. . . . The representatives of the Yishuv's
> institutions as well as the "Joint" people and the

19. THE GREEK COAST WAS RICH IN WELL CONCEALED HARBORS.

American Committee for Refugees all feel as we do and are prepared to give us their full cooperation so that we can continue our program, which holds out hope for thousands. We deeply regret that there is no alternative at present. . . .

They continued in their work, fully aware that to stop at that point would be tantamount to bringing the rescue effort to a permanent halt. After the Mafkura disaster, the Salah-ad-Din brought 547 refugees to Palestine in November of 1944, and the Taurus, 958 in December of that year.

At the end of December, however, activities in Istanbul were terminated abruptly. The British Government, appalled at the sudden influx of Jews into Palestine, nullified the Cranborne Declaration. The Turkish authorities immediately informed their police outposts on the land and sea borders that Jews were no longer to be allowed to enter Turkey without special visas. The first people to be affected by this new ruling were 700 refugees who arrived at the Turkish border a few short hours after the order was put into effect. They were forced to return to Bulgaria.

So it came about that the sea route was closed once more. The emissaries of the Istanbul base can be credited with the rescue of 842 Greek Jews—312 in 1943 and 530 in 1944— out of thousands sent to extermination in the death convoys. At that time, when the borders could scarcely have been guarded more closely, as much effort and energy were expended in saving one life as went into rescuing a large group in more "normal" times. The rescued people trickled into Istanbul a few at a time, arriving in the small boats of Greek fishermen.

The Greek coast, rich in harbors so well concealed that even the sharp-eyed Nazi patrols could not detect them, provided hiding places for the boats of experienced sailors and fishermen of the Greek resistance movement, who worked in the ranks of the Allied underground. The young men of the Bureau, in their search for rescue methods, reached agreements with the captains of these small boats, first in connection with the transfer of letters and funds, and later in connection with transporting people. The representatives of the Allied forces that employed the boats did not even know to what uses they were being put. A small island about one hour's distance from Izmir served as a starting point. Through the aid of Shabtai Shaltiel, head of the Jewish community of Izmir, contact was made with a Greek captain who worked for the British Intelligence and with his two assistants. After lengthy negotiation, he agreed to smuggle Jews out of the country at a price of six gold Turkish pounds per adult, and two pounds per child.

So began the effort to which Agami in particular devoted himself. At first one boat was sent on a trial run. Soon a smoothly functioning system was in operation. After a while, similar arrangements were worked out with boat owners employed by the Americans. A boat built to hold ten people would take on twice and even three times that number; one even took on 37 passengers for one trip. Contact was established with a Jewish merchant in Athens, and he served as a coordinator. The emigrants would leave Athens by bus and would arrive at the shore opposite the island of Euboea. There a motor boat that had been purchased by the Bureau waited to convey them from the shore to the island. On the island they were transported by hired trucks or carts from the western side to the eastern, to the encampment of a partisan brigade which helped the refugees and in exchange were given food and medicine by the young men. This arrangement was mutually beneficial and the Greeks expressed their gratitude to the emissaries from Palestine in official letters still in the archives of the Bureau.

The effort continued for ten months. Moshe Agami made ten visits to Izmir and spent one week there each time. He would come with the gold in his possession and would wait at night in remote corners of the city to meet secretly with the Greeks. Later, Saul continued these visits.

There were instances of extraordinarily humane treatment of Jews on the part of the Greeks. There were men among them who worked with the emissaries not merely out of self-interest. One such was the tall Captain Frangolis, who was genuinely interested in the fate of the Jews. He befriended the men of the Hebrew underground and frequently invited them to his house in Izmir. The small, warm Jewish community of Izmir did its best to provide food and lodging for the refugees who came to the island.

The Turkish authorities were highly displeased with the whole affair and opened fire on the boats on more than one occasion. However, United States officials intervened on behalf of the refugees. The American Ambassador in Ankara, Laurence A. Steinhardt, was especially sympathetic and understanding. The attitude of the British and American newsmen, however, was another thing entirely. After a while it became impossible to deceive them with stories of strange groups of Jewish refugees who "just happened to arrive" on the coast. The newsmen realized that a guiding hand was at work behind the scenes.

Through the offices of A. Hirschman, President Roosevelt's personal envoy for the rescue effort, the Americans in 1944 proposed joint activity. Moshe Agami left for Izmir with Hirschman's assistant in order to meet with the representatives of the American Information Service, to make the necessary arrangements. However, on the next day, he

received a telegram calling him back to Istanbul at once :
"Red Army has entered Bulgaria."

At the same time that the emigration base in Istanbul was renewed, the foundations were laid for another headquarters operated by only two emissaries, Venia Pomerantz (Zeev Hadari) and Menahem Bader. Their goal was to establish links with persons behind the enemy lines and to help the persecuted Jews there. At that time, the Jewish community of Istanbul, as well as the Yishuv in Palestine, did not know what to make of the frightful reports that came in from beyond the front lines. There were no established lines of communication with Jewish centers in Europe. The Jews in Nazi-dominated lands were completely cut off from the outside world.

The ominous rumors were verified in a letter from Rumania smuggled into Istanbul via the Balkans by a Swiss citizen. The letter, which described conditions that seemed utterly incredible, was circulated widely, and gave direction to the emissaries' efforts. They realized that the first thing they had to do was establish way stations leading to Poland in Rumania, Slovakia, and especially Hungary, which until March 26, 1944, did not come under the full control of the Nazis. They began looking for messengers to transport letters and gold. The envoys were, for the most part, Hungarians who worked for the Nazis and who, for large sums of money, also served the Jewish underground organizations. They would slip across borders and military checking points bringing urgent pleas for help and they would return with information and gold. On March 2, 1943, Venia reported to his colleagues in Palestine :

> We hired a messenger this week and sent him off on a
> trip to Sofia, Bucharest, Budapest, Bratislava, and

20. The Jews in Nazi-dominated lands were completely cut off from the outside world.

other places that he will visit on his way back. We gave him letters to deliver to the people in the above-mentioned places, including brief reports on what has been going on in Palestine. We wrote to Bratislava primarily concerning possibilities of sending medical supplies to Poland.

This letter contains the first hint of negotiating for the rescue of the Jews of Hungary:

We have also requested that they inform you at once about the suggestions concerning a go-between. As you know, this idea originated in Bratislava. The messenger will return in another month and only then will we get replies to our letters.

Another section of the letter reveals the ultimate goal which the members of the Bureau always strove to attain under all circumstances. Even though no boats were available to them and the sea route was blocked, they did all they could to get the Jews to the coast, in hopes that something might turn up that would make possible their sailing to Palestine. "The coast" was the magic phrase. A motto then popular with the members of the base in Istanbul was: "To lift a man from the seventh level of hell to the fifth."

Every time they managed to effect the transfer of a packet of letters to their contacts in the Balkans, they felt that a small miracle had been accomplished. They would spend hours in making up the packet, cramming together the brief letters that were written on thin paper so that they would not take up too much space and could be hidden on the smugglers' persons. On more than one occasion the emissaries would all take turns sitting on the packet in order to compress it with the weight of their bodies.

On July 17, 1943, their envoy came from Theresienstadt, having succeeded in getting to Bendin (Bandsburg), in Upper

Silesia, bringing with him the first letter to the emissaries from the Bureau representatives in that area. The letter was signed by the leaders of the pioneer youth movement, including Fruma Plotinitska of Hehalutz headquarters in Poland.

"When this letter reaches you—we will no longer be alive . . ." So begins one of the noblest and most tragic documents of Jewish history of our time. The letter, addressing itself to "the headquarters in Istanbul and to all our friends, wherever they may be" expresses the writers' "great joy" in being able to communicate for the first time since the outbreak of the war with their movement friends after years of hoping in vain, and describes the life they led and the struggle that they carried on.

The tale begins at the outset of the war with the organization of a large network of training farms and youth movements; both were stronger and more numerous then than during the preceding period of peace. In short order, however, the letter begins to describe the Nazi genocide with all its horrors. It tells of 80,000 Jews poisoned by gas in Lodz and of the extermination of the Jews of Lithuania who were shot down in Punari. The letter proudly tells of "the glorious chapter in our struggle"—the Warsaw rebellion. The gentile envoy, stirred by the magnanimity of the group of young Hehalutz leaders, offered to smuggle Fruma and a few of her friends out of the country, but they refused, saying: "We choose to die with our brothers."

On August 6 of that year, a letter was sent from Istanbul to the Histadrut Executive in Tel Aviv, signed by Venia (Hadari), Menahem (Bader), and Danny (Shind), unfolding the entire tragic episode:

> . . . That our messengers have finally broken through to Poland is a very encouraging development.

We could give you a lengthy account of the great difficulties that this involved, but we will leave such matters
for more peaceful times. On Tuesday our messenger
will set out once again, and this time he has promised to
reach Warsaw and Lwow too. We have the addresses
of two "Christians"—these being our friends with
assumed names—who are hiding in those two cities.
This arrangement will enable our messenger to accomplish his mission. We have recently been informed by
our other messenger, who smuggles money into Poland
for us, that an appreciable amount of money was given
to our friends. . . . We cannot know how many of
our brothers still remain in Poland. The last letter from
Bandsburg and Cracow is a tragic, first-hand verifica-
tion of the reports that have reached us thus far of the
number of survivors in Poland. We now know that
there are almost no Jewish children remaining in that
country. We now know that many of the ghettos no
longer exist, but nevertheless, we who are here, you
who are in Palestine, and our friends who are in the
United States and in the rest of the free world, must
not lose hope. We must strengthen the resolve of those
who are proudly holding their own in the ghettos of
Poland.

The members of the Bureau took an active part in the
complex and ill-fated negotiations between Eichmann and
the Jewish delegation in Istanbul concerning the exchange of
1,000,000 Hungarian Jews for 10,000 trucks. Only twenty-
four hours after Joel Brand arrived from Hungary in a
special plane, accompanied by a Gestapo officer, Venia
Hadari arrived in Palestine to report to David Ben-Gurion
and Moshe Shertok (Sharett) and to take part in the confer-
ences of the institutions of the Yishuv. Sharett flew to

London and met with the heads of the British Government. Anthony Eden said to him:

"What will we do with a million Jews?"

Sharett replied heatedly:

"Will you stand by and let them be sent to the ovens?"

Accompanied by Saul Avigur, Sharett hurried to Aleppo, the place British Intelligence had chosen to meet with Brand. The members of the Immigration Bureau stood by expectantly. A million Jews! However, it was not long before they learned that the entire transaction had fallen through.

When all efforts proved futile, the emissaries once more returned to their wearisome and dangerous everyday tasks. At times they looked upon themselves as people trying to break through walls with their bare hands. They were particularly disturbed by the intense factionalism that divided the Zionist youth movements, including the Hehalutz pioneer youth movements, with whom they stood in a special relationship. No matter what dangers and calamities befell them, each movement retained its own framework, almost until the very last moment before their annihilation. Even among the handful of emissaries in Istanbul who singly and together underwent the greatest dangers and risked their very lives in the service of the rescue effort, tensions arose due to differences in party affiliation.

Then, one morning, on August 26, 1944, as the young men of 48 Istiklal Street were walking toward the railroad station with one of their number who was to return to Palestine to confer with leaders there, someone ran into the street and yelled:

"The Russians have crossed the Black Sea; Rumania is liberated . . ."

At once they knew that they had to leave the country.

16

Meeting the Ghetto Fighters

On September 14, Venia Hadari, posing as a reporter for the "Jewish Telegraphic Agency," left Istanbul and headed for Bulgaria, which had been liberated only five days before. His first destination was the Svilengrad station on the Turkish-Bulgarian border. As far as the Jews of the Balkans were concerned, Svilengrad at that time was the boundary-line between torture and freedom, between life and death.

The young men of the Istanbul base were prepared to risk their lives in an attempt to open up that border no matter how slightly. For a long time they had kept contact, through letters, with some Jewish survivors behind the enemy lines and had ardently desired to meet their anonymous correspondents face to face; now one of them was finally headed for Svilengrad.

The entire group accompanied Venia to the railroad station in Istanbul, only to discover at the last minute that in the excitement of the departure, he had left his reporter's identification papers back at their quarters. Moshe Agami, who had just returned that day from Greece, grabbed a taxi, hurried back and got the papers, and overtook the train at the next station, outside the city. In the interim Saul reiterated to Venia the necessity of concentrating on the practical goal of his mission—getting Jews to the border at once. It stood to reason that in the confusion and tumult of the first days of the Russian occupation, at least a few thousand Jews could be saved.

Venia crossed the border on September 15, arriving in Sofia just as the liberating army of 100,000 men, with their commanding General Tolbochin at their head, entered the city with shouts of victory. The population was hungry, cold and half-naked, and the city was partially destroyed. In one section of Sofia the hands of all the clocks pointed to 12:45, at which time a terrific blast must have occurred. In another section, all hands pointed to three o'clock. The hotel had no water and there were no panes in the windows. The emissary hurried to the slum section of Ich-Bonar ("Three Wells") where the Jewish ghetto was located, and there met barefoot, ragged, and abandoned children, but no Jews. The city was jubilant—and there were no Jews. That night he hurried to Varna and there met a Russian officer who revealed to him that there were no Jews left in Odessa, either.

The first thing that Venia did was to search for ships. However, he soon learned the futility of this endeavor, as the entire Bulgarian navy had been sunk by the Nazis. His second project was opening up an escape route across the border so that Jews from Rumania might get through. Two days after his arrival in Sofia he appeared with a reporters' delegation before the Bulgarian Propaganda Minister Kassof, and asked him point blank what was the attitude of the new regime toward the emigration of Jews to Palestine. The minister replied by reading a statement to the effect that Jews were to have equal rights with all other citizens and were invited to return to Sofia from their hiding places and places of exile. He added that he would not oppose Jewish emigration to Palestine.

On the day following this official proclamation, Jews began to gather together and come to the capital. The country was in an anarchic state. An Allied commission was in charge of everything, but had no address and so could not be contacted. Even as the young Communists began to raise the cry of freedom and liberty, the Government began drafting Jews into the armed forces.

In the midst of this pandemonium the first group of emigrants left for the border. However, that very night a message was dispatched from Istanbul stating that the British had nullified the decree giving Jewish refugees the right to enter Palestine, and that the Turkish Government had accordingly withdrawn the right of transit to would-be emigrants. One group of 800 to 900 refugees, who had left Rumania by train, reached Bulgaria and were detained one month in the railroad cars.

Venia was cut off from Palestine as well as from the base in Istanbul, and had to make decisions independently and swiftly. It was not long before he left for Yugoslavia at a time when that country had not yet been completely liberated and the Hungarian border was still a military front. On December 18 he set out in a truck of the Macedonian Brigade and after a series of adventures he arrived in Nish and Skoplje. Upon asking a passerby where he could find the Jewish quarter he was directed to a clean and quiet street, where curtains covered all the windows as if the people behind them were sleeping peacefully. However, every house that he entered was empty and desolate.

Heavy-hearted, he continued his journey in a train that had no windows or water. Seated near him were a group of partisans, young men and women traveling barefoot in the December cold. Upon his arrival in Belgrade he was stopped and was asked incredulously:

"How in the world did you ever get here?"

Presenting his journalist's identification papers, he asked to see Tito at once, and was told to report to the Ministry of Propaganda on the following day. The problem of where he would spend the night then arose. He asked for directions to the building of the Jewish Community Council, only to learn that it had been converted into a hospital. He finally met the head of the Council, who, although he had not been executed like his colleagues, seemed only half-alive.

On the following day Venia met with Moshe Pijade, the leader of the Communist Party in Yugoslavia, and a Jew. Pijade sat in his room, surrounded by a large library wherein his own translations of Lenin stood out prominently on the shelves. They spoke for hours in Russian. The well-educated and assimilated Jew showed no interest whatever in Jews and Jewish problems. When the Palestinian "journalist" asked him whether survivors of the holocaust would be allowed to emigrate to Palestine, he answered evasively:

"I realize that this is the crucial question . . ."

In reply to another question that hinted at the idea of settling the remnants of the Jewish people, including the Jews of Yugoslavia, in Palestine, he said:

"The Fascists tortured me not as a Jew but as a Communist. . . ."

Finally the emissary played his last card and said:

"I am an officer in the Hebrew underground movement; we are fighting the British Government."

The Communist leader replied:

"I'm tired now; come back in two days and we'll talk some more."

"But I have no permit to stay here."

"I'll see to it that you'll be able to stay here for two or three days."

Before he left, Venia repeated a question which troubled him greatly and which his host had not answered:

"Whatever happened to the volunteers of the underground from Palestine who parachuted into Yugoslavia in military uniform and were never heard of again?"

"Only the general can answer that question for you," said Pijade wearily.

This conversation marked the beginning of a new relationship between the Hagana underground on the one hand and Moshe Pijade and Yugoslavia on the other. The relationship was continued the following year when Venia was replaced by Ehud Avriel.

The story of the Hebrew parachutists is one of the most dramatic chapters in the history of Yishuv bravery during the Second World War. Plans for the parachutist project crystallized over the years. The young men began to speak of the plan when they first heard of the Nazi genocide, and fervently hoped that they would be able to implement it. After long and wearisome negotiations between the Political Department of the Jewish Agency and the underground forces of the British Army, the parachutists were selected from among hundreds of the best of the Yishuv's youth, who almost literally beat upon the doors of the Hagana offices to volunteer for the dangerous mission. The volunteers for the most part came from the Balkan countries and eastern and central Europe, and as children had become familiar with the terrain of the occupied regions as well as with the languages and customs of the people. Finally, after long delay, 32 young Hagana members, including three women, were dropped by British Intelligence behind enemy lines into Slovakia, the Balkans, and northern Italy, as the war was drawing to a close. They came at a very late date, almost during the last stage of the Nazi extermination program, but they nevertheless accomplished much by bolstering Jewish morale, organizing resistance, and rescuing Jews. Seven of them did not return.

Many groups were responsible for carrying out the program—the Political Department of the Jewish Agency, which cleared the path for the project; branches of the Hagana and the Palmach, which selected the volunteers and gave them the requisite military training; and the Immigration Bureau, which organized the effort, prepared the parachutists, and sent them on their way.

David Hacohen, Reuben Shiloah, and others representing the Jewish Agency and the Hagana, and emissaries of the Bureau in Istanbul took part in the last stages of the negotiations with British Intelligence in regard to the project. Commander Wolfsohn, officially a naval adjutant at the British Consulate in Istanbul but actually in charge of one of the Intelligence services of the Allied Forces, turned to Eliahu Epstein (Elath), the Jewish Agency's official representative in Istanbul, and suggested joint activity with the underground of the pioneer youth movements in the countries occupied by the Nazis. The Intelligence officer revealed to Eliahu that for a long time he had been following closely the undercover activities of Zvi Yehieli and Danny Shind, the two young men in Istanbul who were active in sending Jews to Palestine illegally, and that he was aware of their telephone conversations with parties in enemy territory, which were technically illegal.

The night that followed this discussion the two emissaries had a difficult decision to make. Hour after hour they debated with themselves and with each other as to what course they should follow. They realized that by going before the British they would be walking into the lion's den, so to speak, but they decided it was worth the risk, since there was a fair chance that it would lead to the rescue of Jewish lives.

The next morning the two men nervously entered the offices of British Intelligence. They had decided that if the meeting should give rise to a plausible suggestion, one of them would return to Palestine at once to confer with their colleagues. Wolfsohn was polite and friendly. He explained that he was in charge of Intelligence and of rescuing and aiding wounded or captured British pilots who had landed behind enemy lines.

The young men emphasized that they were primarily concerned with rescuing Jews, and that they were not willing to become involved in activities that might endanger their underground network. Wolfsohn explained that the interests of both the British and the Hagana could be served. He suggested the possibility of smuggling emissaries of the Hagana underground behind enemy lines by ship, train, and even submarines. At that time no one even dared suggest parachuting.

Zvi Yehieli returned to Palestine to find the Yishuv's representatives at loggerheads with the representatives of British Intelligence, and the Bureau's members debating heatedly as to whether or not the British offer to engage in joint activities was to be trusted. In the end they decided that Zvi would leave for Cairo with Reuven Shiloah, and there meet with Colonel Tony Simonds, a friend and student of Orde Wingate. At that meeting the matter was settled and terms were laid down. It was agreed that the parachutists' tasks would be to get in contact with partisan groups, to organize intelligence, and to help in the rescue of Jews and escaping Allied prisoners of war.

On October 1, 1943, the first two emissaries, wearing British uniforms, jumped into Rumania—Lyova Gokovsky, a member of kibbutz Yagur, and Arye Fichman, a member of kibbutz Bet Oren. They had been instructed to say, in the event of capture, that they were air force officers whose plane had been damaged.

On the night preceding their flight, the two men walked along the banks of the Nile. Zvi, who as soon as he had heard of the formation of the parachutists group, began to study Red Cross regulations concerning prisoners of war, tried to explain to Lyova precisely how to behave the moment his foot touched enemy soil. Lyova had trained himself to use the compass that was disguised as a button on his sleeve, but Zvi pointed out how dangerous that would be, as the light of the luminous dial might give his position away, and that he would be better off relying on the stars. As they walked, Zvi began explaining to his companion the position of the North Star, which was always a reliable guide. For a moment Lyova paid close attention, then burst out suddenly:

"What is this—the boy scouts? Am I going to summer camp or something?"

Later, Lyova jumped straight into the arms of the Rumanian police, breaking his leg in the process. Nevertheless, within two days time, and in spite of the fact that he was being carefully guarded, he succeeded in contacting the Jewish underground youth movement through a non-Jewish nurse in the hospital where he was being kept.

In March of 1944 the second group of parachutists set out, consisting of Reuven Dafni, Hanna Szenes, Abba Berditchev, and Yona Rosenfeld. They jumped into Slavonia, worked very effectively with Tito's partisans, and then infiltrated Rumania and Hungary. In May of that year they were joined by more parachutists.

The very fact of their appearance among the masses of downtrodden and persecuted Jews, who were on the threshhold of despair, heartened the people considerably. In the short period of time that they worked in the underground during the Nazi regime, they managed to imbue the people with the Zionist faith and to organize emigration to Palestine. After their arrival in the different countries the members of the local Zionist centers would express their opinions in every important matter in the name of "The Voice of Jerusalem"—which was to say, the voice of the Hebrew parachutists from Palestine.

The 32 parachutists were chosen from 250 volunteers. One hundred and seventy of them were trained for the role and were prepared to set out on the dangerous mission, and many others were in the process of volunteering, when the war ended. The few emissaries who did get to their destination were oppressed with the thought of how many more lives they could have saved had they arrived sooner. But while their achievement was small statistically, it bolstered Jewish morale and Jewish pride the world over.

Seven did not return.

Hanna Szenes, born in Budapest on July 7, 1921, was a member of kibbutz Sdot Yam, near Caesarea. She flew from Bari on March 14, 1944, and was dropped into Yugoslavia with orders to cross the Hungarian border and get to Budapest. On June 9, three months after Hungary was taken over by the Germans, she set out for the Hungarian border, but did not reach her destination. She was captured, imprisoned, and tortured in Budapest, and finally shot on November 7, 1944. She endured her torments courageously, refusing to explain the code book that she had in her possession or to betray her mission in any other way, even when she was put to a vicious ordeal in the presence of her own mother. Prior to her death, she wrote, among other things, the poem "Blessed is the Match."

Enzo (Haim) Sereni, born in Rome in April, 1905, was a member of kibbutz Givat Brenner, a leader of the Bureau, and an organizer of the parachuting project. In the face of the sharp opposition of the majority of the members at headquarters, he insisted upon participating in the dangerous venture. In spite of his age and the fact that he had a wife and three children, he felt obligated to go, both as a Jew and as a socialist. "A person who enlists others has to be ready to enlist himself," he maintained. On May 15, 1944, he left by plane for the Nazi-occupied territory in northern Italy together with an Italian officer, and there was taken prisoner. He gave hope to the tortured Jews in the concentration camps where he lived and suffered. He was killed in Dachau on November 18, 1944.

Peretz Goldstein, born in a small town in Transylvania on July 24, 1923, was a member of the youth group in kibbutz Afikim. On April 13, 1944, he jumped into Yugoslavia with Yoel Palgi. After he spent two months there with partisan groups he went on to Hungary. He met his parents in a camp of Jews who were about to be sent to Palestine via Spain. He would have joined them, but his companion had been captured and he stayed behind to help free him. In the end, however, he himself was captured. He was sent to Germany and was last heard of in the Oranienburg camp in December of 1944.

Haviva Reik, born in Slovakia in June, 1914, was a member of kibbutz Ma'anit. She was flown from Bari on September 20, 1944, her destination being an area that held a concentration of Jewish partisans and refugees: Banska-Bystrica in the Carpathian Mountains in Slovakia. She set up a broadcasting station in a nearby village and contacted the high command of the Allied underground. After a few days her parachutist colleagues arrived and together they began to work with Jews who had been liberated by the partisans from the concentration camps. They organized them in a fighting Jewish unit.

Raphael (Rafi) Reiss, born in Budapest in 1914, and a member of kibbutz Hulyot, and Zvi Ben-Yaakov, born in Bratislava in 1922, and a member of kibbutz Hahotrim, were dropped into German-occupied Slovakia a few days before Haviva Reik, on the night of September 14. After a nine-day journey on foot that included many narrow escapes, they reached the partisan encampment in the Slovakian Carpathians. There they met survivors of pioneer youth movements and other Jews who had come there from near and far. Some had escaped from concentration camps and prisons, and others had jumped off death trains. They gathered around Haviva Reik and Abba Berditchev (the latter arrived in late September), both of whom had brought weapons, medicine, and money in a plane of the Allied underground. Every two days a British plane would pass over the camp and drop food to the partisans and the Jewish fighting unit headed by the five Palestinian parachutists, who, along with the British major who accompanied them, were the local representatives of the British Intelligence. After their first efforts at organizing the refugees met with success, the parachutists set up a network of way stations from Poland to Slovakia, to expedite the escape of prisoners and pilots of the Allied underground.

Haviva, Rafi, and Zvi were captured when the temporary camp of the Jewish resistance unit which they led was attacked by the Nazis. Haviva and Rafi were executed in Krynica at the end of November, 1944. It seems most likely that Zvi was executed at the end of December. Only one of the group remained alive—Haim Hermesh.

Abba Berditchev, born in December, 1918 in Galati, Rumania, came to Palestine as an illegal immigrant, and was one of many who were kept in the Atlit prison for one and a half years. On March 14, 1944, he left Bari by plane with Szenes and her friends, and was dropped into Yugoslavia. His task was to reach Rumania via Hungary. However, since the Nazis had taken over Hungary in the meantime, it was decided that he should try to reach Rumania directly. He got as far as the Papuk Mountains, but at that point was turned back by the British agents who were his superior officers. He worked as a wireless operator in Yugoslavia and gathered Allied fliers together in partisan areas. In August of 1944 he returned to Bari. He was offered the opportunity to leave the service, but he chose to go on another mission. At the end of September, 1944, he was sent to Banska-Bystrica with three radios for his parachutist friends, who had already arrived there. On October 18 he set out for the Hungarian border, driving a truck that concealed a British sergeant and a major. Near the Polish border in northern Slovakia they were caught by a Nazi patrol, and on January 15, 1945, he was executed in Bratislava.

The Jewish parachutists arrived in Rumania in the darkest days of that country's Jewry. The Rumanian Government had decided to stop fighting. The Germans became aware of this and the Jews expected to be wiped out at the last moment, as had been the case with Hungarian Jewry. The Jewish population was terror-stricken, particularly those Jews who had stolen across the border from Hungary. The parachutists decided that they would have to rescue the Hungarian Jews first.

From the very outset of their work, the emissaries noticed the pathetic factionalism of the pioneer youth movements, even during the periods of greatest adversity. Each movement concerned itself solely with its own members. The first

21. ANY JEW CAUGHT TRYING TO GET ACROSS THE BORDER WAS TO BE SHOT.

task that the parachutists set for themselves, therefore, was the fusion of the rescue organizations in Rumania and Hungary.

They worked through messengers who took their instructions to Budapest and managed to return safely. The groups of refugees leaving Hungary began to arrive without mishap, with few exceptions, and even though only a few thousand people were saved in this fashion, it gave some comfort to the Hungarian Jews, who in the course of a few months had suffered at the Nazis' hands what the Jews of Poland had undergone in a period of years.

The parachutists also gave their attention to organizing a Jewish resistance effort, no matter how small, and to getting together a small supply of weapons for such time as it should be needed. When the Germans bombed Bucharest, in the period between the surrender of Rumania and the entrance of the Red Army into the city, young Jews organized themselves and fought back with these weapons. Even though a genuine program did not develop, the fact that the various groups were brought into one organization was in itself encouraging. The youth movements now gathered about the parachutists, who worked secretly and indirectly through the few people who knew their true identity.

Two parachutists, N. and M. were dropped on the Hungarian-Rumanian border in the spring of 1944. After undergoing many hardships, they managed to arrive at the courtyard of a synagogue of the Jewish community in a Rumanian village. The emissaries were driven by one burning desire—to get to Bucharest and begin their work at once. But that presented a problem, as Jews were forbidden to ride the trains. While the genocide program had not yet been initiated in Rumania, according to the emergency laws any Jew caught trying to get across the border was to be shot. Furthermore, their very appearance was enough to get them in trouble—being healthy young men, how would they be able to explain why they were not at the front?

After they became somewhat familiar with the area, N. learned that in that same courtyard, young men and women of pioneer youth movements were arranging to send secretly to Bucharest those few Jews who had saved themselves and had somehow infiltrated the country from Hungary. N. naively believed that he would now encounter no difficulty in getting to Bucharest. Upon learning which young man was in charge of pioneer youth movements' rescue effort, he went to see him and introduced himself as a Jewish refugee from Hungary; he did not reveal his true identity for security reasons. He was stunned when, upon asking that he be included in the group being sent to Bucharest, he was asked in turn which movement he belonged to.

In this manner he learned of the extreme factionalism that prevailed among the pioneer youth even when the destruction of all of them was imminent.

For eleven days and nights the two parachutists hid in the courtyard, having no way of getting to their destination. One day the wife of the *shamash* (sexton) of the ritual bathhouse attached to the synagogue came to them, frightened, with bad news: on the following day the city was to be searched for two parachutists who had come from across the border. That morning the papers had disclosed that two parachutes had been found in the field, and that anyone giving information leading to the arrest of the two parachutists would be given a big reward. Having no choice, the two men once more turned to the representative of the youth movements and pleaded with him to get them to Bucharest by means of his underground organization; but it was useless. They were forced to devise a scheme that would bring them through the next day safely. They could hit upon nothing better than hiding in the small pool of the ritual bath itself. There they lay in water up to their necks from six in the morning to nine at night; every so often the *shamash* would quietly walk by and open the transom so that they might not suffocate for lack of air.

The day of the search passed uneventfully. After a few days, the two men went to the railroad station, having made arrangements for which they had been forced to pay exorbitantly, and boarded a car filled with crates of chickens. For 34 hours they traveled without moving, jammed between the crates and the wall of the car.

When they finally arrived at their destination, the first thing that they did was to reveal their identities to the young man who had refused to include them with the other refugees who were to be rescued. He was dumbfounded. The emissaries, in discussing his role with him, explained that Jews could not be rescued on percentage systems, but that every Jew had an equal right to be saved. The young man became one of the very few people who knew their identities, and even he did not know how they had arrived. They even kept their secret from the leaders of the Zionist federation. Only the Zionist leader Zisso, a writer and man of letters who cooperated with them in bringing Jews out of Hungary and in renewing the emigration to Palestine from Rumania, knew their true identity.

At the end of July, 1944, on the eve of the sailing of the three ships, the Bulbul, the Marina, and the Mafkura, word got about that German submarines were cruising around in the Black Sea between Constanta and Istanbul. The leaders of the Zionist underground, headed by Zisso, remembering the Struma tragedy, opposed the ships' sailing in light of the information that they had. The two emissaries from Palestine, however, insisted that the ships sail, maintaining that no one knew what would happen to the Jews of Rumania on the next day. They knew well that the Fuhrer in his visit with Premier Antonescu had taken the latter to task sharply for not having liquidated the Jews of Rumania. Also, on other occasions, Antonescu had boasted of his accomplishment in slaughtering the Jews of Bessarabia, who were not "his," and had said, concerning the fate of "his own" Jews, "We shall see . . ." For these reasons the emissaries maintained their position stubbornly.

When the Zionist leadership of Rumania met to come to a final decision on the sailing of the three ships, the emissaries felt that the future of the effort hung in the balance. They left their hiding place and by taking a roundabout route, arrived at the building where the meeting was being held. N. somehow got in the back door and sent a note to Zisso calling him outside. There he told him that they had received a tele- gram from Ben-Gurion demanding that the ships sail. He also threatened on the spot that if the Zionist leaders should come to a negative decision nevertheless, he and his companion would be forced to reveal their identities and organize the sailing on their own. Zisso was impressed, for he felt responsible for the emissaries' safety and had always looked out for their interests. He hesitated for a minute and returned to the meeting. From behind the door the emissary heard him announce vigorously:

"The ships have to sail before tomorrow!"

When asked what had happened to have made him change his mind, he answered shortly:

"The Voice of Jerusalem."

The ships sailed, and on the next day news was received of the sinking of the Mafkura.

In addition to this being a national tragedy, it was an

especially pathetic individual calamity. The emissary M. had parents in Bucharest. During his four month stay in that city he did not meet with them or make his presence known to them. They received his letters from Istanbul, where they assumed he was living. On the night before the ships were to sail, the emissaries decided that M. should visit his parents and suggest that they take advantage of the opportunity to go to Palestine. That night was the occasion of a heavy attack by American and British bombers. The two emissaries made their way carefully across the city and arrived at the home of the astonished parents. They spent a few hours with them, and on the next morning the elderly couple were on board the Mafkura. As fate would have it, they were among the hundreds of victims who drowned when the ship went down. The son bore his sorrow in silence. He did not stop working and won everyone's admiration by his behavior.

The Mafkura tragedy elicited a widespread reaction of terror. The emissaries began to fear that Jews would no longer be willing to leave the country by sea, and that even the young people might have disturbing second thoughts. Once more they turned to Zisso for help, and convinced him to appear before the Jewish youth publicly and urge them to emigrate to Palestine. At a large youth rally held in the synagogue, Zisso revived the enthusiasm of his listeners, while the emissaries busied themselves with arrangements for another ship to Palestine.

Then, at the very last stage of preparations, a new development arose—the Red Army entered Rumania after a fierce struggle with the Germans. This turning point came at a critical time for the 70,000 people who inhabited the Jewish quarter in Bucharest. The forests surrounding the city concealed Nazi troops who were prepared to annihilate the Jews.

Under the leadership of the two emissaries from Palestine the Jewish youth organized to defend themselves as best they could. When, on the night of August 24, 1944, King Michael announced the overthrow of the Antonescu regime, young Jews stood ready to fight with the meager supply of weapons they had managed to accumulate.

For four days the battle went on around the city. Anti-Fascist cells and Jewish Communists met with representatives of the Zionists and argued that the Jewish youth should come and take part in the fighting, but the emissaries from Palestine replied that the Jewish youth belonged in the Jewish quarter, defending their people.

After the German Army was defeated, and the Red Army, whose lines were only 155 miles away from Bucharest, announced that it would enter the city within three days, representatives of the various Jewish organizations assembled, and at the urging of the Jewish Communists, began preparing a festive welcome for the liberators. At this meeting the representatives of the pioneer youth movements infuriated the Communists by announcing that they would appear with the Zionist flag and slogans.

The procession that took place on the following day turned into a Zionist demonstration the likes of which had never been seen in Rumania. At first only 800 Jewish boys and girls in the various pioneer youth movements appeared on the street, carrying one blue-and-white flag and one motto —"Emigration to Palestine." Soon, however, tens of thousands of Jews began to pour out of their homes and hiding places in the Jewish quarter to join the demonstrators. The procession continued late into the night, with the marchers carrying torches in their hands and spreading over the streets to dance the Palestinian hora.

The emissaries decided to take advantage of the transition

period to send an additional ship from the Russian-occupied area, as all the necessary arrangements had been made. They placed on board the ship hundreds of children from an institution that had already been taken over by the Russians.

In the meantime the emissaries were joined by their colleague, Moshe Agami. In his search for a center of operations, Moshe realized that he would not achieve his goals by continuing to pose as a journalist. He needed an office and the machinery that would enable him to overcome the many obstacles that constantly blocked his path. As luck would have it he learned that the local office of the Red Cross was breaking up, as its Nazi supporters had abandoned it. He compensated the employees generously and set up his own office there. He set to work at once to avoid interference on the part of the Russian authorities. Within a few days, it still being November, 1944, the first ship, the Salah-ad-Din, left for Istanbul with 547 persons aboard. When Moshe saw that the Russians still paid no attention to the matter, he relayed this information to Ehud in Istanbul and urged the latter to bring to a hasty conclusion the negotiations over the acquisition of another and larger vessel with a capacity of 900 tons, and to send it off immediately to take on a second group of refugees. In December the Taurus arrived in Istanbul with 950 persons aboard.

So ended the episode of the eight vessels. The Turkish Government announced that since the Germans were no longer in the Balkans, no refugees from the Balkan countries would be allowed to enter Turkey.

During Moshe Agami's first steps in Rumania something happened that made all the heartaches and troubles that he had endured worthwhile. One day, prior to the sailing of the first boat, a young girl arrived in Bucharest dressed in the uniform of the Soviet Army and, speaking in Hebrew, introduced herself as Rushka. She told Moshe of a group of Jewish partisans in Poland, young members of the labor movement, who had gathered in Chernovtsy and were looking for a way to break out of there and emigrate to Palestine. On the very next day the partisan Rushka was on board the underground vessel headed for Palestine.

This was the Bureau's first contact with Jewish youth from the ghettos of Poland who had taken up arms to fight the enemy. Rushka told again that the idea of active resistance came to the leaders of the pioneer youth immediately after the first mass execution of Jews in Vilna. From the very start it was clear that the Jews were not being taken from the ghetto to work elsewhere, and were not being transferred to a "third ghetto," as the Nazis claimed, but were being conveyed to the "Punar"—an area located five miles outside of the city, set aside for the execution and burial of the Jews of Vilna and the nearby ghettos. The extermination of Jews in this area began in the summer of 1941 and continued on into mid-1944. It is estimated that 80,000 to 100,000 Jews were killed in "Punar."

With the first reports of these executions, the pioneer youth decided that they would not be led as sheep to slaughter, but rather, as conscientious Jews, would do all in their power to take an active part in the fight against the Nazi murderers.

It was not easy to carry out such a decision. They were isolated, far removed from the front, and had no weapons. However, their strong determination gave them the strength to overcome all these difficulties. They broadcast secret messages to the Jewish youth, stating that it was better to die like men than live by kind permission of the despised enemy. Many who heard the broadcast joined the resistance effort, even though it was clear that the final outcome of the struggle could only be the utter annihilation of the underground fighters. However, when the partisan organization was formed, a sudden upsurge of confidence swept over the young people and feverish preparations were secretly gotten underway.

First we had to get weapons, related Rushka. We turned to the Polish underground. In the beginning they promised to help us, but they did not keep their promise. So we waited, isolated and shut up in the ghetto. We stole a few weapons from German supply depots, but we paid dearly with our blood. One day, our members who smuggled the weapons into the ghetto were killed, and on the next day others went to face the same danger. We knew that we had no alternative and that we were doing the right thing. Escaping from the ghetto or forging papers would have saved only a few individuals, but not the masses of the people. We wanted our idea to spread to other ghettos. We sent our first delegation to Warsaw, at a time when Warsaw had not yet thought of organized resistance. We sent people to the Bialystok ghetto and to Ushmina, where the extermination program was going on, to urge the Jews to organize, fight back, and escape to the forests. We felt responsible for the Jewish people, not just for ourselves.

Our first units went to the forests, to the partisans. We escaped through cellars and sewers. In leaving the ghetto we did not think of our own welfare, we did not think we would be able to hide in the forests and save ourselves. We only knew that we had to continue our struggle in surroundings where we could accomplish more than we could in the ghetto, which by then had been completely destroyed. Every one of us left behind him the graves of dear ones. One driving force kept us alive: Revenge! The very name "Revenge!" was later given to the first Jewish fighting brigade that was formed.

Life in the forests was very difficult and dangerous. Every day we were given military tasks—to find the enemy and destroy him wherever possible. And we did as good a job as any of the other partisan brigades. In fact, our members volunteered for the most dangerous missions, without worrying whether or not they were adequately armed. We carried out missions that should have won us the respect and admiration of the non-Jewish partisans. But we had a harder time of it than the others, because we were Jews. We had to fight both the Nazis and the Lithuanian farmers who received weapons from the Nazis and used them against the Jews. On top of everything else, we had to be on guard against nationalist Polish partisans, who wandered about the forests, ostensibly to fight the Germans, but actually to hunt down the Jews. Not a few of us were killed in this manner. . . .

We took part in the conquest of Vilna by the Red Army, and entered a city that had no Jews. Only later did a few begin to crawl out of the holes where they had been hiding for three years. Singly, however, because there were no families, none whatsoever. A similar situation existed in other cities—in Ravno, Lwow, Stanislawow. Wherever we went the story was the same: of thousands of Jews, only scores had survived. At times we came into a city that once was a bustling center of Jewish life, and found not a single Jew remaining.

22. ONLY LATER DID A FEW JEWS BEGIN TO CRAWL OUT OF HOLES,
WHERE THEY HAD BEEN HIDING.

Meeting with the Jewish partisan from Poland, a representative of the Jewish youth who actively resisted the Nazis, and sending her to Palestine on an underground ship, compensated the emissary somewhat for the years of frustrated efforts.

The Taurus, the second boat sent by Agami, carried a group of children and a second Jewish partisan who had succeeded in getting across the border like Rushka, and whose story was similar. He told of a group of fifteen young Jewish partisans, boys and girls from pioneer youth movements located in the Russian-occupied sector of Chernovtsy, who were trying to devise a means of getting to Istanbul by train. He also told of other similar, small groups who were wandering about, trying to find a way of getting to Palestine.

In January, 1945, Abba Kovner and L. Lidovski, arrived in Warsaw with a letter signed by Zivia Lubetkin of the organization of ghetto fighters. Zivia had written the letter after hearing that there were Palestinian emissaries in Bucharest who might help them emigrate to the Homeland. Agami obtained a sum of money from the "Joint" and in the widespread chaos that typified the first days of peace he prevailed upon the representatives of the International Red Cross to engage in an unusual undertaking. They hired a Rumanian train and equipped it with doctors and medical supplies, and sent it off to collect Jewish displaced persons from among the camps in Poland. The train went as far as Auschwitz. At the same time the emissaries began to open up an escape route and to organize a chain of way stations stretching from Rumanian to Poland and passing through the Carpatho-Ukraine and Slovakia. In this way a ceaseless stream of refugees began flowing from Poland to Bucharest with the help of the NKVD, the Russian secret police.

At first this underground escape movement had no connection with the illegal transport of Jews across the Mediterranean by the Jewish Brigade in Italy. Thousands streamed from Poland to Bucharest, including groups of partisans, young refugees, the remnants of the pioneer movements, and Jews of all sorts.

Agami's work in Rumania became increasingly difficult due to the lack of communication with Palestine and his colleagues at the Istanbul base. In a letter dated April 13, 1945 (which arrived in Istanbul only on June 7), he writes:

It is almost two months now that I have not received a letter from Istanbul. Slowly but surely I am coming to the conclusion that under these circumstances it will be impossible for me to continue our work here. Imagine how angry I felt when I read in the February 16 edition of "Davar" (the Palestinian Histadrut Hebrew daily), which arrived here late, Moshe Shertok's announcement that 1,000 refugees from Rumania would receive Palestinian visas upon arriving in Istanbul. If I had known of this in time, I would have tried to arrange for a Turkish ship for them, in spite of the fact that the Turkish Government has forbidden such activities over the protests of the Zionist Federation. However, the Zionist Federation would now be in a different position if it had been able to guarantee that the refugees would receive visas from Palestine upon their arrival in Istanbul. Had I known about the matter then, I would have tried to come to some agreement with the local authorities. Now it's too late, since the affair has passed into the hands of the British delegation, and they still do not know how many immigration certificates have been set aside for the Jews of Rumania. As a result, no progress is made. . . .

In 1946 all the emissaries' energies were bent toward organizing the b'riha ("escape"), the mass flight of Jews from Europe, a movement that reached immense and unexpected proportions. From the middle of that year, the stream of would-be emigrants to Palestine was channeled from Rumania through Yugoslavia to ships that bore the names of Hagana, Knesset Israel (The Congregation of Israel), and others. At the end of 1946 another ship was sent that had been readied in Greece. Its name was the Nesinit (from Nesia, the name of the wife of one of the organizers of the transport, Yani Avinadav), which arrived in Palestine during the meeting of the Zionist Congress in Geneva. The Congress had gathered to rally the forces of the Jewish people in the wake of the war. Once more the members of the Bureau assembled in Geneva to review their past activities and lay plans for the future.

This was the beginning of a new period wherein tens of thousands of refugees streamed from Europe to Palestine on board the huge ships of the underground movement.

17

The Eight Ships from Italy (1945)

At the tail end of the war, the Jewish Brigade—
part of the British Army—located near the port of Bari
in Italy, saw as its main task the rendering of aid
to the remnants of European Jewry. A small group
of Bureau emissaries within the Brigade wearing soldiers'
uniforms, carried on their underground work in strict
secrecy. Very few of their comrades in arms knew of
their activities. Two of the emissaries, who had gone to Italy
in the thick of the war, were Misha Neta and Israel Sapir,
who had worked at the Teheran and Basra bases two years
before. In this instance too, their departure had taken place
suddenly, even though they had looked forward to the
mission for months. When it became known that the Jewish
Brigade was about to be sent from Egypt to Italy, Bureau
headquarters seized the opportunity to get some of their
men to Europe.

At the time, Misha was sick and bedridden in his home
in kibbutz Givat Haim. Unexpectedly, the door to his room
opened and in walked Saul, who told him in a few words
that an opportunity had arisen to send some people to
Europe, and that he had been chosen.

Misha gave his consent at once, but Saul was not yet satisfied. He asked to speak with Sonia, Misha's fiancee, since the mission in question would mean the emissary's complete isolation from Palestine for an indeterminate length of time. He went to the field where she was working. She listened quietly but anxiously to what he had to say and her response was:

"If he has to go—he has to go."

On the following day Misha went to Bureau headquarters in Tel Aviv to make the arrangements for his departure.

Israel Sapir too was taken by surprise, having been informed of his departure for Europe only three days ahead of time.

On Sunday morning the two men went to the railroad station disguised as Palestinian soldiers who had just returned from home leave. However, they had no papers for the transport train. When they arrived in Egypt they were sent to Burg-el-Arab, near El Alamein in the western desert, where the Brigade was stationed.

Soon they were on board one of the ships transporting the Jewish Brigade to Europe. British military police counted the embarking soldiers and checked them against lists in their possession. However, with so many people milling about the count became confused, and no notice was taken of the two extra men.

When a call went out for volunteers to serve as military police on board the ship, Misha stepped forward at once, and so became preserver of law and order on board the large vessel, which was also carrying British units. He could scarcely repress his laughter when a British major came over and asked his permission to hang wash out to dry.

He was impressed by the sight of thousands of men engaging in self-defense exercises on the deck of the 24,000-ton ship. Being an MP, he did not participate in the exercises.

Tension was high on board all the ships all during the voyage. A rumor spread that enemy submarines would attack the convoy in order to strike at the contingents of Jewish soldiers. The military authorities had taken precautionary measures before the sailing. Among other things, they had publicized in Egypt a soccer match in which the Jewish Brigade was to participate and which was to take place six days after the convoy's departure. Nevertheless, everyone was nervous.

When they arrived in Italy, Rome had already been liberated (on June 4, 1944). The young men knew that there were Jews in Nazi-occupied Italy, and began devising means of bringing them across the border and sending them southward. It proved a difficult undertaking. The Jews who were in hiding were disguised as Christians. The emissaries began to collect addresses and track them down. Italy was divided, the Nazis holding the north, and the Allies the south. In addition, mine fields were scattered all over, making communications extremely difficult. and chaos and ruin were everywhere.

The emissaries contacted Jews and non-Jews and set to work. They got in touch with the partisan regime in the city of Carrara, not too distant from the coast, knowing that there were many Jews among the partisans. They tried to make other contacts through the British army The first people to extend help to them were the Jewish Palestinian members of the transport units.

One of the tasks that had been given the emissaries was locating Enzo Sereni, whom the Bureau had lost track of a short time before. Toward this end, Misha established contact with an Italian woman, the daughter of a well-known professor. With her help he got in touch with an Italian refugee behind enemy lines. Even though their search was unsuccessful, they continued their efforts until Ada Sereni arrived from Palestine and took charge of the project herself. They also tried to uncover the whereabouts of the parachutists and airmen of the Allied forces who had been captured behind enemy lines.

However, they did not look upon such activities as their central task, but spent most of their efforts establishing a base for Aliya-Bet. They assumed that as the front advanced, large numbers of refugees would stream into Italy. After establishing contact with Rumania, they learned that there were thousands of refugees in that country and they set to work at once to open up an escape route for them via Yugoslavia.

At that time the military had confiscated all vessels that weighed eight tons or more. In the opinion of experienced seamen, professional smugglers included, there was no chance of organizing an illegal emigration effort. In the meantime the first Jewish refugees began to arrive, following the liberation of Florence and then Pisa. The emissaries realized that the time to work had most definitely arrived. They also realized that they would have to adjust to operating under conditions that could change from one day to the next. From the start, they were seriously hampered, having no tools with which to work. In addition, their efforts were not appreciated by their friends in the Brigade, who devoted themselves to helping the Jewish refugees in Italy, and did not believe that the Bureau emissaries would ever be able to obtain the means to promote emigration to Palestine. Even Moshe Shertok (Sharett), who visited Italy at that time, told the emissaries that in his opinion, their underground activities endangered the work of the Jewish Brigade.

This period was perhaps the most difficult for the emissaries, but Misha was not a man to be discouraged. With renewed energy he began to arrange for wireless communications with Palestine. The equipment that had been smuggled into Italy from Palestine up to that time was too weak. Eventually they set up their own workshop and began to "draft" parts for wirelesses. Contact was made with Palestine. Later the workshop supplied the ships with wirelesses, and built sets for the Bureau's European communications network.

By that time, Israel Sapir had contacted members of the party of Count Sforza, leader of the expatriate "Free Italy" movement during the war. Sforza had returned from exile in the United States with the intention of overcoming the Communists in his country. He organized volunteer groups within his party to aid the Allies. Israel met with one volunteer, Enzo Tardini, who was about to leave for Milan, explained the Jewish problem to him, and convinced him to help them in their efforts. Israel, along with Yehezkel Saharov (Sahar), turned to the "Joint," and J. Schwartz gave Tardini a large sum of money to help any Jews he might find. Israel met the Italian once more, after the Nazis were defeated and the north was liberated, and heard him tell how many synagogues and Torah scrolls he had saved from destruction.

Immediately following the liberation, the emissaries began to ferret out Jews. Bologna was liberated in the morning and the two emissaries arrived there that same afternoon. They immediately began calling to the Jews over loudspeakers, urging them to come out of hiding. However, no one appeared. They stood for hours in the city's central square, while the fighting was still going on in the suburbs. After they gave up in despair and walked away from the crowd that had gathered around them, a little boy came up to them and tugged at their sleeves. He led them to the second story of a ruined building. There, in one of the desolate rooms sat a man and his wife with their three small children under a picture of the "Holy Family" and the cross. The boy said:

"This is my mother and father, they're Jews."

The parents looked about them in terror and closed the door.

Israel tried to calm them. "Don't be afraid," he said, "we're Jews, too."

The man's face lit up. He jumped up and said to his wife: "Give me the knife."

He cut the lapel of his coat and took out a mezuza scroll (a piece of parchment inscribed with Biblical passages and attached to the doorpost of Jewish homes), then kissed the insignia of the Brigade on Israel's sleeve. However, he was still reluctant to go outside and said to his wife:

"Don't take off the cross yet. We still don't know what might happen."

Through that family the emissaries managed to find another family. Very slowly they accumulated a list of addresses of Jews hiding in convents. Israel arrived at one nunnery with the name of a Jewish woman. The nuns, however, claiming that no such person lived there, sent him wandering from one office to another and did not let him contact the woman. In another instance he came to a woman, bringing with him the address of her brother, but she denied that she was related to the man. Only after repeated urgings did he prevail upon her to admit to her identity.

The work was exhausting and they progressed at a snail's pace. There seemed to be no possibility of procuring any kind of boat. Finally, in one port, they found a boat that was in the process of being built and had not yet been legally registered. They decided to buy it, even though at the time they had no way of getting the materials needed to complete its construction. They began to enlist the aid of military units in acquiring what they lacked—wood, fuel, iron, and other materials. They also took it upon themselves to bring an engine down from the north. An experienced seaman from kibbutz Sdot Yam was sent from Palestine to supervise the proceedings.

A Jew was found who agreed to have the boat registered in his name. Materials that could not be acquired from Jewish Palestinian units were obtained with the help of other armies.

The young men worked with redoubled energy at completing their boat, which was only an ordinary fishing smack. There were many such unfinished skeleton boats scattered throughout Italy, whose owners were not interested in completing them, knowing that as soon as they did, the boats would be confiscated. Prior to this, the young men had made a study of Italian maritime law and had learned that after a vessel was completed, permission could be obtained to take it out for a few hours for testing purposes. It was then that they decided to buy the boat, finish the construction work, and send it off to Palestine on a "trial run." They began searching for the right man to finish the boat and be its captain.

They found their man in an Italian Jew named Enrico Levi. When the young men came to him and explained their plan, he thought they were insane. Their enthusiasm finally won him over, however, even though they did not share a common language: he hardly knew a word of English. At Misha's suggestion, he left his job as captain of a tanker in the British Navy, and began working on their small vessel. At once he showed himself to be a man of boundless loyalty and dedication, one who was prepared to handle any difficult or dangerous situation. He slept on the floor with the young men, ate the same dry biscuits that they did, and gave himself unsparingly to the backbreaking job.

The work progressed. Since they were unable to obtain an engine, they tried to convert a tanker's engine to meet their needs, but did not succeed. In the end they had no choice but to buy another engine in Milan, then still behind enemy lines. They borrowed money from a Jewish refugee in Yugoslavia, promising to return it to him in Palestine. In the meantime, Milan was liberated (April 21, 1945) and they were able to transfer the engine without difficulty.

The last stages of preparing the boat were even more difficult than the first. They still lacked guides and a radio. One afternoon Israel appeared in the port of Monopoli, southeast of Bari, took a wireless out of a military car, and brought it on board the vessel. That night they learned that there was no water in the boat's tanks, and they had to awaken the mayor so that he might put the water works into operation. The workers employed to help construct the boat demanded higher wages every day and their demands had to be met.

Everyone who saw the boat said: "This will never cross the Mediterranean." Thirty-five people were squeezed on board, quite literally: each person had twenty inches of space to call his own. The young men named the boat the Dalin, one of the underground aliases of Eliahu Golomb, taken from his daughter's name, Dalia. His sudden death, a short while before the boat's sailing had upset them deeply.

Not only did the Dalin bring the refugees safely to Palestine, but she also brought back a group of emissaries of the Bureau, sent to help handle the new upsurge of emigration. The young men had boarded the boat secretly near the coast of Caesaria, where the first immigrants to arrive from Italy since the renewal of the effort, had debarked.

As the boat was in its last stages of preparation, Germany

surrendered, and refugees began streaming to the coast over-night. The little 35-ton vessel, affectionately referred to as "the nutshell," appeared all the more ridiculous in light of the new circumstances. Clearly, much larger means of trans-portation were required.

A while before, Yehuda Arazi arrived in Italy. He had been a British police officer in Palestine and was a daring member of the Hagana. One day Misha was told that some-one was asking for him in the Jewish Community Council building in Bari. Upon his arrival there he met a sergeant of the Polish Air Force. The sergeant was accompanied by a British Air Force officer, Harry Fredin (Freddy), who re-quested that Misha give him a receipt stating that he had delivered "one living body," as he had been instructed.

Freddy told the emissary that Eliahu Golomb, before he died, had given him the task of smuggling Yehuda Arazi out of Palestine since it was no longer possible for him to hide there. A high price had been put on his head when he dis--appeared after having been tried and found guilty by a British court. As a result, the searches carried out by the British police became so frequent and thoroughgoing in nature that he could no longer remain in the country.

In the first seven months that followed the conclusion of the war in Europe, 1,036 people were brought to Palestine on board the Bureau's boats. In the following year the number of immigrants reached 21,788. And in 1947 Aliya-Bet was responsible for bringing over 40,000 immigrants to the Homeland. Yet the path for this massive migration was broken by the eight small boats that made their way across the Mediterranean between August and December of 1945. Thirty-five people to a boat, 40 people, then 80, 170, and 250—so the numbers grew from one month to the next.

After groups of Jews were found in the camps in Austria

and Germany, Jewish refugees began streaming into Italy with the intention of reaching the coast and sailing from there to Palestine. At first this movement was spontaneous, but soon it was organized by Jewish Palestinian units, who put their trains at the disposal of the refugees and established a "Diaspora headquarters."

They assisted the emissaries from Palestine; established transit camps, agricultural training centers, children's houses and many other projects; and did all that they could to help the refugees reach the coast and emigrate to Palestine.

At the same time the emissaries of Aliya-Bet were busy acquiring ships. In the south, near Bari and Taranto, the nearest ports to Palestine, an underground network was created to deal with all that concerned emigration to Palestine. Broadcasting stations and weapons depots were set up. However, the problem of getting ships was not easily solved. The next boat they bought was the Natuna, which was only slightly larger than the tiny Dalin. At the same time, in the north, near Genoa, they bought the Pietro, into which they were able to squeeze 180 people.

At that time Shmarya Tzameret, known as "the privileged one" because he was an American citizen, arrived in Italy. He, too, came in military uniform, after having spent a month in Egypt. In Italy he was given the identification papers of a sergeant in one of the transport units. He was assigned to engage in welfare (occupational training) work, so he enjoyed greater freedom of movement than was usual. At that time soldiers were being offered the opportunity of acquiring different skills before returning home. The centers for the training programs were in Bari, in the South, in a non-Jewish area. There were few Jewish soldiers there, too, as most units had gone north. For this reason the underground had a difficult time working there. It carried on its activities mostly in the soldiers' club and the office of the Jewish Community Council, which also served as the office for the refugees. Here Shmarya worked, while living in the house of the Jewish army chaplain. Misha and Israel returned to Palestine and Shmarya and Yehuda Arazi divided the work between them on a geographic basis. Shmarya took the south and Yehuda, the north.

Italy was desperately impoverished. A department was set up to obtain the necessary equipment and provisions for the emigrants headed for Palestine. Groups of soldiers got food supplies and other necessary materials in a variety of ways, even by donating their own rations for the sake of the refugees. After a while it became customary for all sergeants-major and officers to set aside the bottles of whiskey and gin distributed to them in order to form a special supply that served as an exchange fund for refugees' provisions. One case of whiskey got them a truckload of canned meat. The young men also equipped themselves with letters of recommendation from Jewish chaplains and passed through different army camps that were in the process of disbanding, such as Australian and South African camps, and received from the officers blankets and other equipment for the refugees. It was no wonder that the young men would become furious upon learning from time to time of refugees selling the blankets that they had received.

After the war Italy was occupied by the British. It was impossible to engage in any serious undertaking without their intervening. Therefore the young men found it necessary to work in complete secrecy. All sailings were carried out at night. As a security measure, they arranged to send boats off from different places simultaneously. The first captain, Enrico Levi, helped them find a suitable anchorage that was readily accessible to the boats and the refugees. Still it was clear that they would not be able to carry on their efforts indefinitely without being discovered by British Intelligence. The British response in Palestine to the growing influx of refugees was to increase the patrols along the coast, and in Bari the security agencies of the British Army began to exhibit an unusual interest in the Dalin and Natuna, which were anchored there. At that time the Pietro, too, was anchored in Bari, having arrived there for its first trip, Shmarya feared that the Pietro might be prevented from sailing, so he met with the British agent involved and by generous bribery (tens of thousands of lire) the investigation was suppressed. The Pietro sailed, and on its return trip brought back 22 additional emissaries.

One morning, when the young men were busy preparing for the Pietro's second trip, they were informed that British Intelligence was once more taking an interest in the Bureau's vessels. In a search made on board one boat, Hebrew newspapers had been found. Again bribes were employed to dull British curiosity. However, after two days had elapsed, the British arrested the Bureau's representative in Taranto, a Jewish refugee, and his wife summoned Shmarya from Bari. At the same time, the Italian police, following orders of the British authorities, arrested the Italian crew of the Pietro in Gallipoli, a small port southeast of Taranto, where the boat lay at anchor. The owner of the ship was an Italian who lived in Genoa. He had a brother in Bari, Arizio by name, who was also his partner. Arizio was frightened and upset, and Shmarya returned to Bari so that the two of them might go to Genoa and confer with the ship's owner. However, when Shmarya arrived at Arizio's residence, and the latter's wife opened the door for him, he found himself face to face with a member of the British secret police, dressed in the uniform of a sergeant of the tank corps.

"Follow me," said the sergeant.

Shmarya then recalled that on his way to the house he had seen a military car in the street, which should have warned him that the house was surrounded. On their way out, British soldiers were ordered to take along some suitcases with them —they contained Arizio's belongings. They walked on foot through the city streets. As they passed the club of the Jewish soldiers, Shmarya saw a few of the men with whom he had worked. One of them started to approach him, but the emissary winked, and the man fell back.

They finally arrived at the Intelligence office. They walked up to the second floor and entered a room filled with shelves and briefcases. Seated at a desk was a sergeant typing something, and beside him sat Arizio. Shmarya greeted him, but the Italian did not say a word. They sat in silence and waited. After a while a captain appeared and the sergeant said:

"I brought him here."

The two men entered an adjoining room and called for Arizio to come in. Shmarya began to reflect upon what was happening. He saw clearly that this marked the end of their activities in the south. Moreover, he was afraid that Arizio might reveal the names of the men with whom he had come in contact as well as the centers of the effort. While it was true that the young men had met him in different places and had told him very little, there was still the possibility that he might divulge information which would lead to their arrest. And what would become of himself, Shmarya?

Already there had been many robberies and frauds perpetrated by civilians dressed in British Army uniforms, and the military authorities had decreed that anyone caught wearing a uniform that he was unauthorized to wear, would be sentenced to five years in prison. To make matters worse, Shmarya had in his pocket a small booklet containing the addresses and telephone numbers of the centers of the effort. He knew that if that booklet were to be found, the entire network of Aliya-Bet might be uncovered. However, since there was a sergeant sitting in the room with him, he could not dispose of it. He sat smoking his pipe and pretended to read the English newspaper, put out by the Allied armies, that he had with him.

Finally Arizio came out of the adjoining room and Shmarya was told to come in. Seated behind the table was the English captain, with the sergeant at his side. They politely asked him to be seated. The captain offered him a cigarette and asked to see his identification papers. They were in order; even the pay record listed in the ledger was properly drawn up. The unit to which he ostensibly belonged was then stationed in the north of Italy on the Austrian border, and he had leave papers in his possession. They began the interrogation:

"What are you doing in the south?"

"I'm on leave."

"And what brings you all the way down here from up north?"

"Our unit's moving slowly and I wanted to visit some friends during my leave."

"How many people do you know here?"

"Not many."

"Who are they?"

"I came to visit a girl friend."

"Who is she?"

"I'm sorry, but I can't tell you. She's married."

"I suggest that you tell us. You're in a rather tight spot . . ."

"No, I can't tell you. You know what an Italian would do to his wife if he found out about something like that."

The captain listened sympathetically and told the sergeant to discontinue that line of questioning.

"Whom else do you know here?" he asked.

"The Jewish chaplain."

"Where's he?"

"He's not here anymore."

"And you don't know anybody else?"

"No. This is a private visit."

"When did you get here?"

"This morning."

"How did you come?"

"I hitchhiked from Rome."

"And where are you staying here?"

"I think I'll stay at the soldier's club."

"Have you signed in there?"

"Yes."

"You're in welfare, I see. What is it exactly that you do?"

"I'm trying to set up training programs for our farmers."

Suddenly the captain halted the sergeant's interrogation and said:

"Let me get to the point. According to information in our possession, boats carrying Jewish refugees are sailing from small ports in this country for Palestine, and these refugees are being brought to the coast in military trucks driven by British soldiers. Do you know anything about it?"

"I heard about it, but I don't know any details."

"We have good reason to believe that you have been taking part in this activity . . ."

"Believe me, you're mistaken."

They began to interrogate Shmarya as to details—whether he had heard of a place called Monopoli, a small port, from which the boats had sailed. He replied:

"I think so . . . I don't recall exactly . . ."

Again they asked him what he knew about the refugees and again he gave a vague and non-commital reply:

"Someone mentioned something once . . . but I can't think of what it was . . ."

They asked him about the Jewish refugee who worked for the Bureau in Taranto and had been imprisoned.

After scores of questions had been put to him, Shmarya realized that his interrogators had no clear concept of what they were talking about. That gave him courage.

The captain said:

"This business of smuggling Jews into Palestine is giving us no end of troubles, but you probably aren't interested . . ."

Shmarya decided that that was the right time to pretend to speak openly. He replied:

"Right, I'm not interested in troubles, but I won't be quiet when it comes to stopping emigration to Palestine."

The captain was irritated and said, "It's a small country and it can't hold any more Jews. Why do you people have to go about it this way?"

They embarked upon a discussion of Zionism. Shmarya asked the captain if he had ever visited Palestine, and it turned out that the sergeant had been there.

"Well then, you saw what's been done there. We don't have any doubts that given the right conditions we can absorb millions of people. The problem is a political one— it's not a question of room. You saw how the settlements are thriving there. I myself come from a settlement in the Valley of Jezreel. For generations only a few groups of

Arabs lived there—and today thousands of Jews live in that same area and on a much higher level, too."

"But the Arabs have their rights . . ."

Finally Shmarya steered the conversation toward the question of the refugees. He asked the captain if he knew what had happened to the Jewish people.

"Yes, I know."

"Do you know that six million Jews were killed?"

"I know."

"You heard about the death camps?"

"I heard. I've just come back from Bergen-Belsen and the Nuremberg trials."

"Well then, nothing has to be explained to you."

"Yes, yes, I know all about the refugee problem, but they're all going to be sent back where they came from."

"How is that possible? Where will they go? To their wrecked houses, to the graves of their relatives? What's to be done?"

"I don't know."

"That's the difference between you English and we Jews. We have a solution—Palestine. And anyway you, as a member of the Secret Service, ought to know how the Jewish soldiers serving in the British Army feel. As for myself, I have nothing to do with it, but those people who are organizing the illegal immigration have all my sympathies. And I'm not the only one who feels this way; most of the Jewish soldiers feel the same way I do."

The captain brought the discussion to a close:

"We've listened to what you've had to say, but I still intend to do everything I can to prevent all activities of this sort."

"Well, here's hoping you fail," replied Shmarya.

The captain was rather confused by the Jewish sergeant's

outspoken manner, and sent him to wait in the adjoining room. Shmarya looked at the grim-faced Arizio and smiled to boost his morale.

Once more Arizio was called in for interrogation. One problem perplexed Shmarya: how to get rid of the booklet that was in his pocket. He realized clearly that if he were to be imprisoned, the booklet would be discovered. He looked about the room. It was an ordinary office: the walls were covered with maps and there were cabinets all around. He thought of swallowing the booklet, but it was too large. There was the bathroom—but they would surely search him before allowing him to leave the room. He would have torn it up, but for the presence of the sergeant seated at the typewriter.

There was only one remaining alternative—to hide the booklet where no one would find it. In the room there were two metal filing cabinets standing next to each other, with a very narrow space between them. He saw that he had found his solution: no cleaning woman would ever get into that crack. He waited for the moment when the sergeant would leave the room. Fearing that they might look at him through the keyhole or by some other means, he got up and pretended to examine the maps on the walls, and as soon as the sergeant left for a minute, he thrust the booklet between the two cabinets, resumed his seat, and waited.

After a few moments had passed, Arizio left the room and Shmarya was called in again.

No sooner had he entered the room than he heard the captain tell him:

"You may go."

He could not believe his ears.

"But," the captain added quietly, "you have to report back here tomorrow at nine o'clock."

"Certainly," said Shmarya, his heart pounding.

"Where do you intend to spend the night?"

"In the Jewish soldiers' club."

His identification papers were returned to him.

"Are you freeing the Italian, too?" he asked.

"Don't worry about him; that's none of your affair."

Shmarya turned to go. Suddenly, however, the sergeant whispered something in the captain's ears, and the latter said to the emissary:

"Wait one minute in the next room."

He did as he was told. It was already evening by that time. Once more he was called in to see the captain, and once more he was told that he was dismissed.

He left seemingly calm, and soon noticed that he was being followed by two men—a parachutist and an Italian in civilian dress. He understood at once that while he had been delayed, the two agents had been summoned and had been instructed to keep track of him.

Realizing that under the circumstances he could not return to the soldiers' club or the refugees' office, he sat down in a military bar at an empty table, and after a few moments someone came over and took a seat beside him. As Shmarya sat there smoking his pipe, wondering who his new companion might be, he saw that the man was carrying two folded newspapers. When the soldier spread the papers out to read them, he recognized the papers he had left in the interrogation office: "The Union Jack" (British) and "The Stars and Stripes" (American).

In the meantime a waitress came over and they ordered wine. Shmarya asked where the washrooms were. He left the room as though for a moment and did not come back. He walked along the beach. After he had covered a few hundred yards he stopped, leaned on a fence, and looked around to see if he was being trailed. No one was in sight. He stood there a while, trying to determine what his next step should be. He realized that he would have to discontinue the effort in that area and move elsewhere. At the moment, however, his problem was where to spend the night. He could not go to the club and endanger the safety of the others: agents would be on the lookout for him there. The same applied to the refugee office. He therefore decided to go to the camp of the small military unit of mapmakers, where there were only fifteen soldiers stationed, all of whom were Jewish. One of their officers, who was a confidant of the Bureau's emissaries, lived in a villa alongside the unit.

He set out to cover the few miles distance that lay between him and his destination. Still uncertain that he was not being followed, he took a roundabout route and stopped at a crossroads ostensibly to light his pipe. He walked along for one more block and again stopped and turned about abruptly. He finally began to walk quickly toward the villa. Once there, he contacted his friends back at the club, who immediately brought him his civilian clothing. He told them what had happened during the day, and they all decided that he should wait and see how things would develop. He put on his civilian clothes and went to Naples. When he learned there that Army Intelligence was looking for him, he continued on to Rome, to meet with representatives of a navigation association.

Within two weeks time he had acquired a boat and had found a new base of operations. All was in order. However, at the last moment Italian friends in the local government advised him not to operate in the Venice-Trieste area, since relations between Italy and Yugoslavia were very strained, and Jewish emigration might suffer on that account: the

Italian authorities might see a connection between their effort and the activities of Communist Yugoslavia.

Before long he came across Arizio, who had been freed after having spent a number of weeks in jail. The Italian told Shmarya that when he had seen him go free after the British had interrogated him, he, Arizio, was sure that bribery had been employed. He had then turned to the sergeant and said:

"Can I go, too?"

"No," the sergeant had answered, "we're holding on to you until you tell us who's responsible for all these activities . . ."

Arizio, stunned, said:

"But you know him as well as I do."

"Who is he, then?"

"That sergeant you let go a minute ago . . ."

The two Englishmen jumped out of their seats and dashed out the door to bring him back, but he had already disappeared.

Shortly after his narrow escape from the British, Shmarya was sent to work in France, leaving Yehuda Arazi in charge of the entire effort in Italy.

Yehuda Arazi, who was known in Europe at the end of the war as "Alon" ("Oak"—his underground alias), came to Italy after having been very active in the Hagana underground in Palestine for a long time. Upon his arrival in Italy he plunged into his work with a will. He was not pleased with the system of the "Diaspora headquarters" and the emissaries who had preceded him. He was especially opposed to the accepted custom of making up emigrant groups on a party percentage basis. Yehuda was also interested in bringing about a fundamental change in one aspect of the operation. Up to that time all the ships had been run by non-Jewish sailors, some of whom were professional thieves. The emissaries only organized the trips and were not involved in any nautical activities. Yehuda was all for achieving autonomy. "Let's run the ships ourselves," he said, and chose as his slogan the words of the prophet Isaiah: "With great mercies will I gather thee."

He always carried on his person a note from Eliahu Golomb to the commanding officers of the Jewish units in the British Army. The note requested the officers to help Alon in his mission and to obey his orders in all that pertained to the illegal immigration effort.

In the meantime, however, Eliahu died. Yehuda, disturbed by the death of his friend and teacher, was deeply immersed in his work at the time, and realized clearly what he had to do. He gathered about him a group of industrious soldiers, whose main task was to obtain food and equipment from army depots.

One of the most difficult problems was getting gasoline because there was not an open market yet in Europe for that commodity; it was distributed only to the armed forces. Alon assigned gasoline quotas to every Palestinian unit. Privates, sergeants, officers—all were made to realize that they were inseparable parts of the Hagana and the emigration effort. In this way gasoline, blankets, food, and equipment were obtained. Everything was gathered into hidden storehouses, where the various articles were tallied and set aside to be used by refugees or to be exchanged.

In the meantime the Palestinian units in Italy began to disband with the conclusion of the war, and headquarters was concerned over the future of the effort. The young men managed to "enlist" a few trucks and jeeps, and formed a false unit of their own. To all outward appearances it was a real army unit with all the trimmings. They rented a large courtyard in Milan, hung up military signs, and whenever inspections were held everything was found to be in order. Since it was standard procedure in the army to denote everything by initials, they called their own unit JDC—the initials of the Joint Distribution Committee—and put those three letters on the vehicles and at the top of their drivers' licenses and documents.

On the strength of those initials they were able to obtain gasoline and service at military stations. In addition they built their own garage which contained twenty vehicles, all painted the same color; posted guards around the area; hung up signs; and set up a pay office, as was done in all army camps. The Italian mechanics who worked there never imagined that they were not employed by the army. One day an M.P. came by and asked for gasoline. Not only was his request granted, but he even had to sign the standard receipt form. They had their own pumping station that required an enormous quantity of gasoline for the ships. Once they sent off a convoy of 37 trucks—and no one thought for a moment that it was not a real military convoy.

After the army disbanded the question arose of where to keep the scores of Aliya-Bet emissaries. They were forced to buy houses. They also bought a villa 40 miles out of Milan; it had a secret passageway wherein they set up a broadcasting station.

Another project that occupied Yehuda Arazi's time was the collection of food, and especially canned food, for the sea voyage. Canned food was ideal, as the ships were unable to stop off at ports along the way and were likely to spend a good deal of time at sea. Every military unit was obligated to obtain a certain amount of food, and bring it to the special storehouses in the vicinity of Milan, in the north, and Bari, in the south. When army units began to disband Yehuda would send trucks whose drivers were equipped with falsified credentials, in order to pick up provisions. Things did not always run smoothly, however. Once one of their men was sent to a bakery in his military uniform to exchange flour for certain biscuits that they would need at sea. The man aroused suspicions and was placed under arrest. He remained in prison for six months, but not a word could be gotten out of him. In the end he had to be released in accordance with the law.

Sometime prior to this, in May and June of 1945, when the Jewish Brigade was moving through Northern Italy and part of its number was already in Austria, a parachutist returning from Austria brought back a report that there were Jews in the vicinity of Ebensee. Up to that time no one had even known whether or not there were any Jews left alive in the European camps. The leaders of the Jewish Brigade, who belonged to "Diaspora headquarters," met with Yehuda Arazi, and together they organized a party, to be headed by Captain Hoter-Yishai, to search for Jews. The commander of the Brigade, Brigadier Benjamin, an English Jew, was opposed to such illegal operations being conducted within the framework of the army. Hoter-Yishai, in an angry talk with him, threatened that if the group were not given official permission to leave, soldiers would begin to desert in order to carry out the mission. Faced with this alternative, Benjamin withdrew his opposition. Jews began to stream to the camps of the Brigade. Army officers who were members of "Diaspora headquarters" set up a special reception camp alongside the border. The first group taken across consisted of 180 sick, broken people, skeletally thin. The women were afraid of every stranger. They seemed terrified at the sight of a man, any man, as though they were gripped by a primal animal fear.

The soldiers fed and clothed the refugees, and gave kind and considerate attention to every man and woman among them. After a while the latter began to recuperate somewhat and regain the appearance of human beings. Unpleasant dissension and instances of talebearing began to crop up. Quarrels broke out as one refugee after another was accused of having served as a *kapo* (headman) or in a similar capacity in the concentration camps. A lynching atmosphere was created, and many difficult situations arose.

One camp was not capable of containing all who streamed to the Brigade. "Diaspora headquarters" began renting areas suitable for more camps, so that as many Jews as possible could be transferred to Italy and be taken care of until their departure for Palestine. The members of the "Diaspora headquarters" began to argue among themselves whether it was best to let the people remain where they were in the existing camps—Dachau, Ebensee, and so on—and take care of them there, or to send them straight to Italy. In the end the opinion of the Bureau prevailed, namely, to send them all, down to the very last Jew, to Italy as quickly as possible, illegally as well as legally, in order to get them near the coast and create pressure for emigration to Palestine.

At the conference of "Diaspora headquarters," there appeared a representative of the refugees, Ratner by name, who spoke in Hebrew and made a strong impression on his listeners. He convinced the Palestinians that it was necessary to get all the surviving Jews out of Germany at once. He said:

"If you don't want us to go on despairing, get us out of the death camps and maybe we'll be able to free ourselves of memories that are so horrible that, if I were to tell you only a few of them, you would not be able to laugh again, just as we have forgotten what it is to laugh."

They began to transfer the refugees. One of the largest camps, which they called "Camp A," was located near Milan. At first they transported hundreds of people there in an orderly fashion. However, after news of the Jewish soldiers and their activities got about, hordes of refugees began streaming to the camp and the organized transfer was discontinued. Vast numbers made their way there by train, or on foot over the mountains, or by whatever means they could.

One after another, fifteen camps were established near the large cities—Genoa, Naples, Bari, and others. In the north, in the interior of the country, a large camp, with a capacity of 3,000 people, was established. The number of refugees increased by leaps and bounds; more camps were set up; and the tempo of the emigration to Palestine was stepped up. All this was accomplished in an amazingly short period of time.

This was a period of active cooperation with the "Joint," which played a very important role in supplying the "exodus" with food, clothing, and other necessities. A central storehouse was set up in a Jewish school building in Milan, and from there supplies were distributed to the various camps. Prior to this, arrangements had been made for joint activity with UNRRA (United Nations Relief and Rehabilitation Agency), which included in its ranks a special unit sent from the Yishuv. With the help of the heads of the Brigade and UNRRA the ties between the Bureau and the "Joint" were more firmly cemented. Prior to that period the "Joint" representatives had been reluctant to participate in the underground illegal immigration effort. The change in attitude was due in large part to the appointment of J. Schwartz as director of the "Joint" in Europe; Schwartz was very sympathetic to the rescue effort.

When the flow of refugees continued to swell, a house was

bought in Milan to serve as a special headquarters for the drivers who, in setting out to transport groups of refugees at odd hours of the night, were likely to appear suspicious. When it became evident that the exodus was to continue to swell, another house was bought in Rome. However, in all their undertakings they were always careful not to operate within the refugee camps, so as not to disclose their activities. In addition, the refugees were not told ahead of time when and where they would board the boats.

Yehuda Arazi, together with Ada Sereni, who had arrived in Italy at the end of 1945 to search for her husband, Enzo, and then entered into the service of the Bureau there, negotiated with shipowners for their ships. By that time the emissaries themselves took charge of fixing the boats. Yehuda and the young men would go down inside the ship to construct sleeping facilities. They built layers of wooden shelves and set aside small sleeping quarters for each person barely large enough to contain a narrow hammock. They arranged for ventilation on each ship, and set up water tanks, a kitchen, and a bathroom, with the greatest of difficulties.

One of Yehuda Arazi's favorite vessels was the Pietro, which he spoke of almost as though it were a living creature.
I had my first sight of her during the middle of summer.I stood on the shore looking out at the Italian Riviera and saw her sparkling in the sun, with the dash of the white spray about her. It was her first day on the water and she looked completely different from all the other boats—buoyant, slender and graceful . . .
Her name, Pietro, was given to her by her owner, who stood next to me, ready to sell her. He was fifty years old and sported a typical Italian beard on his prominent chin. He was a shrewd fellow. Even though

he was not Jewish, he wore a gold Star of David on his lapel for the sake of the business at hand. He looked the Pietro over, praised her good points, and almost reached out to hug her, so caught up was he in his own glowing description.

We came to a price and the "bearded one" took it upon himself to prepare the ship for its first voyage within a very short period of time. In fact, no sooner had she returned to the dock when I heard the sound of hammering, iron striking iron, and the sawing of wood, and I saw showers of sparks thrown off by the welding guns. The ship was also repainted. The white coat with the green stripe was replaced with a pale blue-gray color that would make the ship hard to distinguish against a background of sea and sky.

The Pietro was not the first boat sent from Italy by the underground movement after the war, but when compared with the Dalin and the Natuna, was the first *large* boat. She weighed 150 tons and her engine was strong and functioned well. She was twenty-eight yards long, seven and a half yards wide, and traveled at approximately nine knots.

After a few weeks of involved negotiations with the crafty owner, the Pietro was making her way along the coast toward Crotone, an isolated spot at the heel of the Italian boot. The only building in the vicinity was a small railroad station in the heart of a large forest. Here the refugees that were to embark were brought in trucks of one of the Palestinian military units that was stationed in the vicinity of Bari. At that moment Yehuda was standing on the shore alongside the "bearded one" and the latter's friend and partner, a colonel in the Italian Intelligence.

The night was pitch black. In the distance all that could be seen were the flickering green and red lights of the Pietro approaching the shore. The silence was suddenly broken by the noise of clanking chains, as the anchor was lowered. At that moment the humming of the motors of the approaching trucks became audible.

The refugees made their way from the trucks to the boat by a backwoods route marked off by white strips of felt tied to the trees. They advanced slowly and silently carrying their baggage with them, while in front of them and behind them young men of the immigration underground stood their posts with submachine guns in their hands. The sea was peaceful. Not a sound marred the silence. With the help of fishermen hired especially for the occasion, the 170 refugees boarded the vessel.

Group after group slipped out of the thick woods and entered the fishing smacks. From the smacks they climbed up the rope ladders hanging down from the Pietro's sides. Every person was taken to the hammock whose number corresponded with the number he or she had been given. Blankets were spread on the hammocks, and knapsacks served as pillows.

The captain was an immense fellow, the son of Italian aristocrats. The crew of seven Palestinian sailors, chosen especially for the occasion, worked quietly and efficiently. Somewhere in the distance, in the direction of the British naval base in Taranto, a white beam of light shot out from the lighthouse and skimmed across the water.

Eliezer was the name of the young man who was to run the boat and be in charge of the refugees. He was one of the first members of the Palyam, the naval branch of the Palmach, to be sent to accompany an Aliya-Bet ship. He knew the shores of Palestine like the palm of his hand, and he also knew how to maintain discipline. In addition, his excellent command of French helped him in his relations with the Italian captain.

The refugees lay in their hammocks without uttering a sound. After Yehuda finished his brief words of farewell and prepared to leave, all eyes followed him in silent gratitude.

As was customary, Yehuda put a pistol into the pocket of each guide and returned to the smack. Once more the night's silence was broken as the Pietro lifted anchor and set sail.

After a few days had passed, and a series of encouraging messages sent from the vessel had come in, Yehuda received a report of the ship's being fired upon in the vicinity of one of the Dodecanese islands, southwest of Rhodes, after not having answered broadcasts from the shore demanding that the vessel identify itself. The Pietro escaped quickly into the darkness of the night.

Eight days after the ship had sailed, the good news arrived that all the refugees had arrived safely in Palestine in the vicinity of the kibbutz Shfayim.

Preparations were begun immediately for equipping the ship anew for a second trip. Food and fuel were stored secretly in the port of Taranto, to remain there until the Pietro would be able to anchor in Crotone under cover of night. On her return trip, the Pietro brought back emissaries from Palestine who were assigned to work in Poland, Rumania, Hungary, Austria, and Germany. They were illegally debarked in Italy, and it was the responsibility of Yehuda and his colleagues to provide them with whatever they needed to continue their journey, and to convey them to their destinations.

Summer passed and fall arrived, bringing storms that stirred up the waters of the Mediterranean. Once again a truck convoy brought 170 refugees to the coast. Because of the storm, boarding the ship was very difficult. However, the Pietro finally sailed under the command of its two captains. This time, too, she arrived at her destination safely. However, on the return trip she struck a reef and sprung a leak and was forced to take refuge in the port of Gallipoli. Prior to entering the port, while still at sea, everything was thrown overboard that might have been incriminating. Therefore, when a British patrol impounded the ship on the following day, thtey found it almost completely empty.

The captain and the crew were ordered to stay on board the vessel. They were charged with smuggling refugees into Palestine and, although they denied the charge, it was obvious that the ship had been employed in an illegal venture.

The "bearded one" was also imprisoned in Genoa and was subjected to a grueling interrogation at the hands of the British Intelligence; he was freed only after generous bribes had been distributed in the proper places.

The Pietro was confined in the port of Bari for months. It seemed that she would never be freed. The Italian captain began to drink excessively; the crew became uncontrollable. However, after a while Ada Sereni managed to obtain the ship's release on the strength of her personal influence and the contacts she had established. In a mock ceremony the ship was sold to different owners. The captain and crew were changed and the ship was given a new name.

During the time that the Pietro was kept in Bari, a few other, larger immigration vessels sailed from the coast of Italy—the Enzo Sereni, the Hannah Szenes and the Orde Wingate.

With the passage of time, it became increasingly difficult to break through the British sea blockade. After the Pietro was released it became an escort boat. It carried the belongings of the immigrants as far as Palestine's territorial waters, where the cargo was transferred to a larger ship. At a later date the vessel was employed to return the Italian crew to Italy as the men of Palyam began to operate the large ships.

In this way the Pietro received a new, unofficial name, the Escort, and witnessed the loading of many ships in different parts of Italy—the Brakha Fuld, the Shabtai Luzinski (both of which commemorated Palestinians killed in the service of the immigration effort), the Palmach, the Sh'ar Yashuv (The Remnant Shall Return), and the Ghetto Fighters. At all times the Pietro hurried to the aid of the other ships that needed provisions. And when the immigration ships from Italy needed fuel, it was the small Pietro that would sail to France and smuggle out a load of fuel for her "big sisters."

18

The Hagana and Exodus

In the beginning of November, 1945, Leibel Abramovski, wearing a British military uniform, set out for Egypt on his way to Europe. Bureau headquarters in Tel Aviv had not come to a clear-cut decision as to where he was to go. As for himself, he planned to go to Yugoslavia, not merely because other emissaries had already renewed the illegal immigration effort in France, Greece, Italy, and other European countries, but primarily because Yugoslavia was, in his opinion, an ideal country for underground work from a geographical point of view. Since it bordered on the sea, as well as on Rumania, Hungary, Austria, Greece, Italy, Albania, and Bulgaria, it could serve as a direct or indirect route to Palestine.

In Egypt Leibel lived an unsettled existence, awaiting the first opportunity to be on his way. One day he received a secret communication through the group of Jewish women soldiers of the ATS (Auxiliary Territorial Service) who lived nearby, telling him to go to Cairo. He took his haversack and boarded the first train for that city. There he was met by Efraim Schultz, a member of religious kibbutz Tirat Zvi, who told him that a Jewish unit returning from leave in Palestine would be taking the train that night to Port Said and from there would continue by ship to Italy. Someone would meet him at the port, give him the necessary equipment, and help him get aboard the ship.

Leibel was quite happy to be told this, although he was well aware of the dangers that lay ahead. Only recently four emissaries—among them Abba Kovner and Haggai Uberal—had boarded a military transport bound for Italy. After the ship put out to sea, they were called before the convoy's commanding officer and put into the brig. It was rumored that an informer had been at work.

Leibel was ready. Having studied his military identification card, and obtained emblems of various Italian units and unit shoulder patches to put on when the need should arise, he left for the railroad station. There he saw crowds of soldiers of different nationalities, with many Jews among them.

"Where are the Jews going?" he asked.

"Port Said—Italy."

He joined the Jewish soldiers, being careful not to speak with anyone, and wherever they went—he went.

As soon as the train started moving, most of the soldiers fell asleep, but not Leibel, who was busy devising a plan of action. As dawn broke and the train pulled into Port Said, he kept a sharp lookout for the man who was to help him. For some reason he could not stop thinking of the anecdote of the British paratrooper whose chute failed to open. Before he hit the ground he managed to yell to his companion: "I say, George, look here—not only won't this blasted chute open, but there's no car waiting by the tree to take us to lunch like they promised . . ."

The same fate was Leibel's—no "someone," no military gear, and no one to help him. There he stood, alone in the railroad station, the contents of the small haversack that

THE GATE BREAKERS

hung from his shoulder being all that he had. Nevertheless, he was determined to board the ship at all costs.

As ill luck would have it, the ship was anchored at sea and the soldiers were to be taken to it by tug. Only after he had already gotten in line to get on board the tugboat was he approached by the man who was supposed to have helped him. It turned out that the latter had been unable to accomplish anything. He as much as told Leibel to forget about the whole thing. The emissary turned his back on the man and paid him no more attention. He looked around and saw some Jewish soldiers loaded down with luggage. In order not to appear conspicuous—he had no gear—he offered to help. The soldiers were glad to accept his offer and in a few moments he was loaded down with baggage and was indistinguishable from everyone else.

After a half hour's ride, the tugboat arrived at the side of the ship. More trouble lay ahead, however. A large float was attached to the ship, and on it was a table surrounded by an inspecting team consisting of officers and military police; they were going over the soldiers' identification papers very thoroughly, handing each soldier a meal ticket for the duration of the trip and helping him up the ship's ladder. Leibel felt sure that the game was up. He was at a loss as to what to do. Were he to jump overboard he would be noticed and captured at once; besides which, with his clothes on he would never be able to swim the long distance to shore. Of necessity he was pushed forward. When he arrived at the table, he "accidentally" slipped and fell, and his bundles tumbled all over him. He got up, only to fall again beneath the heavy load. He was covered with sweat and was breathing heavily. In the meanwhile, some soldiers behind him had already gotten their meal tickets, and wanted to get on board the ship, but he was blocking their path. Cursing and shouting, they began to push him aside. An officer and an MP, thinking in the confusion that his papers had been checked and that he had been given a meal ticket, got him on his feet and helped him up the ladder.

When Leibel reached the deck he was shaking. He wiped the sweat off his face and breathed deeply.

He found out the reason for the rigorous check—there were Italian prisoners in the hold below who were being taken to Italy. The check was also a precautionary measure taken against British soldiers who were looking for a free ride home for the holidays; some had been caught in the attempt on two or three occasions. Finally, since the capture of Abba Kovner and his colleagues, officials were on the lookout for like-minded stowaways.

After Leibel got on board the ship, the same sergeant who was supposed to have helped him approached, showed his amazement by clapping the emissary on the shoulder—and disappeared once more.

Leibel's troubles were by no means over. In order to be given food, every soldier had to pass through a narrow doorway and have his meal ticket punched by an officer. After receiving his ration, each soldier would continue along the narrow passageway, which led into the dining room. Leibel observed this procedure during his first day aboard and decided to forego his ration rather than risk discovery. Before long, however, hunger pangs and dizziness compelled him to head for the kitchen. He somehow managed to bypass all obstacles and get a meal, but he did not dare endanger himself a second time.

As soon as the ship set sail, an announcement over the loudspeakers called for volunteers to serve as MPs. The volunteers' main job was to keep order on deck, and to prevent the men from coming too close to the spot where some Jewish ATS soldiers (women) were quartered. Leibel was among the first to volunteer. He pinned the MP armband onto his sleeve and started to work. He made it a point to be clean-shaven and neat at all times. His new role was not especially difficult, since he had served in Wingate's Commando units and in British units in Palestine during the riots and attacks of 1936-1939.

On board ship he met a Jewish soldier who came from a neighboring kibbutz. The latter looked at him a long while and said:

"Tell me, do you have a brother in kibbutz Mishmar Hayam, guards the fields, rides a horse, name of Leibel?"

"Why, yes," replied Leibel quickly, "that's right, my twin brother. We look exactly alike."

The kibbutz member was looking for a chess partner. Leibel suggested that they try a game. So it was that the emissary found a friend and a pleasant way to pass the time during off-duty hours. Later he told his friend of his food problem and from then on he had an easier time of it.

On their third day out they ran into a storm and many soldiers were too sick to eat. Leibel used the opportunity to good advantage, eating enough to banish all memory of hunger.

After four days they arrived at Taranto, in southern Italy. Here too all had to undergo a rigorous examination. The orders of each group of soldiers were checked and then each group was counted prior to walking through the port's gate. The soldiers did not carry their bags with them on the march to the transit camp, and no one wanted to guard the baggage or serve as a porter. Once again Leibel was quick to spot his opportunity. Loading the bags onto the trucks was no easy task, but by so doing he got into the transit camp without any difficulty. That night he was on a military train headed north, not knowing the train's destination. Within 24 hours he arrived in an army camp not far from Venice, and from there he went to Milan.

In Milan he met two Palestinians who had already been in Yugoslavia and had made contacts there. They gave him addresses in Zagreb and Belgrade. He was also given some money to get the program started. A truck heading toward Trieste stopped to give him a lift, and he was on his way. There he forged papers identifying him as Jacob Leibovitz, a refugee from one of the exodus centers. He put a small amount of food into his haversack, and by nightfall he was on a freight train, heading for Yugoslavia.

It was a cold November. Leibel blew on his fingers while he tried to make out the route that they were following and determine how he would get back to Italy. The farther they traveled from Trieste, the colder it became. Daybreak found the emissary huddled in a corner of the car, so preoccupied with combatting the cold that he did not pay attention to where he was. After half an hour had passed he heard the sound of approaching footsteps. The door opened and they were ordered outside. The car which he was in was filled with Yugoslavian refugees returning to their homeland. When the latter went outside, Leibel took his haversack and went with them. He hid his face in his hat, hiked up his scarf around his neck, and did calisthenics to keep warm.

After a ten-minute walk under partisan escort, they arrived at the partisans' camp, which consisted of a few barracks. Leibel felt secure. He had seen no instances of intimidation or physical harassment up to that time; on the contrary, the soft-spoken partisans had even helped an old man struggling with a big bundle. Leibel thought it most unlikely that he would come to any harm at their hands.

The men were lined up and made to pass in front of a

window, single file, to have their papers checked and certified. Occasionally someone would be taken out of line with
his baggage and brought into a small room to be searched.
Leibel's turn arrived. He was asked who he was.

"A Jew," he replied.

"Where are you coming from?"

"From a concentration camp for political prisoners in
Ebensee."

"How did you get here?"

"I escaped from a camp in Padua."

"Where are you going?"

"Home, to find what's left of my family."

"Where's your home?"

"In Poland."

"Passport, please."

Leibel handed him the refugee papers.

"That's all you have?"

"Yes, comrade."

The man questioned him in Yugoslavian and Leibel
answered in Russian, a very respected language at the time.
Nevertheless, they took him out of line and made him wait
on the side. After everyone else had been checked, they
searched him. He was afraid that they might discover his
money, but they found nothing. They put him into a small
jail where there were nine prisoners besides himself—
Bulgarians, Hungarians, and others. There was a Jewish boy
among them who made a good impression on Leibel; the
boy introduced himself as an emissary of the pioneer movement in Hungary. The others presented themselves as
partisans or as prisoners on their way home. The jail was a
small room in a barracks that contained wooden, double-
decker bunks without matresses along the walls. Each man
was given a deep bowl in which he received, every morning,

23. **The boy introduced himself as an emissary of the pioneer movement in Hungary.**

an unsweetened chicory beverage and half a loaf of black bread. For lunch the prisoners received a bowl of soup which they searched in vain for tiny fat-particles. At night it was chicory again.

Seven days passed in this manner, with no questions being asked of them. Leibel grew a beard, his clothes became shabby, and he looked like a wild man. However, he did his best to act properly and constantly tried to hit upon a scheme for winning release from his wretched confinement. He finally resorted to a tried-and-true method—he complained that he was sick: he said that he had pains in his stomach and could not eat, and wanted to see the doctor. Before noon a partisan came and took him to the city.

The sign hanging over the physician's door read "Dr. Berkowitz"—as Jewish a name as one could find anywhere. Instead of relating to the doctor his aches and pains, the emissary told him what he had told his interrogators at the border. The search for missing relatives had become at that time the main topic of discussion among Jews. The doctor began to ask his patient whether he had met his (the doctor's) brother, rumored to have been in camp at Ebensee. Leibel explained to him that the people in the camp changed their appearance and names from time to time, in order not to be recognized and thus to avoid punishment. The doctor was considerate; he told the emissary of the situation that existed in the country and assured him that things would soon quiet down, but said that he could not help him for the time being.

That same night, the prisoners were transferred, under partisan guard, to Ljubljana, the capital of the Slovenian Republic. They were led into a large building which had not yet been completed. Wooden boards took the place of windows, and straw strewn about the floor did for beds. It was much too cold to sleep. The prisoners feared that they would freeze. All night long Leibel walked up and down, rubbing one leg against the other, rubbing his hands together, and exercising in an effort to keep warm. In the morning, when the partisans responsible for the prisoners arrived and saw what the situation was, they served them hot coffee and moved them to a room that was heated with an iron stove with many tin chimneys. Leibel, exhausted, fell asleep at once.

Finally, he arrived at the refugee camp in Zagreb, the capital of Croatia. The camp had formerly been used by the Nazis for prisoners; now it served as a center for the Yugoslavian refugees. Prior to their going home, the refugees underwent an investigation to determine their past activities and economic status. Leibel had the address of a person who lived in that city, and he knew of the existence of a Jewish community there; the problem was one of making contact. The camp was not too closely guarded, but Leibel was apprehensive because of the tense political situation in the country. However, when he saw some Yugoslavian refugees obtain permission to go to the city, he too went before the camp authorities and asked for permission to turn to the Jewish community and seek their help before he should continue his journey to Hungary. He was given a two-hour pass.

They gave him directions for getting to the Jewish community and he started out. He met the man whom he had been told to get in touch with, one of the chairmen of the community council, but the latter was very cold and un-cooperative; he said that every day he was approached by people claiming to be emissaries from Palestine and asking for help. Disappointed, Leibel turned and left. He walked about the streets a bit and went to the railroad station to find out about connections between Zagreb and Belgrade. The next morning he again received permission to leave the camp, and upon his arrival at the Jewish community he was informed that an Ehud Uberal, a newspaperman from Palestine, had been there the night before. Leibel tried to contact him, but with no success. Once again he went to the railroad station to study the timetables. Upon his arrival at the camp he was told that they would be leaving that night at nine o'clock. He and ten others were taken by the partisans to the station a good while before the train was scheduled to leave, and were put into a railroad car.

Leibel knew that at eleven o'clock an express would be leaving for Belgrade. At 10:30 one of the prisoners asked permission to go to the washroom, located at the end of the car. Leibel too asked permission and went in the opposite direction. The guards did not imagine that anyone would try to escape—where could one go without credentials or money?—but Leibel walked out of the car and made for the express on the other track.

The express train was so packed that he could not get in. The stairs as well as the platforms between the cars were completely filled; people were even climbing onto the tops of the cars. Leibel was desperate; this was his last chance to escape. He had to get on that train at all costs. He ran until he came to a car that had written all over it in large chalk letters, "For Invalids Only." He tried to open the door, but an officer who was posted there told him angrily that he could not get in, and then slammed the door in his face with such violence that Leibel almost was hit. Then the officer banged the door open again, his jaw tight with anger. Leibel shouted past him in Russian:

"No room for a Russian here?"

That did the trick. The adulation of Russian war heroes was then at its height. The officer mumbled, "Of course, of course."

A space was cleared for "the Russian" among the wounded soldiers who, with bandaged arms, legs, and heads, and blood-stained uniforms, were on their way to Belgrade for treatment. They bore their pain quietly, almost as if they were not wounded. It was not long before Leibel was on friendly terms with them. They offered him bread and cream which he ate with relish. Someone started humming a partisan tune, and they asked him to sing a song in Russian for them. He complied.

The next morning they arrived in Belgrade. Leibel got off the train with the wounded and invalid soldiers and continued on foot to the upper section of the city. On the way he asked traffic policemen if they knew where the Jewish community was located. Some of them knew and told him, and those that did not stopped passersby and asked them. Some people were kind enough to walk with him to the nearest corner and point the way.

Leibel's appearance was not one to inspire confidence. He seemed worn; he wore the shabby winter coat of a German refugee which he had acquired in one of the camps; and his beard was thick and wild. All in all, he looked like a derelict. When he asked for a Moshe, people looked at him suspiciously and said that they knew of no such person. Leibel would not move, however, insisting that his intentions were of the best and that he had an important message to deliver. Finally he met Moshe, one of the two heads of the local underground. He was a former refugee, had been a member of the Gordonia youth movement, and was an artist by profession. With him was a boy, quite young, whom the war had aged prematurely. Moshe had come from Carpatho-Ukraine and had quickly learned the local language. Later on he took charge of the emigrant groups. On the same day, Leibel met Ehud Uberal, who had already made connections with some Government officials and some Belgrade Jews. It was he who introduced Leibel to the leaders of the Jewish community and to David Alkalay in particular.

With the assistance of the heads of the Jewish community, Leibel and the young fellow found quarters: the attic of the Jewish orphanage and the wine cellar of the synagogue. Both rooms were very damp and were not conducive to good health, but they had to do. What mattered was that they were safe and suitable places for the emissaries to work in at night, preparing false identification papers for the emigrants. As for themselves, the two men carried papers printed on forms of the Jewish Community Council, which stated that they were Jewish refugees under the Council's jurisdiction. Realizing that their papers were worth very little, they carefully avoided meeting any military patrols. At nightfall they would enter the house, cook a meal, and prepare the next day's work. Their main function at that time was sending off groups of emigrants to Greece and Italy. They established bases at the borders and at points along the way. Wherever the emigrants went, they were received by members of the Bureau, who arranged for stopovers, food, lodging, and transportation.

After the project was established in Belgrade, Leibel left for Budapest to make connections with people on both sides of the border, in order to coordinate activities; set up aid stations and stopping points along the way; print papers that would get the emigrants across the border, and so on. He reached the town of Szeged, just inside Hungary, without experiencing any difficulties. From there on, however, his troubles were many. Budapest was only 100 miles away, but it was dangerous to travel by train. Leibel phoned Yona Rosenfeld in Budapest, who urged him not to take the train and sent him a car. Thirteen miles out of Szeged a tire blew out. Before Leibel could change the tire, a huge Russian truck bore down on him and knocked the tiny automobile into a ditch alongside the road. It was a miracle that the emissary was not killed; the auto, however, was wrecked beyond repair. Leibel stood freezing on the Szeged-Budapest road, moving his thumb from side to side as the vehicles passed by. Some people shouted at him unintelligibly and someone tossed him a stale chunk of bread—but no one stopped.

Suddenly a motorcycle with two riders roared into view. An empty sidecar was attached to it. Leibel raised his hand and the motorcycle stopped. Speaking in Russian, he asked the riders to take him to Budapest, and promised to pay anything that they would ask. He had on his person 750,000 pengö and offered it to them. It was, however, a very small sum. He promised to give them a million and a half more, as well as a few good drinks, upon their arrival in Budapest. The riders' faces lit up. They seated him in the sidecar and started off. The ride was incredibly cold and the emissary might well have frozen had the travelers not stopped off occasionally for some liquid refreshment, and for bread and sausages. In the process they spent much more on Leibel than he had agreed to pay them, but they refused to let him pick up the checks. They spent millions. In those inflationary times some people in Hungary paid their bills with baskets of money.

They finally brought the emissary to "smuggling" headquarters in Budapest, where he paid them what he owed them. All three were decidedly tipsy by that time, and the "boys" were more than a little surprised to see Leibel, a non-drinker, in such a state.

A short while after his arrival in Budapest, Leibel left for Yugoslavia with 70 men. En route, in the city of Kiskunhalas, he met an emigrant group that had been viciously attacked; Hungarians had beaten them and thrown them out of their railroad cars. Leibel made for the city with his group, which now numbered 100 members, went to the Russian commander of the local garrison and told him in Russian that he had with him Yugoslavian refugees who were on their way home after having been released from concentration camps; that Hungarians had thrown them off a train and had beaten them; and that he needed his help. The Russian officer was hesitant. He went out to confer with others, and upon returning said:

"Listen, comrade, I don't have very much food here because we're only a small post. There are ten loaves of bread in the storeroom, each loaf about half a table long, and ten kilos of sausage—you take half."

Leibel explained that the food was not as important as transportation to the Yugoslavian border. The officer got onto his motorcycle, set Leibel down behind him, rode over to the station, and rattled off some orders to the station-master. Before two hours had elapsed, they had been given a locomotive and three cars and had reached the border. Leibel and the officer had a drinking contest "by fingers"—having no glasses, they placed their fingers against the bottle for measurement and drank. The Russian was highly pleased, and Leibel discovered once again that a bottle of vodka constituted the best provisions for a trip of that sort. When they arrived at the border, they were taken by special train to the city of Subotica in Yugoslavia. Here the emissary felt at ease. Nowhere in Europe could Jewish refugees feel more secure than on Yugoslavian soil, and none could compare with the Yugoslavian partisan, who would share his bread and help a Jew in any way that he could.

Leibel did his best to reach Greece and make it a center for

Jewish refugees, even as Italy was. Being acquainted with the work of the members of the Bureau before the war, Leibel knew that originally Greece had served as the principal base of the illegal immigration effort. He also knew that there were many professional smuggling rings in that country and that much could be accomplished there. For these reasons he concentrated upon getting to Greece and initiating a program. At the start he did very well, bringing hundreds of Jews into Greece. His success was short-lived, however. On one occasion he set out with a picked group of 35 members of Hehalutz. In the early morning hours they crossed the border in the Macedonian triangle, Albania-Yugoslavia-Greece, at the Yugoslavian city of Bitola on their way to Florina in Greece. Here for the first time they were confronted by the British, who had enlisted the help of local farmers. The pioneers were forcibly and roughly turned back. Once more they set out, by a different route, 62 miles away, and with the aid of Yugoslavian partisans crossed the border at Zhyoslia, in the other triangle: Greece-Bulgaria-Yugoslavia. In Greece they arrived at a point 30 miles away from Salonika. Leibel sent a host of telegrams to Salonika and Athens, to every address that he had, but he received no replies. He presented his group as citizens of Palestine who were trying to return home; the sentries, however, did not know what to do with them. They remained in Greece three days, and on the fourth were requested to go back where they had come from. When they refused, a British officer appeared, looked them over, scowling the while, and said to the Greeks:

"These are Moscow agents sent by the Yugoslavs to help the Greek partisans."

The Greeks needed no more incitement than that; they set upon the pioneers with a will.

The group returned to Yugoslavia with two of their number wounded. So ended the "Greek experiment." From then on, all refugees who came from Hungary and Rumania to Yugoslavia were sent to Italy.

Every day they would send off a group of 40 to 50 people, until they began running into difficulties in Trieste. Many refugees were captured by the British, and days would pass before Leibel would hear of it. In the meanwhile, more people would arrive in Trieste daily, only to be captured and then confined in the building of the Palestine Office under British guard. A British protest was lodged with the Yugoslavian Government concerning aid extended by the Yugoslavs to the illegal emigration to Palestine—and the Government knew nothing about it. They launched an investigation to discover how so many people could have passed through the country without certification. The British pressed for the return of 400 people. The Yugoslavs did not know what to do. In the meanwhile, things were happening in Italy. While British sentinels stood outside the door of the building, preparing to return the Jews where they had come from, all 400 were silently lowered by ropes out of a rear window. When the British police arrived in a truck to take their prisoners back to Yugoslavia, they opened the door and found an empty building.

Upon returning to Belgrade, Leibel learned that the police had found out about their activities and were looking for them, and for Moshe in particular. It seemed that two war criminals wanted by the police were halted at the border in an attempt to escape from Yugoslavia; they possessed papers forged by the Jewish underground. Through those papers the underground activities of the pioneer youth movements were uncovered. Moshe had managed to get across the border into Italy within 48 hours; Leibel remained alone. The leftist

leaders of the Jewish community, who were opposed on
principle to all Zionist activities, forced him out of his room
in the orphanage attic; but he was determined to remain in
Yugoslavia. He received a note from Saul Avigur, urging
him not to leave the country. With his pursuers hot on his
heels, he found two hiding places: in the house of Rabbi
Alteretz and in the home of the leader of Yugoslavian Jewry,
the well-known lawyer, David Alkalay. The latter protected
him and helped him in every way that he could. Leibel soon
had the greatest respect for Alkalay, and the stronger their
bonds of friendship became, the more Leibel pressed him to
take bold steps to change the situation.

One of the first things that Leibel demanded of him was
that a delegation from the Jewish community should go
before Moshe Pijade and explain to him the problem of
those Palestinian Jews, who, having been imprisoned at the
outbreak of the war and having survived the horrors of the
Nazi concentration camps, were seeking a way of returning
to their country. They wanted permission to sail from a
Yugoslavian port in a ship sent especially for them by the
Bureau. Alkalay, who would have to make such a move
entirely on his own, was very reluctant to comply. Leibel,
however, continued to demand it of him, until he almost
came to blows with the man upon whom he was wholly
dependent. He accused the Jewish Community Council of
lacking a conscience and threatened to inform the Jewish
press around the world that they refused to help Jewish
refugees. Finally he closed himself up in a corner of Rabbi
Alteretz's house and declared a hunger strike in hopes that
it would produce results. Alkalay, who sympathized with
Leibel all along, was finally won over. It was not long before
he approached the emissary with a big smile on his face and
told him that he had asked to see Pijade and that a meeting

had been set for the next day. The two men embraced each other. Leibel was never to forget that day. Like a caged animal he paced back and forth in the corner of the room, until Alkalay returned and told him that he had been well-received, but that the Yugoslavian Government was well aware of the true intent of the request. Pijade, who then served as Vice Premier and Minister without Portfolio, said that he was not authorized to handle the matter and referred them to the Assistant to the Minister of the Interior, General Stepovitz. The next day, when the representatives of the Jewish community went to see the general, he already knew what they had to say, and without discussing the matter, told one of his secretaries, a young Jew, to sign the permit. At Leibel's request, the document was short and very inclusive:

> To His Eminence, the Minister of the Interior of the Government of Croatia, Zagreb.
>
> We should have no objections should you give assistance to Jewish refugees who wish to pass through this country and sail to their homeland from one of our ports.

It was an unbelievable stroke of luck. Alkalay was as happy as Leibel. From then on, the situation grew increasingly brighter.

One day, as Leibel was sitting in his room in the building of the Jewish Community Council, the door suddenly opened and a man came in and asked him:

"Is there an emissary here from Palestine?"

Leibel, taken aback, said that he knew of no such person. The man left. After half an hour he returned, accompanied by Alkalay, and without saying a word thrust into Leibel's hands a packet of letters written in Hebrew.

Leibel looked at the signatures and his hands clenched involuntarily. They were the last letters of the two parachutists, Zvi Ben-Yaakov and Rafi Reiss, who had volunteered to jump behind the enemy's lines and had died in Slovakia. The man who brought their letters had been a political prisoner in the same jail in which they were kept in Banska-Bystrica. On the eve of their execution they gave him letters to their families, which he faithfully delivered.

The conditions under which the Palestinians worked in Yugoslavia were completely different from those in other countries. Bribery was commonplace elsewhere, but not in Yugoslavia. There, all dealings were aboveboard and honesty was the rule. It once happened that Leibel was sitting in the room of a military officer of high rank who was in charge of allocating the permits. While the officer was writing, his pen broke. Leibel handed him his own fountain pen, and the officer continued writing, praising the merits of the pen the while. After he finished, Leibel got up and left, leaving his pen behind. He had only gone a short distance when he heard his name being called. He saw the officer running up to him, pen in hand. Leibel asked that he keep it as a gift, and added that he could very easily obtain another. The Yugoslavian officer put the pen in Leibel's hand and said:

"If I didn't know you so well, I would be deeply offended. This time I'll forgive you."

Leibel was warmly received when he presented himself to the Croatian authorities, who were fully sympathetic to his cause. He was given a liaison man with a great deal of authority, one of the top officers in the secret police. The one condition that they laid upon him was that the program be carried out quietly, so that the city's population should not be aware of the movements of the emigrants. Permission was granted for only one ship, so that no more refugees would converge upon them; they had more of their own that they could handle.

Yugoslavia abounds in natural and man-made harbors, and Leibel's first step was to visit some of them. He finally decided upon the port of Bakar for a variety of reasons: it was an ideal spot from a geographic point of view; connections from the train to the ship were good; fuel and supplies could be obtained without much difficulty; and it was only seven miles away from the two large cities of Susak and Fiume, and connected with both places by a good road. In addition he chose the port of Novigrad to serve as an anchorage for the ship, since a fair amount of time would pass before the sailing. He made arrangements with port and municipal agencies, the army and the police, and in every instance was given the assistance requested. He then returned to Zagreb and his plans bore fruit.

After he had chosen the ports, he obtained the Government's permission to make a tour of army camps in the area. At his request a barracks camp formerly used by the German Army and located in a thick forest near the city was placed at his disposal. It soon was filled with thousands of refugees.

One of the chief problems was obtaining provisions to maintain 2,700 people both during their stay in the camp and during the sea journey. The one source of supply, the municipal storehouse, was none too full itself. The lack of food was felt by the general population. But thanks to connections with the administrators of government food depots, their needs were taken care of. Furthermore, when funds were lacking, they would be loaned food supplies, and in large quantities.

Refugee headquarters put at the disposal of the effort Palestinian trucks, free of charge, for the transport of the emigrants from the train directly to the camp. Also, the

Government provided them with a police unit to stand guard around the clock. The guards were more than courteous; they directed the work that went on in the camp, and often lent a hand themselves. They refused to accept any payment —not even so much as a camp meal. A special door was installed in the railroad station so that the refugees would be able to pass through it from their own railroad cars to the trucks, without mingling with other travelers.

An agreement was reached between the organizers of the effort in Rumania and Hungary and the respective governments of those countries, whereby 100 to 150 people at most were to be sent off daily. However, the pressure for emigration to Palestine was so strong among the masses of Rumanian Jewry that the agreement could not be adhered to. Finally, fearful lest they endanger the operation by being unable to take all the refugees on board one ship, they were forced to close the border to the emigrants.

Life in the camp was orderly. Leaders of the pioneer movements kept discipline; the army lent the refugees a field kitchen unit which included fifteen army stoves; the kitchen was well run; and the distribution of food was well organized. Also, a cultural committee was chosen, and they arranged to have nightly programs which included dramatic readings, telling stories of the forest and the partisans, and group singing. Until late at night echoes of their songs were to be heard in different corners of the city. A considerable number of soldiers and policemen were very impressed with the order and the atmosphere in the camp, and attended the parties regularly.

As soon as the emigrants arrived, preparations for the embarkation got under way. The forest was placarded with numbered signs which served as addresses. Everyone had to remember two numbers: his own and that of his unit. Without a number it was difficult to get food, since the camp received its rations in accordance with a prearranged plan. One hundred young men were appointed to keep order. A medical unit was formed, which included doctors, nurses, and stretcher bearers. Sanitation squads were set up, as well as squads to distribute food and water. The old, the weak, and the sick were grouped separately. The camp was divided into units of 30 each, with one unit taking up the rear. The arrangements were tested out during a practice session prior to the sailing, and everything went smoothly.

July 20, 1946. The day that all had waited for had arrived. As the ship approached the shore Leibel went out to meet her accompanied by the port authorities and the mayor of Bakar, a thick-bearded fellow who had been most helpful during their activities in that city. As their little rowboat neared the ship, Leibel grew more and more apprehensive, not knowing who constituted the crew. He was overjoyed when, upon boarding the vessel, he met his close friend from Ginnosar, Yehoshua Rabinowitz. He was so overwhelmed that he failed to notice the young, broad shouldered, suntanned sailor who was standing to the side, dressed in a smart, white uniform, and puffing away on a pipe. Finally Leibel felt an iron hand grip his shoulder. As he turned his head, he heard the sailor say in Hebrew:

"You don't remember Aryeh, from Sdot Yam?"

Here was another pleasant surprise!

That night he met with the crew over a drink, described local conditions for them as well as the structure of the community, and told them to behave properly during their off-duty hours ashore. The gathering broke up at a late hour and everyone went to bed in good spirits. However, they had not been long asleep when they were suddenly jarred awake by what felt like an earthquake. Some were thrown out of bed; all were frightened. In a matter of seconds the engines shut off and the ship was covered with a blanket of black ash. It turned out that the stoker had fallen asleep and had failed to put in the necessary amount of water, with the result that the engines were seriously damaged. All the passengers were furious. Some were for putting the stoker on trial before a military tribunal. However, debate was inappropriate at the time. The engines had to be repaired, and at once. They soon learned that they would have to wait a full 24 hours for the engines to cool off, before they would be able to approach the furnaces. Leibel spent the day scouring ports and small shipyards until he succeeded in finding the right workmen and the proper tools. Repairs were begun immediately.

After the engines were fixed, two trains were put at the refugees' disposal, each consisting of a locomotive and 45 passenger cars. The trains were situated in a quiet locale, far removed from the railroad station. After the cars were numbered and those charged with keeping order went through them, the signal was given; the whole camp moved forward to the large trucks, in accordance with the prearranged schedule. Everyone had an assigned place in the trains and on the ship. In two hours' time the transfer was effected in a quiet and orderly manner. Police officers and representatives of the Government who were present were highly impressed.

At daybreak the train left.

Just before the ship was to sail, Leibel was informed that a woman in the camp was about to give birth. He tried to persuade her to stay behind, promising to put her on the next ship or to get her to Palestine by a more comfortable means of transportation; but in spite of her condition, the woman refused, and said:

"I don't care what happens—I can't stay among strangers any longer."

The train had not passed three stations before the woman began to scream with the onset of her birth pangs. The doctor did not know what to do. They stopped the train at the next station and asked the stationmaster for a mail car. After a short conversation with the railroad's board of directors in Zagreb, an affirmative reply was received. A clean, neat mail car was attached to the train, and the woman was taken into it by the medical team, who had made all the necessary preparations.

The port of Bakar is situated between two tall mountains, at the bottom of a valley. It was necessary to divide the train, as the locomotive would not be able to stop on the steep incline. The descent to the harbor took longer than the rest of the trip. Those who stood below witnessed four trains inch down the mountainside.

Before they even reached the harbor word spread that the woman had given birth to a son. Immediately Leibel jumped off the train, which was creeping down the hill, and rushed to the bottom on foot. He went straight to the ship, and before the mail car arrived in the harbor, he had managed to prepare the captain's room, which the latter had put at the disposal of the new mother. Leibel had made a matress out of mats and had put it on the bed. They brought the woman and her baby to a neat, clean room, and a doctor and nurse were placed in charge of the mother and child.

At Leibel's request, the authorities had closed off all roads leading to the port. A curfew had been put into effect in the surrounding area, and a police detail had been assigned to prevent citizens from coming near the harbor. The boarding of the ship began according to schedule. One hundred people charged with keeping order guided their fellow passengers along the paths, helped them with their luggage, and showed them to their places on the ship After the descent of the first 500 refugees the large bundles began to block the road and it seemed likely that the sailing would be delayed. The refugees were requested to go down to the ship without their baggage, but not one of them was willing to do so. After all warnings and pleas proved futile, stern measures had to be taken. Then many opened their bundles, took out whatever they could, and pulled one garment over another. Some sat on their bundles and refused to move. In the meanwhile, the people on board had begun to get organized, and it was possible to begin taking the bundles aboard.

Two weeks of exhausting work, without any let-up, had weakened Leibel greatly; he suddenly collapsed unconscious.

In the morning, the Hagana put out to sea to the sound of jubilant singing. Permission for another ship was granted without difficulty, and the young men began preparations at once.

From the beginnings of the organized illegal immigration effort in the summer of 1934, until the arrival in Haifa of the last group of refugees from the detention camps in Cyprus in January, 1949, 115,000 people immigrated into Palestine "illegally." Of these, 105,000 were organized and brought over by the young men of the Immigration Bureau, while 10,000 were brought over by the Revisionist Party organization and private agents.

Most of the illegal immigrants came from Europe by sea, and only a minority of them, from Arab countries, came by land. The number of vessels used by the young men of the Bureau was 96: 18 before the outbreak of the war, 13 during the war, and 65 after the end of the war.

The vessels varied greatly in size and nature, ranging from

the tiny Poseidon in 1938, which held 65 people, to huge ships like the Kibbutz Galuyot (Ingathering of the Exiles) and the Atzmaut (Independence) ten years later, on the eve of the establishment of the State of Israel, with a capacity of 7,500 people each.

From 1946 on, the Mandatory Government stepped up its efforts to combat the ships of the immigration underground. Ships were fired upon, immigrants were deported immediately upon their arrival in Palestine and were imprisoned in camps on the island of Cyprus for months and years.

World opinion was especially aroused by the episode involving the Fedeh in the port of La Spezia in Italy. The ship, with 1,014 survivors of the death camps of Europe aboard, was prepared to sail on April 4, 1946. After it was detained through the intervention of the British authorities, a fierce struggle commenced. Among other things, the refugees, led by Yehuda Arazi of the Bureau, declared a hunger strike which lasted for days and terminated only in its 74th hour, with the arrival of the British Labor Leader, Harold Laski, who gave his personal assurance that the ship would be released. Finally, after having been held captive for 33 days, the refugees continued their journey to Palestine on board two ships, the Eliahu Golomb and the Dov Hoz.

Another of the 96 Hagana ships which attained world-wide fame in its courageous struggle against the British was the Exodus 1947.

Originally the Exodus was an American passenger liner known as the President Warfield, and sailed in Chesapeake Bay. Danny (Zeev) Shind, of kibbutz Ayelet Hashahar, who ten years before had arrived in Athens and had discovered the tiny "nutshell," the Poseidon, bought the large, wooden vessel. The ship was well built, had strong engines, and contained spacious dormitories that were to accommodate 4,500 men, women, and children. The loading of the ship had been accomplished in a remarkably short time. Within a period of four days special trains and scores of trucks had brought the passengers to secret farms near Marseilles in southern France.

At the same time, hammers were being wielded inside the ship at a furious rate, day and night, in final preparation for the sailing. The six young emissaries from Palestine, who were supervising the repairs, were to be in charge of the passengers, the distribution of food, the medical service, and the study, cultural, and social programs to be conducted during the trip.

They built a kitchen from which they would be able to feed each of the 4,500 passengers in forty minutes. Signs and arrows were hung up to prevent confusion and delay. A large supply of fresh food, including eggs, fruit, and vegetables was stocked for the young children and babies. On July 10, 1947, truck convoys bearing groups of emigrants from the farms began to arrive in the corner of the harbor near Marseilles where the scrubbed-down ship waited to receive them. The young men had scrubbed themselves too and were wearing spotless white clothing in honor of the occasion. Among them were Yossi Hamburger (Harel), who was to be in charge of the refugees, and young Yitzhak Rabinowitz (Ike), who was to serve as captain. On shore, taking care of last-minute preparations, were Shimon, who had helped organize so many transports since the sailing of the very first boat of the illegal immigration effort, the Velos; and Abi Schwartz from kibbutz Dafna, who joined the effort at a somewhat later date. Seated by the telephone in Paris at the nerve center of the entire operation were—as usual—

of every phase of the final preparations, and waited for the ship to sail that night.

Saul Avigur and his colleagues. They anxiously kept track

Most unexpectedly, during the morning an official delegation from Marseilles arrived in the harbor to determine whether or not the ship was seaworthy. The British had evidently been at work behind the scenes. What is more, a British plane appeared and photographed every movement in the harbor area. The young men stepped up the tempo of the operation. Finally, during the afternoon, the last refugee was taken on board the ship, and the tug boats got ready to take the packed vessel out to sea. Suddenly a voice shouted: "Halt! This ship cannot sail."

So began the life-and-death struggle between the survivors of the Nazi holocaust on board the Exodus and the Bevin Government and its policies.

At midnight, July 10, Saul Avigur in Paris phoned Yossi in Marseilles, and speaking in Hebrew told the latter that the Bureau's negotiations with the British authorities to get permission for the ship to sail had fallen through, and that from there on they were on their own.

Yossi imparted Saul's message to his colleagues and they all decided at once to do everything in their power to sail.

When zero hour—2 A.M.—arrived, the helmsman who was authorized to take the ship out of the port had not yet appeared. The clock moved to 2:15, to 2:30—and still he was missing. The young men decided to take the ship out by themselves, despite the weather's sudden change for the worse and the strong wind that had risen. To their dismay, no sooner did they put the ship in motion than the propeller fouled on some cables and could not function. The young men, despairing, sat down on the gangplank used in boarding the ship, and tried to decide what to do.

Meanwhile, the engineer was trying to move the ship backwards and forwards, until the whole vessel shook and seemed about to fall apart. It was only due to the strength of the 3,600-horsepower engine that the cables were finally broken. It was now almost 4 A.M., and fishing boats began to appear on all sides, endangering the entire operation.

When they finally managed to turn the ship around, the young men were overjoyed. However, many anxious moments still lay ahead. The more progress they made, the more obstacles they encountered. Once the ship was severely jarred in bumping into a pier. The Exodus finally approached the principal opening of the harbor, difficult to negotiate because of its narrowness. When the ship finally passed through she ran onto a reef. It seemed that all was lost. In their despair, the young men began to calculate how many boats would be required to debark the thousands of passengers sleeping peacefully below, unaware of the danger that they were in.

As a last resort they decided to run the engine at full speed. Ninety revolutions per minute . . . one hundred revolutions . . . one hundred and five . . . one hundred and ten . . . almost one hundred and fifteen. The struggle continued for an hour and a half. It seemed that in another moment the engines would explode. Then, at that very instant, they realized that the ship was moving; within minutes they were afloat once more.

The emissaries could not contain themselves. They hugged and kissed each other. The engineers inspected every corner of the ship and reported that no damage had been sustained. Having learned this, the young men sank to the floor on the spot and fell asleep—for the first time in four days.

However, no sooner did the ship get three miles away from the shore than she was met by a British destroyer. The next day, a four-engined bomber flew overhead. Soon after, there appeared the famous destroyer Ajax, that had sunk the "Graf Spee," and joined the "honor escort" which did not leave the Exodus until she arrived in Palestinian waters, where the second phase of the struggle commenced.

At 2:30 A.M. on Friday, July 18, when the ship was 22 miles away from the coast of Palestine, the British destroyer "36.7" radioed her that she had entered territorial waters and had to stop at once. The captain of the Exodus radioed a reply to the commander of the British fleet, wherein he said, among other things:

There are 4,500 men, women, and children aboard, whose only crime is the fact that they are Jews. We are going to our country because it is our right, not because someone has seen fit to extend us a kindness . . . The last thing we want is bloodshed, but you must understand that we will not go to a concentration camp, even a British one . . . You will be personally responsible if any shots are fired into the crowds of these unarmed adults and children. I regret to say that such incidents have occurred in the past . . .

There was no moon that night and it was very dark. The few defense groups that had been organized worked at fortifying the ship. The young captain, Ike, serving in that capacity for the first time, had deliberately slowed the ship's engines with the intention of arriving within the territorial waters when it was morning. However, the British disregarded the very laws that they themselves had set up, and before it was dawn the Exodus was surrounded by six destroyers. The attackers used rifles and submachine guns, clubs and gas bombs, and two of the destroyers opened fire with heavy artillery. The defenders met the first group of armed soldiers with cans of preserves, with screws, and with potatoes, the only "weapons" that they employed. The ship became a battlefield. Blood flowed on the deck.

Three men were killed; Mordecai Baumstein, Zvi Jacobovitz, and William (Bill) Bernstein. Bernstein was a native of San Francisco who had served as a captain in the United States Merchant Marine. After he met the young men of Aliya-Bet in Baltimore, he joined their effort. He was an unaffected and good-natured fellow who, although he felt his Jewishness deeply, was not affiliated with any group, religious or otherwise. From the minute he boarded the ship he mingled with the passengers and became one of them. He shared his possessions with everyone. He worked unflaggingly and with great enthusiasm, although no one demanded it of him. Many were the times he put refugees in good spirits by his contagious cheerfulness. When the Exodus' propeller had fouled on some cables prior to the ship's sailing, he had volunteered to swim ashore and disentangle the cables. Often at night he talked about his plans for organizing the immigration effort in such a way that nothing the British could do would be able to stop it. He said on more than one occasion that he would like to help the illegal immigrants for at least a few years longer.

Bill became close friends with the 28-year-old Protestant minister from America, John Grauel. The minister made the young men's cause his own, and helped them in all that they undertook to do. He even washed dishes and scrubbed floors with the rest, and his influence on the morale of the American volunteers among the crew was inestimable. He never preached or scolded; he had only smiled.

The ship was taken into Haifa, and that night the thousands of passengers, some of whom had been wounded in the fighting, were transferred to three British destroyers assigned the task of deporting them. Included with the deportees were the young men of the Hagana, who stayed with the refugees and shared their lot to the very end.

A member of the Hagana, the nurse Sima, related:

When I went down into the hold of the Empire Rival I almost fainted at the sight that met my eyes. The people were actually wedged together in a mass. They scarcely had room enough to stand; moving was out of the question. The room was filled with screaming and shouting, and here and there fights broke out over spaces for standing or sitting. The English did not come below. A group of men, who had previously searched the clothing of all the refugees and taken whatever was of value, looked in from time to time. Everyone was weak and exhausted, but no one could sleep because of the terrible congestion . . .

Their troubles were far from over, however. They were stunned when they heard a statement informing them that they were to be returned to Europe. When the full realization of the meaning of the announcement had sunk in, cries of despair and the sound of weeping filled the ship.

Out of their sorrow and suffering a decision arose: not to get off the ship in France! They greeted the French delegation sent to meet them at Port-de-Bouc with a short statement: "We will not get off!" On the deck of the deportation vessel a terrible demonstration took place. The members of the delegation beheld women in torn clothing holding in their arms infants covered with open wounds. One pregnant woman had only a towel to wear. The Frenchmen could not contain themselves; they wept like children.

The days slipped by and became weeks. Every day the deportees waited to hear some announcement that would tell them of any change in their fate, but no such announcement came. In this manner, 24 days passed. The critical hour arrived. The refugees learned that they were to sail for Hamburg and that nothing could be done to prevent it. They were to return to the same country where they had undergone untold torture and suffering. The young men of the Hagana did all they could to bolster the morale of the despairing deportees. They were aided by the secret wireless which they smuggled on board. In the same broadcast that informed them of their forced return to Germany they were charged by the Hagana command not to rest until the last refugees on board the Exodus returned to Palestine.

In order to assure the refugees that the Hagana would keep its promise, the young men decided to distribute certificates of their own making to them. Immediately they set to work. They took the rubber heel off Sima's shoe and carved into it the insignia of the Hagana—the olive branch and the sword —and proceeded to stamp out 4,500 certificates. For hours they sat in the hold and affixed their signatures to the pieces of paper which every man, women and child received and guarded zealously.

The promise was fulfilled. After several months of anguish on German soil, the refugees of the Exodus 1947 were brought back to Palestine in different groups and on different ships.

On September 7, 1948, a telegram arrived in Israel from Immigration Bureau headquarters in Paris, then already preparing to disband. It read:

"We have sent off the last of the Exodus passengers from Germany. Except for some sick persons, no one remains . . . We have kept our promise."

The illegal immigration effort continued until the gates of independent Israel were opened to every Jew wishing to return to his Homeland. Only then did the group disband. The members, some of whom had been engaged in the

24. WE HAVE SENT OFF THE LAST OF THE EXODUS PASSENGERS.

dangers and labors of Aliya-Bet for fifteen years, returned to their various tasks. They had set out as youths, and returned as men who had experienced much, met many severe tests, and were proud of having served their people faithfully. Today they are to be found in all walks of life in the growing State of Israel. They are farmers, artisans, army officers, and captains of the large and handsome vessels of the Israeli merchant marine. They are also to be found among the leaders of the State, holding important positions in the Government and the Knesset (Parliament), and representing Israel among the nations of the world. Israel will ever be in their debt.